WINDOW SHOPPING

CINEMA AND THE POSTMODERN

ANNE FRIEDBERG

UNIVERSITY OF CALIFORNIA PRESS   BERKELEY   LOS ANGELES   LONDON

University of California Press

Berkeley and Los Angeles, California

University of California Press, Ltd.

London, England

Copyright © 1993 by Anne Friedberg

First Paperback Printing 1994

Library of Congress Cataloging-in-Publication Data

Friedberg, Anne.

Window shopping : cinema and the

postmodern / Anne Friedberg.

p.   cm.

Includes bibliographical references and index.

ISBN 0-520-07916-7 (alk. paper)

ISBN 0-520-08924-3 (pbk.: alk. paper)

I. Motion pictures—

Philosophy.   2. Postmodernism.   3. Motion

pictures—Social aspects.   4. Feminism and

motion pictures.

I. Title.

PN1995.F743   1993

791.43'01—dc20   92-30917

                                   CIP

Printed in the United States of America

   2   3   4   5   6   7   8   9

The paper used in this publication meets the minimum
requirements of American National Standard for
Information Sciences—Permanence of Paper for
Printed Library Materials, ANSI Z39.48—1984. ⊚

CONTENTS

For my parents
Arthur L. Friedberg (1919–1984) and
Marian Davis Friedberg (1920–1991)

This book is a product of its context, both historical and geographical. In 1985 its author moved from New York City, the quintessential *modern* city (Capital of the Twentieth Century) to Los Angeles, the quintessential *post-modern* city (Capital of the Twenty-First). Living in Southern California, one learns rapidly about machines that mobilize the gaze; the lessons of the everyday are learned through an automobile windshield.[1]

But for this author, the major shock of living in motorized culture was its effect on the habits of urban cinephilia. On a previous trip to Los Angeles, I had to leave a Westwood movie theater in the middle of a film in order to feed a parking meter. On that particular afternoon, as I emerged from the theater's dark comfort, balancing the price of a movie ticket against the price of a parking ticket, I realized some basic things about spectatorship. I had been watching the garish color "remake" of Jean-Luc Godard's 1959 *Breathless*. Richard Gere was a warped transubstantiation of Jean Paul Belmondo; the film made a twisted return to the Godard of the New Wave—a time travel of reference. Out in the glaring sun of Westwood Boulevard, I was hit with the epiphanic force of the obvious. Cinema spectatorship was not only a radical metaphor for the windshield, it was also a unique form of time travel; parking was a necessary physical prerequisite to the imaginary mobilities of such *flânerie*.

Living in Los Angeles, shopping mall cinemas quickly became my preferred venue, if only because they supplied parking. My initial digust at being forced into the belly of a consumer theme park gave way to a fascination with the shared logic of moviegoing and the shopping mall. The shopper-spectator strolls through a phantasmagoric array of commodified images and experiences; both the multiplex cinema and the shopping mall, I quickly realized, sell the pleasures of imaginary mobility as psychic transformation.

These initial thoughts about mobility and the imaginary "virtual" travel of cinema spectatorship met the (mid-1980s) debates about the "postmodern" at a significant intersection. The book that follows addresses this crossing, taking the spatial and temporal displacements of cinematic and televisual spectatorship and aligning them with the postmodern "crisis" about the past. By providing a cultural history of the commodification of a mobile and virtual gaze, I offer a reading of contemporary culture that encourages us to see the cumulative and wide-ranging effects of cinematic and televisual apparatuses in a newly focused historical light.

In the mid-1980s, new electronic technologies transfigured the network of everyday communication: cash machines at airports, phones on airplanes and in automobiles, computer terminals in libraries, fax machines everywhere. These technologies appeared with a suddenness that made one consider the science fiction future as the present. The momentous shifts in global politics in the late 1980s were, I would argue, produced as much by these new technologies as by political or ideological shifts. What could provide more vivid proof of the spatial and temporal changes produced by new communications technologies than the global political arena of 1988–1992? Consider: the fax-machine-fueled "prodemocracy movement" in China; the "CNN war" in the Persian Gulf; microwave TV signals carrying images of comfortable lifestyles and abundant consumer goods into the meagerly-stocked households of East Germany and the Eastern bloc; satellite beams bringing MTV and the vivid boons of the capitalist West into the fraying economy of the Soviet Union. The boundaries of space and time which were so dramatically challenged by "modernity" have been, again, radically transformed.

Everyday life is a fuel for thought: the private mobility of driving transforms the windshield into a synoptic vista, and the fifty-two-mile commute between the sprawling transurban metropolis of Los Angeles and the university-as-theme-park of the University of California at Irvine became, for me, a consistently speculative analytic hour. While writing this book, the freeways that encircle and bisect Los Angeles were under constant construction; the topography of the road reconfigured itself daily. As the new "Century Freeway" loomed apocalyptically into the future, one could not help but draw parallels between the end of this century and the end of the last.

LOS ANGELES
JANUARY 1992

■ ACKNOWLEDGMENTS

I am indebted to many people and institutions for their generous contributions to the writing of this book.

Career Development Awards from the University of California at Irvine in 1986, 1987, and 1988 provided generous research funding for this project as it developed; the Organized Research Unit on Women and Image at UCI also supplied continued financial assistance. In the summer of 1987, I was an NEH Fellow at the Institute for Study of the Avant-gardes at Harvard University; I am grateful to the Institute and its participants for conversations and debates about many of the issues which inform this book. San Francisco Artspace's "New Writing in Arts Criticism" Award in 1987 lent encouragement to this project in its initial stages.

Two colleagues deserve special thanks for their support. Eric Rentschler encouraged my thinking at all stages of the book's progress. Miriam Hansen was a steady friend and colleague as the book took shape; I am grateful for her careful reading of the manuscript, for her rigorous comments and generous suggestions. Discussions with Steve Hall, Bill Horrigan, Lynne Kirby, Gertrud Koch, Judith Mayne, Tania Modelski, Laura Mulvey, Lesley Stern, Lynne Tillman, and Lindsay Waters were helpful in clarifying my ideas. UCI colleagues John Smith and Linda Williams offered helpful suggestions on the manuscript in its earliest form. Linda Hutcheon provided valuable comments on the manuscript in its penultimate version. William Boddy and Rhona Berenstein were helpful throughout and, in particular, provided careful readings of chapter 3. Steve Simon helped with stills and frame enlargements. Ed Dimendberg, my editor at University of California Press, deserves special thanks for his persuasive judgment and unflagging support. For all of the extraordinary help I've received, any limitations in the book's thought, structure, or scope are, of course, entirely my own.

During the course of writing this book I became more fully aware of one of my important and unspoken intellectual debts. Annette Michelson's eloquent writing on the cinema as a philosophical enterprise was what drew me to film study in the first place. Her work has remained a model of vitality and intellect.

Finally, Howard Rodman's eloquent sense of language and careful logic were inspirations throughout; our many shared *flâneries* have provided extraordinary intellectual and emotional subsidy. And, in its final stages, the book improved thanks to the vigilant support of Benjamin Nemo.

Sections of this book were presented as lectures or conference papers. The essay that became the core of the book, "Les Flaneurs du mal(l): Cinema and the Postmodern Condition," was presented in evolving versions at various conferences and university seminars: SUNY/Stonybrook 1988, Society for Cinema Studies Conference in Bozeman, Montana 1988; Columbia Film Seminar in New York 1988, Art Center Pasadena 1990; "Feminismus und Medien: Perspektiven der amerikanischen feministischen Medientheorie," at the Kunst Museum Bern and the Staatliche Hochscule für Bildende Künst in Frankfurt am Main in June 1990. I am grateful to those audiences for questions and suggestions that were helpful in clarifying and strengthening my arguments. A version of this essay appeared in *PMLA* (May 1991) and was translated into German in *Feminismus und Medien* (Bern: Benteli Verlag, 1991). Another paper which informed the book's earliest stage was presented as "Mutual Indifference: Feminism and Postmodernism" at the MLA in New York 1986; Foundation for Art Resources (F.A.R.), Los Angeles in May 1987; UC Irvine in May 1987; California Institute of the Arts in January 1988; and appeared in Juliet MacCannell, ed., *The Other Perspective on Gender and Culture* (Columbia University Press, 1990).

The past can be seized only as an image which flashes up at
the instant when it can be recognized and is never seen
again. . . . For every image of the past that is not
recognized by the present as one of its own concerns
threatens to disappear irretrievably.

WALTER BENJAMIN, "On the Concept of History"

THE PAST, THE PRESENT, THE VIRTUAL   As the century draws to a close, the cultural
detritus of the last two decades may well be measured by the rhetorical
debates about the social formation called "postmodernity," and the subjective position deemed the "postmodern condition."[1] In a 1983 essay, Fredric Jameson, one of the key diagnosticians of postmodernity, catalogued
some of its symptoms as:

the disappearance of history, the way in which our entire contemporary social
system has little by little begun to *lose its capacity to retain its own past,* has
begun to live in *a perpetual present* and in a perpetual change that obliterates
traditions.[2] (emphasis added)

This "disappearance of history" and its corollary effect, a life in the "perpetual present," has emerged as one of the most profound depictions of
"postmodern" subjectivity. Yet these charges strike a chord that resonates
back to the middle of the last century. In 1859, Charles Baudelaire indicted
photography as being a "cheap method of disseminating a loathing for
history."[3] Baudelaire was an early declaimer of the dangerous transformations of history and memory that the photographic image would produce.
Despite photography's "loathing for history," Baudelaire also recognized it
as a technique that could preserve "precious things whose form is dissolving

and which demand a place in the archives of our memory."[4] In this double-edged reaction, Baudelaire prophetically noted the emergence of a new archive of memory which obscures the past in the guise of preserving it. For Baudelaire, the disappearance of history was a potential consequence of the photographic image.[5]

The debates about the "post" to "modernity" address these same reshufflings of history and memory and are infused with many of the same ambivalences about the cultural effects of these new configurations.[6] Theorists continue to examine the qualitative transformations of time, space, and subjectivity in what has variously been called postindustrial society (Daniel Bell), multinational capitalism and consumer society (Jameson), the society of the spectacle (Guy Debord), the neocolonial (Gayatri Spivak).[7]

In this crucible of philosophic debate, where history and memory are endangered forms, cinematic and televisual apparatuses become readable not just as symptoms of a "postmodern condition," but as contributing causes. A diminished capacity to retain the past is, as I will argue, a loss that has figured as the price of the cinema's cultural gain. Cinema and television—mechanical and electronic extensions of photography's capacity to transform our access to history and memory—have produced increasingly detemporalized subjectivities. At the same time, the ubiquity of cinematic and televisual representations has fostered an increasingly derealized sense of "presence" and identity. Seen in this context, descriptions of a decentered, derealized, and detemporalized postmodern subject form a striking parallel to the subjective consequences of cinema and televisual spectatorship. Where, then, does the "postmodern condition" begin?

Rather than proclaiming a single distinct moment of rupture—when the modern ended and the postmodern began—I suggest a gradual and indistinct epistemological tear along the fabric of modernity, a change produced by the increasing cultural centrality of an integral feature of both cinematic and televisual apparatuses: a *mobilized "virtual" gaze*. The *virtual gaze*[8] is not a direct perception but a *received* perception mediated through representation.[9] I introduce this compound term in order to describe a gaze that travels in an imaginary *flânerie* through an imaginary elsewhere and an imaginary elsewhen. The *mobilized gaze* has a history, which begins well before the cinema and is rooted in other cultural activities that involve walking and travel. The virtual gaze has a history rooted in all forms of visual representation (back to cave painting), but produced most dramatically by photography. The cinema developed as an apparatus that combined the "mobile" with the "virtual." Hence, cinematic spectatorship changed, in unprecedented ways, concepts of the *present* and the *real.*

As a device to organize a critical intervention into the theorization of the "postmodern," I borrow a conceit from social and textual accounts of the nineteenth century—that fundamental paradigm of the subject in modernity, the *flâneur. Flânerie* will serve as an explanatory device to trace changes in representation and the aesthetic experience in the nineteenth century. As a social and textual construct for a mobilized visuality, flânerie can be historically situated as an urban phenomenon linked to, in gradual but direct ways, the new aesthetic of reception found in "moviegoing." As I will argue, the imaginary flânerie of cinema spectatorship offers a spatially mobilized visuality but also, importantly, a temporal mobility. This use of the historical model of the flâneur will also draw attention to the gendering of power and visuality in the configurations of modernity. It is here that we can find the origins of the *flâneuse,* the female counterpart to the male subject in modernity.

By introducing the terms *mobilized* and *virtual,* I hope to widen the historical focus in accounts of the emergence of the cinema, and to extend a consideration of cinematic spectatorship to other activities that supply an imaginary flânerie. Hence, I will argue that to trace the cultural formations that endowed visuality with its ultimately dominant power, it will be necessary also to analyze the cultural contexts for these acts of looking: the social behaviors involved in the examination of goods on display (shopping) and the experience of "foreign" spaces (tourism). The cultural shifts resulting from the organization of the look in the service of consumption, and the gradual incorporation of the commodified experience into everyday life, has, I will argue, profoundly altered the subjective role of memory and history.

In the nineteenth century, machines that changed the measure of space and time (machines of mobility, including trains, steamships, bicycles, elevators, escalators, moving walkways, and, later, automobiles and airplanes) changed the relation between sight and bodily movement. A variety of architectural forms also emerged in the nineteenth century which facilitated and encouraged a pedestrian mobilized gaze—exhibition halls, winter-gardens, arcades, department stores, museums. The pedestrian in a glass enclosed winter-garden or exhibition hall enjoyed an endless summer;

arcades protected against weather; museums brought artifacts of the past into a tourable present. As the technical advances of iron and glass architecture changed the temporal concept of the seasonal, institutional museology changed the relation to the past.[10] And, just as machines of transport (from the railway to the *trottoir roulant*) produced a new experience of distance and time, these architectural spaces were, in a sense, machines of timelessness, producing a derealized sense of the present and a detemporalized sense of the real.[11] Coincident with the new mobilities produced by changes in transportation, architecture and urban planning, photography brought with it a virtual gaze, one that brought the past to the present, the distant to the near, the miniscule to its enlargement. And machines of virtual transport (the panorama, the diorama, and later, the cinema) extended the virtual gaze of photography to provide virtual mobility.

At the beginnings of consumer culture, this gaze became imbued with the power of choice and incorporation: the shopper's gaze. During the mid-nineteenth century, the coincident development of department store shopping, packaged tourism, and protocinematic entertainment began to transform this mobilized gaze into a commodity, one sold to a consumer-spectator. These forms of commodified visual mobility, once only available in the imperial cities of the first world, gradually became a global standard of modernity. And here, at the base of modernity, the social underpinnings of gender began to shift. Women were empowered with new forms of social mobility as shoppers, as tourists, as cinema-goers.

The gradual shift into postmodernity is marked, I argue, by the increased centrality of the mobilized and virtual gaze as a fundamental feature of everyday life. Although the social formations of modernity were increasingly mediated through images, this gaze was initially restricted to the public sphere (within "high" culture in painterly views and theatrical experiences, or within "low" culture in the arcade, the department store, the diorama, or the panorama).[12] In postmodernity, the spatial and temporal displacements of a mobilized virtual gaze are now as much a part of the public sphere (in, for example, the shopping mall and multiplex cinema) as they are a part of the private (at home, with the television and the VCR). The boundaries between public and private, already fragile in modernity, have now been more fully eroded. The mobilized virtual gaze is now available in the video markets of Katmandu and other outposts of the imperial web of technoculture.[13]

The original title of this book relied on a palimpsest of references: Baudelaire, Walter Benjamin, the shopping mall. Unfortunately that title—*Les Flâneurs du Mal(l)*—did little to indicate these sources to an uninitiated reader. Baudelaire's collection of poems entitled *Les Fleurs du Mal* (*Flowers of Evil*) was the cornerstone of Benjamin's massive work on modernity, his uncompleted study of the Paris arcades. *Les Fleurs du Mal,* according to Benjamin, recorded the ambulatory "gaze of the flâneur" on "Paris—Capital of the Nineteenth Century." The title *Les Flâneurs du Mall,* was thus an appropriative double pun (on *fleurs* and on *mal*), locating the flânerie of the postmodern cinema spectator in the shopping mall. *Window Shopping*—a title that came late to the manuscript—is the loosest of equivalents, evoking similar motifs of visuality, contemplation, and pedestrian mobility while remaining a key metaphor for spectatorship, whether it be in the shopping mall multiplex or at home in front of the TV screen.

METHOD   As the above summary indicates, I have drawn from a variety of ongoing debates and several potentially conflicting discourses. It is therefore important to draw these methodological premises to the surface. This book is addressed to three distinct but overlapping discursive fields: 1) the debates about the "postmodern," debates that have already formed an interdisciplinary domain, labeled everything from "cultural studies" to combinations of philosophy, history, literary theory, and art and architectural history, 2) film studies, which include the often-warring methodologies of film history and film theory, and 3) feminist studies, an equally interdisciplinary (and ever-widening) discursive arena. Here then, I will signpost the goals of my argument for each of these areas:

Debates about Postmodernity   Post implies historical sequence, a moment of rupture when the *post* succeeds the *past.* But, as historiographers remind us, history is not only a discourse but a product of discourses.[14] The debates about postmodernity have often been marked by—as if a product of their own discourse—a symptomatic amnesia to the past. I argue the need to reintroduce history into the debate about the postmodern; and I argue that accounts of the cinema and the postmodern require a wider historical focus than simply that of the last two decades or since World War II.

As a historiographical consequence of suggesting a *pre*history to the "*post*modern," the problem of teleology looms large. Attempts to historicize "emergence" can veer toward a narrativized account of "convergences." Here it is important to acknowledge the two potentially conflicting objectives of this study: to show that the cinema (as it "emerged" as a technology and commodity form) was defined by the mobilized and virtual gaze, and to describe the gradual, yet specific, differences in the "postmodern" mobilization of this gaze. If the hidden danger of the first is teleology, that of the second is the unwitting celebration of all that is "new and different" in the postmodern. To negotiate the narrow passage between these perilous straits will require a cautious historiography.[15]

As we will see, the very term *post*—and the periodization it implies—incites discord. I contend that the ever-increasing cultural centrality of the mobilized and virtual gaze produced a gradual change, not an apocalyptic rupture, and that the initial frayings were present at the beginnings of the break into the "modern." This argument places a prehistory of postmodernity in the nineteenth century amid transformations that theorists have otherwise termed the "prehistory of modernity." The emergence of the cinema was, I will argue, a "proto-postmodern" cultural symptom.

Any contemporary work advocating a "return to history" needs to define its relation not only to the "new historicism," but also to history, to notions of the past. The tag of new historicist has been attached to methods that replace the "old" historicism of the nineteenth century, and which resist the bent of neopositivism, facticity, and the myth of historical objectivity—while at the same time rejecting the notions of the autonomous text found in critical formalism. A new historicism insists on reconnecting text with *con*text.[16]

Because this book crosses disciplinary boundaries (architecture, literature, film, consumer culture) and because I insist that the film text be read in the architectural context of its reception rather than as an autonomous aesthetic product, my method may be labeled new historicist. While I will not reject this designation out of hand, I would like to point out the nearly contradictory relation of the methodological principles of new historicism to the argument I am making about film and televisual spectatorship.

I argue that a key component of what has been deemed "the postmodern condition" is found in the simultaneous acknowledgment and disavowal of the idea that the past cannot be reconstituted as it was; and I describe how film and television spectatorship has produced a new relation to the past. The past is, now, inexorably bound with images of a constructed past: a confusing blur of "simulated" and "real."

Debates in Film Studies   The massive flood of literature on postmodernism and postmodernity which spewed forth from conferences and museum shows of the 1980s—a discursive tide that inundated academic journals and art publications—has had relatively little impact on theoretical or historiographic accounts of the cinema.[17] As we will see, if the term *postmodern* has entered into film studies or film criticism, it has been as *postmodernism*—a stylistic term or aesthetic symptom. I will argue that beyond a mere marking of contemporary style, cinematic and televisual spectatorship produces a subject fluidity that bears remarkable similarity to descriptions of postmodern subjectivity. This subjectivity is produced by spectatorship itself—whether or not the style per se is postmodern.

The recent work of a variety of film scholars (Doane [1988], Mayne [1988], Gaines [1989], Petro [1989], Musser [1990], and Hansen [1991]) has argued for widening the focus of social and psychic accounts of cinematic spectatorship to include advertising, illustrated print journalism, fashion, and other modes of "screen practice": in short, the everyday.[18] To continue this revision of conceptual models of spectatorship, it is necessary to include new forms of reception in this age of the VCR and the multiplex cinema.

Taking this route will produce a rather different history, one defined not through the changing forms of film styles and conventions of cinematic representation (modeled on the familiar paradigms of art history) but rather a history that, instead, traces the cultural contexts of these commodified forms of looking and of the *experiences* of spatial and temporal mobility which were first converted into "commodity-experiences" in the nineteenth century. Here I follow work by Kern (1983) and Schivelbusch (1977, 1983) on nineteenth-century transformations of time and space and work by Williams (1982), Bowlby (1985), and Peiss (1986) on women and the origins of consumer culture.[19]

In the nineteenth century, the commodity-experience marketed the subjective spatial and temporal fluidities that have become primary components of contemporary cinematic and televisual spectatorship. Standardized repeatability was an implicit feature of photography and of the cinema, and its features are more pronounced in the exhibition practices of repertory and multiplex cinemas, VCRs, and various forms of television spectatorship. Hence, I argue, we must consider the subjective consequences of reseeing films outside of their historical context and measure the consequences of a contemporary spectatorship that occupies equally the public sphere of the shopping mall and the private domestic sphere of the VCR.

It is here that a discussion of the *post* to modernism and modernity poses a unique dilemma to film historiography. Although each of the arts may produce a certain timelessness, film and televisual media do so with the aid of powerful reality effects, propagating a subjectivity that posits "presence" in a virtual elsewhere and elsewhen.

In the last two decades, as the discipline of film studies has emerged as a fixture in the academy—complete with graduate programs, as well as museums dedicated to its past—technological advances have transformed our access to this history. As the VCR has become a common household appliance, as cable television networks (TNT, TMC, AMC, TBS) acquire and exhibit Hollywood archives, the cinematic past is accessible in ever more direct ways. Even though cinematic spectatorship itself produces viewing experiences that are not temporally fixed, films have even more profoundly lost their historical identity. In this regard, the ascendancy of film historical discourse (and, by extension, the growing academic discipline of film studies) has worked to mask the very loss of history that the film itself has incurred.[20]

As Michel Foucault noted, in a statement about television and cinema as "effective means . . . of *reprogramming popular memory*":

people are shown *not what they were but what they must remember having been*. . . . Since memory is a very important factor in struggle . . . if one controls people's memory, one controls their dynamism.[21] (emphasis added)

Anton Kaes has pinpointed this historiographical concern in the conclusion to his recent study of postwar West German filmmaking, *From Hitler to Heimat: The Return of History as Film:*

A memory preserved in filmed images does not vanish, but the sheer mass of historical images transmitted by today's media weakens the link between public memory and personal experience. The past is in danger of becoming a rapidly expanding collection of images, easily retrievable but isolated from time and space, available in an eternal present by pushing a button on the remote control. History thus returns forever—as film.[22]

Kaes demonstrates how postwar German films reconstitute our sense of the historical past. As the past is disso.᾿ ᾿d as a real referent and reconstituted by the cinematic images that displace it, Baudelaire's cynical prophesy about photography's "loathing for history" meets Jameson's dystopic symptomatology of history's "disappearance."

The book that follows conducts a paradoxical history, one that is designed to restructure cinematic history along a different set of questions: a history of the timelessness produced by cinematic spectatorship, as well as an analysis of the impact on gender and subjectivity of such a interminably recycled, ever-accessible past.

Feminist Studies   As I have indicated, I rely on the flâneur and the work of Benjamin to organize the diverse changes in contemporary aesthetic experience and reception. But, at the same time, pursuing a feminist corrective to previously gender-blind work, I introduce the flâneuse—the female urban subject, strikingly absent from accounts of modernity. The urban mobilities first available to women in modernity are, I will argue, a crucial determinant of the transformations of the role of gender in *post*-modernity.

Although much of feminist film theory has focused on the cinematic representation of the female body and voice, I join the historians and theorists who insist we consider the context for these representations, not only the relation to advertising, publicity, and fashion but also the effects of cinematic and televisual spectatorship on the psychic and social construction of gender in the context of the commercial and the everyday.

As my "Post-Script" attests, debates about postmodernism often took the discursive place of feminist debates in the late 1980s. This serves as a reminder that, as an ever-potent product of postmodern culture, theoretical discourse is not innocent, and if we consider the wider cultural *mise en scène,* every discourse also has its (even if unwitting) political function.

THE "P" WORD   Even though cultural historians may have already begun to write a history of the term *postmodern,*[23] this is not my project here. Yet one cannot enter into a discussion of the postmodern without commenting on the discursive field that has trivialized the word. To date, a persistent factor in the cultural debate about the postmodern is the revulsion the very term invokes. That the terminology of postmodernism has been scavenged by the discourses of advertising and the mass media without regard to its ideological underpinnings may be the worst recuperation of the word—now forced to sell the style of the signifier without the referent. The word *postmodern* has become a slippery polyseme defined largely through its (over)usage; its semantic inflation has increased in direct proportion to the deflation of its referent. As was once the case with the term *modern, postmodern* seems to be invoked to simply refer to the "new."[24]

As the debate continues about the cultural and ideological valences of the postmodern, the term itself has been turned into a stylistic cliché, a fitting example of how *discourse about the object* becomes submerged in *discourse of the object*.[25] Dick Hebdige, theorist of subcultures, has acutely noted:

> When it becomes possible for people to describe as "postmodern" the decor of a room, the design of a building, the diegesis of a film, the construction of a record, or a "scratch" video, a TV commercial, or an arts documentary, or the intertextual relations between them, the layout of a page in a fashion magazine or a critical journal, an anti-teleological tendency within epistemology, the attack on "the metaphysics of presence," a general attenuation of feeling, the collective chagrin and morbid projections of a post-War generation of Baby Boomers confronting middle age, the "predicament" of reflexivity, a group of rhetorical tropes, a proliferation of surfaces, a new phase in commodity fetishism, a fascination for "images," codes and styles, a process of cultural, political or existential fragmentation and/or crisis, the "decentering" of the subject, an "incredulity towards metanarratives," the replacement of unitary power axes by a pluralism of power/discourse formations, the "implosion of meaning," the collapse of cultural hierarchies, the dread engendered by the threat of nuclear self-destruction, the decline of the University, the functioning and effects of the new miniaturized technologies, broad societal and economic shifts into a "media" and "consumer" or "multinational" phase, a sense (depending on who you read) of "placelessness" or the abandonment of placelessness ("critical regionalism") or (even) a generalized substitution of spatial for temporal coordinates—when it becomes possible to describe all those things as "postmodern" (or more simply, using current abbreviation, as "post" or "very post") then it's clear we are in the presence of a buzzword. [26]

In short, the word *postmodern* has acquired a semiotic instability that almost mimetically reproduces its denotation of indeterminacy. The mire of debate about its history and definition has become infused with many of the epistemic assumptions that the theorists of the postmodern themselves would challenge—the ontology of history, the denotative certainty of definition.

Postmodern has been defined as the end of the Enlightenment (Lyotard) and as the site of the Enlightenment's completion (Habermas); it has been seen as radical pluralism, multiculturalism, centralized marginality (Spivak) and as a culture of decentered subjectivity (Derrida); it suggests texts that refer only to texts and authentic experiences replaced by simulations (Baudrillard). The categories of antimodern, late modern, postmodern blur into one another as the debate rages. At this juncture, one is tempted to demand that the use of the word *postmodern* be regulated or, better, that it be dropped from our vocabularies altogether.[27] But when all the semantic dust settles, the valence of the modifier *post* signifies its position vis-à-vis the root word *modern,* indicating either its end or its continuance in a new configuration.

If film scholars have reacted to the term *postmodernism* with a justifiable distrust, it has been because the term was eagerly adopted with the sort of quick "applicationism" that marks intellectual insecurity in any field. In both academic and journalistic film criticism, the "post" word has been used without questioning the concept of modernism or modernity which is its assumed base, or interrogating the problematic oversights in adopting the blithe label *postmodern.*

A ROAD MAP   Beyond this introductory foyer, the architecture of this book is arranged in four chapters—chapters 1 and 2 on modernity; chapters 3 and 4 on postmodernity—linked by "passages" or brief excursuses. These transitional texts are designed to buttress the otherwise abrupt ellipse between the end of this century and the end of last. These three passages illustrate the movement of my argument through a range of interdisciplinary examples from literature, architecture, and film: "Passage 1" is through a literary text (Zola's *Au Bonheur des Dames* [1883]); "Passage 2" is through film texts (*The European Rest Cure* [1904]; *Paris Qui Dort* [1924]; *La Jetée* [1962/1964]; *Alphaville* [1965]; *The Time Machine* [1960]); "Passage 3" is through architectural examples (the Bradbury Building [1893], the Musée d'Orsay [1900/1987], the Westside Pavilion [1985]).

In chapter 1, "The Mobilized and Virtual Gaze in Modernity: Flâneur/Flâneuse," I discuss the historical contexts for the emergence of the cinema and its development from precinematic "mobile" and "virtual" gazes. I propose the dioramic and panoramic spectator as alternatives to the model of structured visuality so frequently associated with modernity—the panoptic gaze. A new social figure—the flâneuse—appeared in public spaces made possible by the new configurations of consumer culture.

Chapter 2, "The Passage from Arcade to Cinema," examines the architectural and social contexts for the mobilized and virtual gaze, and its instrumentalization as a commodity-experience. As I've already indicated, Benjamin's unfinished *Das Passagen-werk* is a key and prophetic text on modernity and urban experience. Benjamin considered the *passage* as a threshold for time's passing. His writing on photography and the cinema, mechanical reproduction and the loss of aura, and the impact of an "unconscious optics" emphasizes the cinema's unique temporality. Hence, I return to arcades, department stores, and exhibition halls to examine the reconfigurations of spatial and temporal mobility; from the timeless spaces where the "mobilized" gaze was situated to the time machines that extended its mobility in "virtual" fashion.

Chapter 3, "Les Flâneurs/Flâneuse du Mall," parallels the historical movement of chapter 2 (arcades and modernity, malls and postmodernity). The shopping mall is the contemporary extension of the nineteenth-century passage, offering a site for flânerie and for a mobilized gaze instrumentalized by consumer culture. This chapter begins with a brief history of the shopping mall and argues that the development of the shopping mall has produced an architectural analogue to the cinematic and televisual apparatus. In this chapter, I also distinguish between the principles of classical spectatorship and contemporary challenges to this model. This chapter also begins a discussion of participant-based "virtual reality" technologies—computer-generated "Toon Town" worlds with no original referent—which are designed to produce the "virtual" effects of the real.

In chapter 4, "The End of Modernity: 'Where Is Your Rupture?'" I argue that even though the term *postmodern* has been used to describe aesthetic symptoms, it can be more profitably used to consider the social formation of postmodern*ity*. As I've indicated, in film studies *postmodernism* has come to be used as a descriptive term for a genre or a period style without an account of how the cultural configurations of postmodernity have been profoundly affected by the very instruments of cinema and television. Cinematic and televisual spectatorship has produced a new form of subjectivity, I argue, a subjectivity that is inherently produced by the apparatus, whether or not the style is "postmodern."

In a brief conclusion, "Spending Time," I summarize the book's argument by supplying the Vidéothèque de Paris as a final illustration. In the Post-Script, "The Fate of Feminism in Postmodernity," I address the role of debates about postmodernity which do not engage in questions of gender. If this early discourse about postmodernity is analyzed, it becomes apparent that these discussions "feminized" postmodernity as an unchartable terrain, as enigmatic as that *other* other—femininity. In this way, debates about postmodernity may have served an unacknowledged ideological agenda—that of displacing feminist debate.

Notes on Terms Used   Modernity: I assume a definition of *modernity* as a social formation coincident with late eighteenth- and early nineteenth-century industrialization and urbanization. Although these changes had their first impact on capitalist, cosmopolitan cities (Paris, Berlin, London, New York, Chicago, Moscow), the rate of development (and decay) was uneven.

Subject: The category of the subject, as Derrida reminds us, is itself a questionable vestige of logocentrism. My use of the term provides an indication of my theoretical premises in the linguistic, semiotic, and psychoanalytic theories that have inflected contemporary film theory. In general terms, film theories that use the term *subject* contain an implicit critique of versimilitude in representation and approach the cinema as a construction that produces *subject*ivity. Lacanian-inflected film theory assumes that subjectivity is structured through visuality. The Lacanian "mirror-phase" implies that the subject only sees itself as whole, *elsewhere*. Although subject-oriented apparatus theories have shifted the debate away from style, theorists have continually questioned the relation between the apparatus and specific textual strategies.

The gaze: I use the term *gaze* to describe mobilized and virtual visuality. While "the male gaze"—aligned with voyeurism and with fetishism—was an early staple of feminist film theory, the gendering of the gaze remains an historical problematic. By questioning the historical paradigms of the panoptic gaze, I wish to reclaim the gaze as a different form of visuality and to continue to interrogate the psychic and physiological relation between body and psyche. Benjamin formulates a description of the gaze of the flâneur ("der Blick des Flaneurs") which relied on physical and psychical mobility.[28] The common contemporary connotation of the "gaze" relies on the (more panoptic) Lacanian description of the "inside-out" structure of a gaze where the subject only sees itself being seen.[29]

The second half of the nineteenth century lives in a sort of
frenzy of the visible. It is, of course, the effect of the *social
multiplication of images:* ever wider distribution of
illustrated papers, waves of print, caricatures, etc. The effect
also, however, of something of a geographical extension of
the *field of the visible* and the representable: by journies,
explorations, colonizations, the whole world becomes
visible at the same time that it becomes appropriatable.[1]

JEAN-LOUIS COMOLLI, "Machines of the Visible" (emphasis added)

In societies where modern conditions of production prevail,
all of life presents itself as *an immense accumulation of
spectacles. Everything that was directly lived has moved away
into a representation.*[2]

GUY DEBORD, *Society of the Spectacle* (emphasis added)

In the nineteenth century, a wide variety of apparatuses extended the "field
of the visible" and turned visualized experience into commodity forms. As
print was disseminated widely, new forms of newspaper illustration
emerged; as lithography was introduced, the caricatures of Daumier,
Grandville, and others burgeoned; as photography became more wide-
spread, the evidentiary means of public and family record were transformed.
The telegraph, the telephone, and electricity increased the speed of communications, the railroad and steamship changed concepts of distance,
while the new visual culture—photography, advertising, and shop display—recast the nature of memory and experience. Whether a "frenzy of

the visible," or "an immense accumulation of spectacles," everyday life was transfigured by the "social multiplication of images."

Yet there remains a historiographical debate about whether this new predominance of the visible produced a crisis of confidence in the eye itself, or whether it was the coincident increase in optical research which produced this frenzy of visual culture. The same historiographic debate pervades the history of the arts; either the invention of photography produced a crisis that led to continued optical research, or the nineteenth-century obsession with optical research produced a crisis that led to photography.[3] In order to organize the vast historical process that led to the emergence of the cinema it is necessary to enter into this debate, a dispute that festers at the roots of modernity.[4]

In this chapter, I begin by describing the "observer" in modernity, situating the emergence of the cinema in the historical framework of precinematic mobile and virtual gazes. Such a "situated" approach to the cinematic apparatus necessitates an account of the imbrication of images in the social relations of looking.[5] The flâneur will serve as a model for an observer who follows a style of visuality different from the model of power and vision so frequently linked with modernity—what Michel Foucault dramatically described as "un régime panoptique."[6] The trope of flânerie delineates a mode of visual practice coincident with—but antithetical to—the panoptic gaze. Like the panopticon system, flânerie relied on the visual register— but with a converse instrumentalism, emphasizing mobility and fluid subjectivity rather than restraint and interpellated reform.

The panoptic gaze has been invoked by feminist theorists to underline the one-way power of gendered looking, where women have internalized the voyeuristic gaze and are always subjectively "objects of the look."[7] As we examine divergent models of the observer in modernity, a refutation of theories of the panoptic gaze will have significant ramifications on accounts of gendered spectatorship. The panoptic gaze may indeed suggest a model for the increased priority of the visual register, but there were alternative gazes that, while still reordering the importance of the visual, produced different—more fluid—forms of subjectivity.

Gender, to follow Teresa de Lauretis's recent formulation, "is the product of various social technologies" that include "*cinema* . . . institutionalized discourses, epistemologies, and critical practices, *as well as practices of daily life*" (emphasis added).[8] And although gender seems a necessary component

of debates about the role of vision in modernity and postmodernity, gene-
alogies of the nineteenth-century observer have, as we will see, retained a
resistance to the gendered subject. Once we establish the flâneur's mobility,
we will see the necessity of charting the origins of his female equivalent,
the flâneuse.

MODERNITY AND THE "PANOPTIC" GAZE   It is in this *episteme*, as Foucault would
have it, that new modes of social and political control were institutionalized
by "un régime panoptique." Foucault places the panoptic model in a pivotal position in the epistemological shift from eighteenth-century empiri-
cism to the invention of a transcendental concept of "man." In a dramatic
passage in *The Order of Things*, he describes this transition as "the threshold
of modernity." Foucault finds the origins of modernity in the reordering
of power and knowledge and the visible.[9]

The Panopticon   Jeremy Bentham's panopticon device (1791) provided the
model for Foucault's characterization of panoptic power and the "disci-
plines" of imagined scrutiny.[10] (*Discipline* has been the common English
translation for Foucault's term, *surveiller*.) Invoked as a philosophic model
for the scopic regime of power through the visual register, the panopticon
was an apparatus—a "machine of the visible," to use Comolli's phrase—
which controlled the seer-seen relation. In the panopticon, an *unseen seer*
surveys a confined and controlled subject.[11] The panopticon produces a
subjective effect, a "brutal dissymmetry of visibility"[12] for both positions
in this dyad: the *seer* with the sense of omnipotent voyeurism and the *seen*
with the sense of disciplined surveillance.

Foucault described the panopticon as an "architectural mechanism,"[13]
a "pure architectural and optical system" that did not need to use force
because the "real subjection is born *mechanically* from a *fictitious relation*."[14]
The panopticon structure was then, in a sense, a "building-machine" that,
through its spatial arrangement, established scopic control over its inhabitants.

The architectural system of the panopticon restructured the relation of
jailer to inmate into a scopic relation of power and domination. The panopticon building was a twelve-sided polygon. Using iron as a skeleton, its
internal and external skin was glass. The central tower was pierced by windows that provided a panoramic view of separate peripheral cells. Light

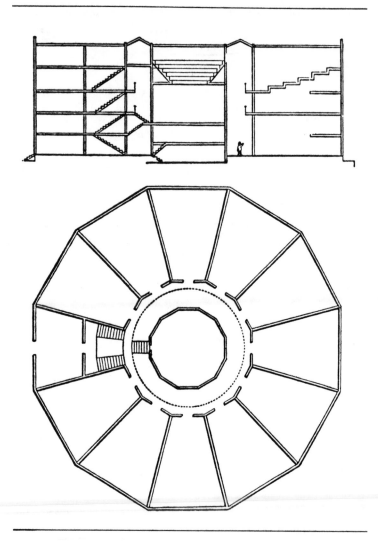

Jeremy Bentham, Section and Plan
of Panopticon building, 1791.

from the outer walls illuminated each cell. The panoptic subject was placed in a state of "conscious and permanent visibility."[15] The panopticon prison was thought of as a spatial reformatorium that could change and "correct" subjectivity by architectural means. As Foucault describes it:

The *seeing machine* was once a sort of dark room into which individuals spied; it has become a transparent building in which the exercise of power may be supervised by society as a whole.[16]

Prisoners were objects of an *imagined* scrutiny, where the internalized sense of surveillance changed the disposition of external power:

He who is subjected to a field of visibility, and who knows it, assumes responsibility for the constraints of power . . . he becomes the principle of his own subjection. By this very fact, the external power may throw off its physical weight; *it tends to the non-corporeal;* and, the more it approaches this limit, the more constant, profound and permanent are its effects.[17] (emphasis added)

Foucault uses the panoptic model to illustrate how, when power enters the visual register, it "tends to the non-corporeal." In the panopticon prison, confinement was successfully maintained by the barrier walls of the prison, but the subjective changes in the inmate were to be produced by the incorporation of the imagined and permanent gaze of the jailer. Bentham's panopticon was designed for other uses than the prison—the factory, the asylum, the hospital—but all of these uses were for institutions where enclosure was a priority.[18]

Hence, the panopticon model has served as a tempting originary root for the inventions that led to the cinema, an apparatus that produces an even more "mechanically . . . fictitious relation" and whose "subjection" is equally internalized.[19] Feminist theorists have invoked the "panoptic" implant as a model for the ever-present "male gaze," while "apparatus" film theories relied more on the immobility and confined spatial matrix of the prison. The prisoners in Plato's cave provide, in Jean-Louis Baudry's emphatic account, an origin for cinematic spectatorship with immobility as a necessary condition.[20]

As an analogy for cinematic spectation, the model of the panoptic guard (the *unseen seer* in the position of omnipotent voyeurism) is not literal, but figurative and metaphoric. Like the central tower guard, the film spectator is totally invisible, absent not only from self-observation but from surveillance as well. But unlike the panoptic guard, the film spectator is not in the position of the central tower, with full scopic range, but is rather a subject with a limited (and preordained) scope. The film spectator's position is one of such *imaginary* visual omnipotence.[21] It is the condition of invisibility which is the premise, in the argument of Baudry, for the spectator-subject's confusion of representation and self-generated perception, what Baudry deemed an "over-cathexis" with representation, a position that guarantees the dependence on the constructed view provided by representation.[22] The panoptic model emphasizes the subjective effects of imagined scrutiny and "permanent visibility" on the *observed*, but does not explore the subjectivity of the *observer*.

In reexamining the emergence of the cinema, one can trace the roots of an instrumentalization of visual culture which is coincident with, but also different from, the paradigm of panoptic visuality. A brief comparison of the panopticon (1791) with two other important devices—the panorama (1792) and the diorama (1823)—will suggest alternative models for visuality.

The panorama and the diorama were building-machines with a different objective: designed to *transport*—rather than to *confine*—the spectator-subject.[23] As we will see, these devices produced a spatial and temporal mobility—if only a "virtual" one. The panoramic and dioramic observer was deceptively accorded an *imaginary* illusion of mobility. In Walter Benjamin's conversely demonstrative rhetoric, cinematic spectatorship functioned as an explosive ("dynamite of a tenth of a second") that freed the spectator from the "prison-world" (*Kerkerwelt*) of nineteenth-century architectural space.[24]

MODERNITY AND THE "VIRTUAL" GAZE

The Panorama

At leisure let us view from day to day,
As they present themselves, *the spectacles*
Within doors: troops of wild beast, bird and beasts
Of every nature from all climes convened,
And, next to these, *those mimic sights that ape*
The absolute presence of reality

Expressing as in mirror sea and land,
And what earth is, and what she hath to shew—
I do not here allude to subtlest craft,
By means refined attaining purest ends,
But imitations fondly made in plain
Confession of man's weakness and his loves.
Whether the painter—*fashioning a work*
To Nature's circumambient scenery

WILLIAM WORDSWORTH, describing the panorama, in the 1805 *Prelude*
(Seventh Book, lines 244–257, emphasis added)

As Wordsworth notes, the panorama was not the "subtlest craft" for presenting "the absolute presence of reality." But its "spectacles/Within doors" of "every nature from all climes" used "circumambient scenery" to create an artificial elsewhere for the panoramic spectator.

The panorama was a 360-degree cylindrical painting, viewed by an observer in the center. The illusion presented by the panorama was created by a combination of realist techniques of perspective and scale with a mode of viewing that placed the spectator in the center of a darkened room surrounded by a scene lit from above. The panorama was first patented by the Irishman Robert Barker, who took out a patent for panoramic painting in Edinburgh in 1787 and opened the first completely circular panorama in Leicester Square in London in 1792.[25] (Recall the years of Bentham's work on the panopticon, from 1787 to 1791.) Barker's inspiration for the panorama came, according to an anecdote told by historian Olive Cook, in a manner worthy of comparison to Bentham's panopticon prison:

> The invention of the Panorama is usually attributed to Robert Barker, an Edinburgh painter. In about 1785 he was put into prison for debt and was confined to a cell lit by a grating let into the wall at the junction of wall and ceiling. One day he was reading a letter and to see more clearly carried it below the grating. *The effect when the paper was held in the shaft of light falling from the opening was so astonishing that Barker's imagination was set working on the possibilities of controlled light flung from above upon pictures of large dimensions.*[26] (emphasis added)

If "controlled light" served to survey and measure the wards in the panopticon prison, in an opposite way it also served to create the visual illusions of the panorama.

68. *Schnitt durch Barkers doppelstöckige Panoramarotunde am Leicester Square um 1798 (Mitchell).*

Cross-section of Barker's

panorama, 1792.

The panorama did not physically *mobilize* the body, but provided virtual spatial and temporal mobility, bringing the country to the town dweller, transporting the past to the present. The panoramic spectator lost, as Helmut Gernsheim described, "all judgement of distance and space" and "in the absence of any means of comparison with real objects, a perfect illusion was given."[27] The panorama offered a spectacle in which all sense of time and space was lost, produced by the combination of the observer in a darkened room (where there were no markers of place or time) and presentation of "realistic" views of other places and times.

The ideology of representation in the panoramic painting must be placed in the context of the concurrent reconceptualization of the idea of the horizon and of perspective (the first hot air balloon was launched in 1783 and aerial balloonists found vistas that radically changed the landscape perspective) and the "cult of immensity" in painting, where scale was a factor in the concept of illusionist immersion. In addition, the panorama developed out of the context of earlier "screen" entertainments.

The "magic lantern" devices of Athanasius Kircher, Johannes Zahn, and others introduced a form of projected entertainment spectacle that relied on controlled light projected through glass slides: drawn figures of skeletons, demons, and ghosts appeared on a screen surface.[28] In his text of 1646, *Ars Magna Lucis et Umbrae,* Kircher (1601–1680)—a Roman Catholic priest—published his procedures for projecting ghostly apparitions. Whether, as Musser argues, Kircher sought to demystify the "magic" of the lantern or whether, to the contrary, he trained a new legion of mystifiers, the eerie effects produced by these luminous projections established an early link between two potentially competing systems of subjective interpellation: religion and optics.[29] Kircher concealed the lantern from his audiences by placing it on the other side of the screen. He could change the distance of the lantern, vary the sizes of his figures. Musser traces the roots of cinema in these forms of late eighteenth-century forms of "screen practice." These entertainments—shadow plays, phantasmagorias, lantern displays—relied on dark rooms and projected light.

Philip Jacob de Loutherbourg, a French-born painter and stage designer who came to England in 1771, had designed a viewing system, the *eidophusikon* (1781), which also relied on spectators in a darkened auditorium viewing an illuminated (ten foot by six foot) translucent screen, with light projected from behind. The eidophusikon spectacle produced simulations of sunsets, fog, and dawn accompanied by sound effects and harpsichord music.[30] In Paris, a device called the phantasmagoria similarly relied on a lantern with lens to project drawings of celebrities from Voltaire to Rousseau to Marat. Étienne-Gaspard Robertson—a self-styled *aéronaute* to whom the invention of the parachute is attributed—devised a magic lantern show set in a Capuchin monastery. The phantasmagoria debuted in Paris from 1797 to 1800, traveled to London from 1801 to 1803, and arrived in New York in 1803.

Phantasmagorias, panoramas, dioramas—devices that concealed their machinery—were dependent on the relative immobility of their spectators, who enjoyed the illusion of presence of virtual figures. These apparatuses produced an illusion of unmediated referentiality. Other optical entertainments that required viewing devices—the stereoscope, the phenakistoscope—were dependent on quite different optical principles and hence produced diverse subjective effects.[31]

Benjamin saw a direct relation between the panoramic observer and the flâneur:

86. Die Panoramarotunden am Boulevard Montmartre mit der Passage, um 1802 (Ceram, Archäologie).

Built in 1800, the Passage des
Panoramas cut between the two
panorama rotundas on the
Boulevard Montmarte.

The city-dweller . . . attempts to introduce the countryside into the city. In the panoramas the city dilates to become landscape, as it does in a subtler way for the *flâneur*.[32]

Before the advent of illustrated print journalism in the 1840s, the panorama supplied a visual illustration of places and events that one could read about in print. The panorama not only appealed to the public interest in battles and historical illustration, but also to a fascination with landscape art, travel literature, and travel itself. As Richard Altick argues, the panorama was the "bourgeois public's substitute for the Grand Tour."[33]

Dolf Sternberger has emphasized that the lure of these entertainments was not in their verisimilitude with reality, but rather in their deceptive skills, their very artificiality.[34] As an early epitome of the lure of artificiality, in 1823 Yorkshireman Thomas Hornor climbed the top of St. Paul's with sketching implements and telescopes and sketched London in 360-degree detail. Hornor's gigantic rendering was housed in Decimus Burton's Colosseum. The building took years to build (1824–1829) but, when finished, encased a panorama of remarkable verisimilitude: a simulated London viewed from the top of a simulated St. Paul's. The rooftop location of this panorama necessitated a new design feature: the first hydraulic passenger lift ("ascending room") carried spectators who did not wish to climb the stairs.[35] The elevator was a mechanical aid to mobility; the gaze at the end of this "lift" was virtual.

The panorama was taken to Paris in 1799 by Robert Fulton,[36] who had purchased the foreign patent rights. Two rotundas for the panorama were built in Paris on Boulevard Montmartre. In the interior were two paintings, one that displayed a view of Paris from the Tuilleries and another that showed the British evacuation during the Battle of Toulon in 1793. The immediate city—the Paris of only blocks away—was presented to itself; but so was a distant city (Toulon) at a distant time (six years before). Sternberger has aptly named these panoramic paintings, "captured historical moment(s)."[37]

In 1800, the Passage des Panoramas was built to connect the Palais Royal to the panorama on Boulevard Monmartre. The cylindrical panorama building was connected directly to the Passage des Panoramas—one entered through the arcade. The panorama was lit from above by the same glass and iron skylight as the arcade. In the next chapter, we will examine the relationship between the passage—an architectural and social space designed for flânerie—and these precinematic devices for mobilizing a virtual gaze.[38]

The Diorama   Louis Jacques Mandé Daguerre, later famed for his 1839 invention of a photographic process he named the daguerreotype, began his career as an assistant to the celebrated panorama painter, Pierre Prévost. In 1822, Daguerre debuted a viewing device that expanded upon the panorama's ability to transport the viewer, an apparatus he called the diorama.[39]

Like the *diaphanorama*—in which translucent watercolors were illuminated from behind—the dioramic illusion relied on the manipulation of light through a transparent painting.[40] Daguerre's visitors looked through a proscenium at a scene composed of objects arranged in front of a backdrop; after a few minutes, the auditorium platform was rotated seventy-three degrees to expose another dioramic opening.[41] The diorama was designed to construct and restructure—through light and movement—the relation of the viewer to the spatial and temporal present. A scene was transformed through the manipulation of daylight, which shifted the temporal mood.[42] The diorama differed significantly from the panorama: the diorama spectator was immobile, at the center of the building, and the "views" were mobilized as the entire diorama building with its pulleys, cords, and rollers became a machine for changing the spectator's view.

When the diorama opened in Paris in 1822, it displayed two distant tableaux: "The Valley of Sarnen," a scene from Switzerland, and "Interior of Trinity Church—Canterbury Cathedral," a scene from England. Of the thirty-two scenes exhibited during the seventeen years of its existence, ten of the paintings were interiors of distant chapels or cathedrals.[43] As a local newspaper account indicated:

We cannot sufficiently urge Parisians who like pleasure without fatigue to make the journey to Switzerland and to England without leaving the capital.[44]

Helmut and Alison Gernsheim extend this description of the diorama as a substitute for travel:

The many foreign views, too, no doubt had a special appeal to the general public who, before the days of Cook's Tours, had little chance of travelling abroad."[45]

Dioramas opened in other cities, in Breslau in 1826, in Berlin in 1827, in Stockholm in 1846, and in Frankfurt in 1852. (Thomas Cook's first guided tours of the continent were in 1855.) There were other variations on the diorama. The *pleorama,* which opened in Berlin in 1832, had the audience seated in a ship and taken for an hour's "voyage," as the illusion of movement was created by the backcloth moving slowly across the stage.[46] This device emphasized the equation otherwise implicit between travel and viewing scenes of the distant and of the past.

In 1839, Daguerre's diorama on Rue Sanson in Paris was destroyed by fire. In that same year, he patented a technique for *fixing* images on copper plates, the "daguerreotype." Few dioramic or panoramic paintings survive.

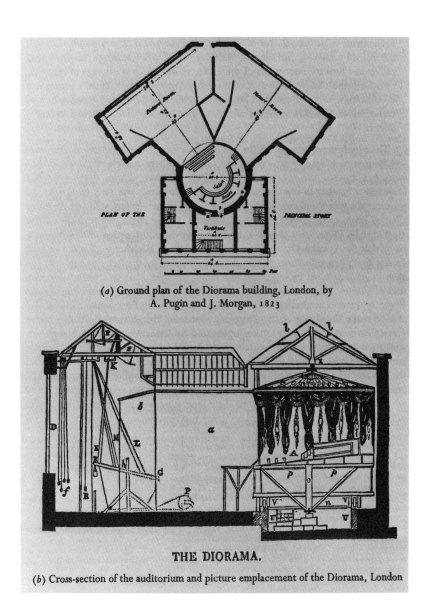

(*a*) Ground plan of the Diorama building, London, by
A. Pugin and J. Morgan, 1823

THE DIORAMA.

(*b*) Cross-section of the auditorium and picture emplacement of the Diorama, London

Cross-section and ground plan of the Diorama
building, London. Louis Jacques Mandé Daguerre,
1822.

The illusions produced were dependent on the effects of artificial light, and many of the paintings, and the buildings which housed them, ended in flames. The "captured historical moment" could be more securely impounded on a photographic plate. Benjamin will remark on this historical coincidence; photography emerged from the ashes of the diorama.[47]

Both the panorama and its successor, the diorama, offered new forms of virtual mobility to its viewer. But a paradox here must be emphasized: as the "mobility" of the gaze became more "virtual"—as techniques were developed to paint (and then to photograph) realistic images, as mobility was implied by changes in lighting (and then cinematography)—the observer became more immobile, passive, ready to receive the constructions of a virtual reality placed in front of his or her unmoving body.

The Panopticon versus the Diorama   Like the panopticon,[48] the diorama-building was an architectural arrangement with a center position for the *seer* with a view to "cells" or "galleries." Yet unlike the observation tower of the panopticon, the diorama platform turned (the auditorium rotated seventy-three degrees) to mobilize the viewer. The diorama had a *collective observer,* a shared audience on the moving platform. Dioramas and panoramas were not directly instruments of social engineering (cf. Fourier's phalanstery) but were, nevertheless, conceived of as satisfying a social desire or curiosity—a desire to have visual mastery over the constraints of space and time. The technology of the diorama relied on spectator immobility, but offered a visual excursion and a virtual release from the confinements of everyday space and time.

But if the panopticon was dependent on the enclosure of the look, the inward measure of confined but visible subjects, the diorama was dependent on the imaginary expansion of that look. Unlike the jailer-surveyor, the dioramic spectator was not attempting mastery over human subjects, but was instead engaged in the pleasures of mastery over an artificially constructed world, the pleasure of immersion in a world not present.

In the diorama, the spectator sat on a darkened center platform and looked toward the brightness of the peripheral scenes: transparent paintings where light was manipulated to give the effect of time passing—a sunset, or the changing light of the day. In the panopticon, the role of light was to indict, to measure.[49] In the diorama, light played a deceptive role. In the panopticon, there was no spatial illusion, no fooling with time.

Both panoptic and dioramic systems required a degree of spectator immobility and the predominance of the visual function.[50] And it is this notion of the confined *place* combined with a notion of *journey* that is present simultaneously in cinematic spectation.

THE BAUDELAIREAN OBSERVER: THE "MOBILIZED" GAZE OF THE FLÂNEUR Baudelaire, of course, provides an eloquent testimony of the observer in modernity.[51] As poet and art critic, Baudelaire positioned himself in the midst of a nineteenth-century city, Paris (and later Brussels), wandering through its panorama of gaslit streets, cafes, theaters, brothels, parks, and passages, collecting images that he would record in newspaper reviews and prose poems. In the famed essay of 1863, "Le Peintre de la vie moderne," Baudelaire extols the work of the artist Constantin Guys as "the painter of modern life."[52] "Modernity," Baudelaire explains in this essay, is that part of art "which is ephemeral, fugitive, contingent upon the occasion; it is half of art, whose other half is the eternal and unchangeable."[53] But the essay was less a celebration of Guys than it was a paean to the flâneur who provides a vivid example of "the impassioned observer":

To the perfect spectator, the impassioned observer, it is an immense joy to make his domicile amongst numbers, amidst fluctuation and movement, amidst the fugitive and infinite. *To be away from home, and yet to feel at home; to behold the world, to be in the midst of the world and yet to remain hidden from the world*—these are some of the minor pleasures of such independent, impassioned and impartial spirits, whom words can only clumsily describe. . . . *the observer is a prince who always rejoices in his incognito.*[54] (emphasis added)

To Baudelaire, this "perfect spectator" was resolutely *male,* an observing "prince" who was allowed the paradoxical pleasure: to be at home away from home, in the midst of the world and yet hidden from it, impassioned and yet impartial, here and yet elsewhere. The Baudelairean observer was a (male) painter or a (male) poet—a flâneur—whose mobility through the urban landscape allowed him access to the public sphere of the streets and to the domestic realms of the home. He had a fluidity of social position, a mutable subjectivity. In *Paris Spleen,* Baudelaire describes the "mysterious drunkenness," the "art" of "enjoying a crowd," as a privilege available only to "*l'Homme des foules.*"[55] Yet, as Baudelaire insists, these pleasures were not available to just *any* man, but to one with "the love of masks and masquerade, the hate of home and *the passion for roaming*" (emphasis added).[56]

While Baudelaire's flâneur is mediated through his textual constructs (vividly central to the *Tableaux parisiens* section of *Les Fleurs du Mal*), the flâneur was not a fiction. An 1841 edition of *Les Français: Encyclopédie Morale du Dix-neuvième Siècle* provides a physiognomy of "Le Flâneur" as "une personnification toute française."[57] To Baudelaire, the flâneur was an archetypal Parisian, a poet whose language traced the texture and chaos of urban life.

Yet Baudelaire's aesthetic is symptomatic of the nineteenth century's ambivalence toward new forms of visual culture. Although he was actively extolling the mobile gaze of the flâneur "always travelling across the great human desert"[58]—celebrating observation and spectation—Baudelaire was equally vehement in his polemic against photography, the new technology for recording these observations. Baudelaire's *scopophilic* preference was for an unaided urban mobility—the pace of the flâneur through the chaos of urbanity; Baudelaire's *scopophobia* was directed at the apparatus for recording these observations.[59] Baudelaire, champion of the flâneur, was polemically opposed to the flâneur's apparatical replacement, photography; he was a partisan of a mobilized but not virtual gaze.

In *The Salon of 1859,* Baudelaire decried photography as "art's most mortal enemy" and suggested that it harms the viewing public to view copies of nature, not works of imagination.[60] Baudelaire's complaint that photography was but a "cheap method of disseminating a loathing for history"[61] underlines his insistence on the fluidity of the (male) urban subject *not* being contained or confined, not fixed.[62] "The passion for roaming" contradicted the "fixing" of the visual image into a photographic record. The movements of the Baudelairean flâneur produced a "mobilized gaze," a moving nowhere, neither here nor elsewhere. Yet Baudelaire did not embrace the visual mobilities offered by photography. Photography offered a mobilized gaze through a "virtual real," changed one's relation to bodily movement, to the act of looking, to history, and to memory. The Baudelairean flâneur was a male whose social mobility was replaced by the virtual mobilities produced by the photograph. As Susan Sontag records:

In fact, photography first comes into its own as an extension of the eye of the middle-class *flâneur*, whose sensibility was so accurately charted by Baudelaire. The photographer is an armed version of the solitary walker reconnoitering, stalking, cruising the urban inferno, the voyeuristic stroller who discovers the city as a landscape of voluptuous extremes.[63]

The photographer, an "armed version of the solitary walker," could produce "virtual" visual records of his flânerie.[64]

Nadar (Felix Tournachon, 1820–1910) was an exemplary prototype of such a flâneur. A caricaturist, art critic, balloonist, the inspiration of the character in his friend Jules Verne's *The Journey from Earth to Moon*, Nadar's photographs captured such "voluptous extremes." Nadar took his camera above Paris in a balloon (1858), into the sewers and catacombs (1861), and coaxed studio portraits from Sarah Bernhardt, George Sand, Alexandre Dumas, and even Baudelaire.

In its rapid global deployment of "armed walkers," photography transformed the "field of the visible." (Between 1863 and 1866, Samuel Bourne took photographic equipment along to record his travels in the Himalayas; John Thompson recorded his travels in China in 1873; Matthew Brady made historic records of the battles of the Civil War.) The fugitive present became a captured virtual presence.

As we consider these changes in the "field of the visible," it is worth addressing Jonathan Crary's recent challenges to the history of "techniques of the observer" in the nineteenth century. In Crary's polemical rereading of the history of perception, the perceptual paradigm of the seventeenth- and eighteenth-century *camera obscura* typified a system of "representation, cognition and subjectivity" which is "fundamentally discontinuous" from the models of perception for the nineteenth-century observer.[65] Crary maintains that the dominant perceptual assumptions surrounding the seventeenth- and eighteenth-century observer—that the camera obscura presented a "real" and "true" representation of the world and that optical apparatuses were the source of their produced effect—gave way, in the nineteenth century, to a physiological optics that describes the subjectivity of vision. This produced, in Crary's account, a dramatic epistemological shift from apparatically-produced subjectivity to a "corporeal subjectivity," where the body was "the active producer of optical experience."[66]

⟨ But to Crary, the "body of the observer" is not a gendered body. He analyzes the discursive context of visual apparatuses, not their social function. He begins:

an observer posited . . . as . . . the autonomous producer of *his or her* own content. This essay seeks to describe some of the features of this new kind of observer and to suggest how *his or her* formation in the nineteenth century was immanent to the elaboration of new empirical knowledge of vision and techniques of the visible.[67] (emphasis added)

Despite the initial and pronounced pronoun inclusion of the gendered subject (his or her), Crary backs away from a sexualized or gendered notion of psychic functioning when he discusses the *body* of the observer. [68]

Crary's observer is in a paradoxical position, simultaneously experiencing the *mobility* of images ("new abstraction and mobility of images"[69]) and the *rigidity* of images ("disciplining . . . the observer in terms of rigidly fixed relations to image and apparatus"[70]). Crary doesn't expand upon the implications of these dialectically opposed forms of observation. And yet, the combination of the mobility and rigidity of images seems to offer the foundation for a paradigm shift to a more fluid subjectivity further from the positioned *body* of the observer.[71]

THE GENDER OF THE OBSERVER: THE FLÂNEUSE

⟨ The moment the look dominates, the body loses its materiality.

LUCE IRIGARAY[72]

And if the eye which moves is no longer fettered by a body, by the laws of matter and time, if there are no more assignable limits to its displacement—conditions fulfilled by the possibilities of shooting and of film—the world will be constituted not only by this eye but for it.

JEAN LOUIS BAUDRY, "Ideological Effects of the Basic Apparatus"[73]

Our society is characterized by a cancerous growth of vision, measuring everything by its ability to show or be shown and transmuting communication into a visual journey.

MICHEL DECERTEAU, *The Practice of Everyday Life*[74]

The above epigraphs imply very different theories of the body and the visual. For Irigaray "the look" replaces the body, separates itself from it, and renders the body immaterial. Baudry describes the cinema as an apparatical prosthesis, a substitute for the eye *without* a body. DeCerteau metaphorizes a social body, victim to the unstoppable growth of the visual function, which has metastasized into all aspects of everyday life. But in each of these cases, the act of seeing—perception through the visual register—is described in terms of its displacement of the body. Although the above theorists may at first seem dissimilar, they all hail from a French "episteme" and their theories converge along the assumption that the body is a fiction, a decorporealized subjectivity sliding fluidly among a variety of positions. I want to pose a historical framework for the origins of this form of subjectivity, whose "mobility" is routed through the "virtual."

As the gendered French noun designates, the flâneur was a male urban subject, endowed with a gaze at an elusive and almost unseen flâneuse. The flâneur could be an urban poet, whose movements through a newly configured urban space often transformed the female's presence into a textual homage.[75]

In "A une passante," one of the most famous sonnets of *Les Fleurs du Mal,* Baudelaire evokes the fleeting sight of a woman in the modern city. Amid the deafening noise of the street (*la rue assourdissante*), a majestic but mourning woman (*a douleur majesteuse*) passes by (*une femme passe*). It is here that the flâneur meets, in an eye-line match, the gaze of a woman. In such a momentary *fascinum* her gaze is returned, but only momentarily, and then lost.

A flash . . . then night! O lovely fugitive,
I am suddenly reborn from your swift glance;
shall I never see you till eternity?

[Un éclair . . . puis la nuit!—Fugitive beauté
Dont le regard m'a fait soudainement renâitre,
Ne te verrai-je plus que dans l'éternité?][76]

In another poem from *Les Fleurs du Mal,* the flâneur meets the gaze of a woman whose presence in urban space is equated with the lure of the commodity:

Your eyes, lit up like shops to lure their trade . . .
Or fireworks in the park on holidays,
insolently make use of borrowed power
and never learn (you might say, "in the dark")
what law it is that governs their good looks.
[Tes yeux, illuminés ainsi que des boutiques
Et des if flamboyants dans les fêtes publiques,
Usent insolemment d'un pouvoir emprunté
Sans connaître jamais la loi de leur beauté.][77]

"Lit up like shops to lure their trade," the eyes of Baudelaire's *femme* "make use of borrowed power." In this imagery, the woman is almost a shop mannequin, whose gaze is made of "borrowed power" seized, one assumes, from the lure of the luxury item in a shop window as if in a triangulated bid for seduction. The flâneur becomes an easy prototype for the consumer, whose perceptual style of "just looking" was the pedestrian equivalent of slow motion. But Baudelaire did not consider the power of the woman's gaze *to* the shop window—a gaze imbued with the power of choice and incorporation through purchase. It was as a consumer that the flâneuse was born.

Les Fleurs du Mal, Baudelaire's collection of reveries on Parisian flânerie, was the cornerstone of Benjamin's massive and uncompleted work on modernity, his study of the Paris arcades. The poems of *Les Fleurs du Mal* recorded "the gaze of the flâneur"[78] on "Paris—Capital of the Nineteenth Century." Benjamin's flâneur was a palimpsestic construct: a textual flâneur taken from the Baudelairean city of the middle nineteenth century as well as an actual flâneur—Benjamin himself, roaming the arcades and cafes of Paris in the 1920s and 1930s. For Benjamin, the flâneur "who goes botanizing on the asphalt"[79] was the quintessential paradigm of the subject in modernity, wandering through urban space in a daze of distraction.[80] The arcades of Paris, dank sites of both the textual and actual flâneur, represented a symptomatic urban space, readable in a *Kulturkritik* of urban subjectivity.[81]

> The crowd was the veil from behind which the familiar city as phantasmagoria beckoned to the *flâneur*. In it the city was now landscape, now a room. And both of these went into the construction of the department store, *which made use of flânerie itself in order to sell goods.* The department store was the *flâneur*'s final coup.[82] (emphasis added)

Traffic and the decline of the arcade killed the flâneur and his perceptual patterns of distracted observation and dreamlike reverie. But it was the (male) flâneur who was at home in this privatized public space. As Susan Buck-Morss has stunningly detailed, if women roamed the street they became "streetwalkers," prostitutes, carnal commodities on sale alongside other items in the arcade.[83] Women were objects for consumption, objects for the gaze of the flâneur, or the poet who, like Baudelaire, would notice women as mere *passersby*.[84]

And as the work of Baudelaire and Crary suggests, most theories of the "observer" in the nineteenth century are either ungendered or resolutely male. Even though nineteenth-century perceptual theories may not have addressed sexuality, once we assess the cultural uses of perceptual apparatuses—the function that they serve in the experience of everyday life—then the question of gender in the "body" of the observer becomes a far more pertinent aspect in the arrangements of social power.

As a familiar idiom of feminist methodology, when the question of gender is posed to (otherwise normative) theories that evade sexuality, a new set of questions begins to appear. It was precisely while these changes in the observer were occurring in the nineteenth century that women were changing their social role and were allowed a new and more public access to mobility through urban space. As consumers, women had a new set of social prerogatives in which their social powerlessness was crossed with new paradoxes of subjective power.

In a challenge to the histories of modernity or modernism which evade the issue of sexuality, Griselda Pollock has argued that any such account of nineteenth-century art history "ensures the normalcy of that position leav-

ing it [sexual difference] below the threshold of historical investigation and
theoretical analysis."[85] In Pollock's critique, a class-aware art critic such as
T. J. Clark may describe modernist paintings that "imply a masculine
viewer/consumer" but, as she points out, Clark neglects to address the
presence of female observers or the *absence* of female artists, both factors
that offer a more precise account of the sexual politics of modernism.

Clark discusses the oscillation between two divergent painterly representations of woman in the nineteenth century—the *fille publique* (woman of
the streets) and the *femme honnête* (the respectable married woman).[86] As
we will see, to find the origins of a female observer—a public woman who
was neither a fille publique nor a femme honnête—one has to turn to new
spaces that appeared in the mid-nineteenth century, public spaces such as
the department store or the amusement park, spaces where women could
exist outside of these two narrow definitions.[87] The flâneuse was the nineteenth-century version of a female observer, whose gaze was mobilized in
these new public spaces of modernity.

The female flâneur, the flâneuse, was not possible until she was free to
roam the city on her own.[88] And this was equated with the privilege of
shopping on her own. The development in the late nineteenth century of
shopping as socially acceptable leisure activity for bourgeois women, as a
"pleasure rather than a necessity,"[89] encouraged women to be peripatetic
without escort. Department stores became a central fixture in the capitalist
city in the mid-nineteenth century. In Paris, Bon Marché opened a store
in 1852, Macy's opened in New York in 1857, and others followed. Only
gradually did these *grand magasins* begin to employ women as shop clerks,
allowing the female to be both buyer and seller.[90] It wasn't until the closing
decades of the century that the department store became a safe haven for
unchaperoned women.[91]

The flâneuse appeared in the public spaces—department stores—made
possible by the new configurations of consumer culture.[92] The flâneuse was
empowered in a paradoxical sense: new freedoms of lifestyle and "choice"
were available, but, as feminist theorists have amply illustrated, women were
addressed as consumers in ways that played on deeply rooted cultural constructions of gender.

The impossibility of a flâneuse has been forcefully argued by Janet
Wolff.[93] Wolff describes a modernity that was predominately identified
with the public sphere of work, politics and urban life—realms that were

exclusively male. In her account, the literature of modernity accepts the confinement of women to the private sphere, and hence fails to delineate women's experience. Certainly the literature that Wolff surveys—Simmel, Baudelaire, Benjamin—describes the experience of men in the public sphere from which women are invisible.[94] Wolff wants to produce a feminist sociology that would supply the experiences of women, but it seems important also to turn to some literary texts by female "modernists."[95] As Pollock has shown with Berthe Morisot and Mary Cassatt, paintings by nineteenth-century women provide vivid illustration of women in urban spaces.[96] And, although Wolff does mention that consumerism is a central aspect of modernity and that the establishment of the department store in the 1850s and 1860s created an new arena for the public appearance of women, she does not consider the female consumer as an important figure.

Yet it is precisely here that I find the origins of the new social character, the flâneuse. Shopping, like other itinerancies of the late nineteenth century—museum- and exhibition-going, packaged tourism and, of course, the cinema—relied on the visual register and helped to ensure the predominance of the gaze in capitalist society. The department store that, like the arcade before it, "made use of *flânerie* itself in order to sell goods,"[97] constructed fantasy worlds for itinerant lookers. But unlike the arcade, the department store offered a protected site for the empowered gaze of the flâneuse. Endowed with purchase power, she was the target of consumer address. New desires were created *for her* by advertising and consumer culture;[98] desires elaborated in a system of selling and consumption which depended on the relation between *looking* and *buying,* and the indirect desire to possess and incorporate through the eye. The department store may have been, as Benjamin put it, the flâneur's last coup, but it was the flâneuse's first.

THE "MOBILIZED" AND "VIRTUAL" GAZE   In the nineteenth century, a wide variety of apparatuses turned the pleasures of flânerie into a commodity form, negotiated new illusions of spatial and temporal mobility. Unlike the confinement of the panoptic system, many protocinematic devices negotiated spatial and temporal illusions. In short, all of these forms depended on the immobility of the spectator, a stasis rewarded by the imaginary mobilities that such fixity provided.

While the nineteenth-century observer may well have been offered the illusion of mobility, it was at first only a spatial mobility. The illusion of temporal mobility became more effectively produced in cinematic spectation. Such imaginary flânerie produced a new form of subjectivity—not only decorporealized and derealized, but detemporalized as well. And these new pleasures—more possible, more public—were available to women for the first time.

Hence, as Crary has indicated, we can trace the subjective shifts produced by apparatuses that separate the referent from the experience and locate perception in the "body" of the observer. In chapter 2 we will examine the even further severing of experience from referent, extending the illusion of spatial mobility into the *illusion of temporal mobility*. For the cinematic observer, the body itself is a fiction, a site for departure and return.

As we turn to a consideration of the architectural and social contexts—arcades, department stores, exhibition halls—the timeless spaces that encouraged flânerie, we can begin to correlate the nineteenth-century instrumentalization of flânerie into "commodity-experiences" with the emergence of cinematic "time machines" that extended this mobility in a virtual fashion.

Modernity is marked by the paradoxes of industrial growth; as the expansion of the city destroyed nature, the desire for parks and gardens increased. The city itself redefined the gaze. New means of transportation provided an unprecedented urban mobility, the broadened boulevards produced unimpeded forms of urban circulation, shop windows invited passersby to engage in imaginative new sites of looking. The flâneur's movements through urban space were, in the rhetoric of deCerteau, "pedestrian speech acts." Such a "rhetoric of walking" was also transformed to the textual constructs of literature of the nineteenth-century city.[99]

Benjamin will serve as our initial guide through this critical passage; his work on flânerie and the arcade, on the commodity and memory, on the cinema and photography as "mechanical reproduction," provides a preliminary Baedeker to the transformations between the nineteenth century and the present.

Appearance / memory traces — past that makes
(Mother's skirt)

prod. use of nostalgia
in order to spark
n rev. potential —

Au Bon Marché was the model for Zola's fictional store, Au Bonheur des Dames. Bon Marché carte postale, circa 1900.

THE LADIES' PARADISE BY ÉMILE ZOLA

Émile Zola's 1883 novel of a grand magasin makes apparent the purpose of the department store: for the pleasure of women. As if an implicit conflation of the pleasures of reading with the newly wrought pleasures available in the public sphere of consumption, the name of Zola's fictional store, Au Bonheur des Dames, is also the name of his eleventh novel. *Au Bonheur des Dames* describes the transformation of Denise Baudu, a young woman of twenty who comes to Paris from the country town of Valognes. In her first moments in the teeming metropolis, fresh from the Saint-Lazare railway station, Denise becomes transfixed in front of the windows of a grand magasin. In the shop windows Denise sees silk stockings and gloves in symmetrical array, silks, satins, and velvets arranged in a spectrum of colors and textures, lace dresses and woolen mantles worn by mannequins with slim waists and long necks. For Zola, the store window makes the equation between women and commodity quite explicit:

The well-rounded neck and graceful figures of the dummies exaggerated the slimness of the waist, *the absent head being replaced by a large price-ticket pinned on the neck;* whilst the mirrors, cleverly arranged on each side of the window, reflected and multiplied the forms without end, *peopling the street with these beautiful women for sale, each bearing a price in big figures in the place of a head.*[1] (emphasis added)

Even before Denise goes to work in Au Bonheur des Dames, she

began to feel as if she were watching a machine working at full pressure communicating its movement even as far as the windows. . . . There was a crowd before them, groups of women pushing and squeezing, devouring the finery with longing, covetous eyes. . . . And all that went on in an orderly manner, with mechanical regularity, quite *a nation of women passing through the force and logic of this wonderful commercial machine.*[2] (emphasis added)

Throughout the novel Zola maintains this description of the store as a "commercial machine," fueled by the masses of women that teem through its doors. The store's owner, Mouret, arranges the objects on display, aware that they produce an almost mesmerizing effect on the women who pass them, the "crowded sea of customers, this sea of bodies, swelling with life, beating with desire":[3]

> Mouret's unique passion was *to conquer woman*. He wished her to be queen in his house, and he had built this temple to get her completely at his mercy. *His sole aim was to intoxicate her with gallant attentions, and traffic on her desires, work on her fever.*[4] (emphasis added)

The department store, like the arcade before it, constructed a sheltered refuge for itinerant lookers, a sanctuary for consumption kept separate from the domain of production. Zola's grand magasin was a consumer empire in which "women reigned supreme,"[5] where shopping was a "new religion," a site for the empowered gaze of the flâneuse. Either as leisured consumers or as working-class *calicots* (saleswomen), women were encouraged to enter this public sphere and, as the sign posted at the entrances indicated, free admission promised a form of liberation: *entrée libre.*

The "paradise" of the department store relied on the relation between *looking* and *buying,* and the indirect desire to possess and incorporate through the eye. Of course, along with the creation of new desires, new disorders emerged: impulse buying, binge shopping, shopping bulimia, agoraphobia, and agoramania. Zola's portrait of female consumer behavior was attuned to these newly produced neuroses:

> Madame Marty, carried away by her rage for spending, took everything at the Ladies Paradise, without choosing, just as articles appeared; Madame Guibal walked about the shop for hours without ever buying anything, happy and satisfied to simply feast her eyes; Madame de Boves, short of money, always tortured by some immoderate wish, nourished a feeling of rancour against the goods she could not carry away; Madame Bourdelais, with the sharp eye of a careful practical housewife, made straight for the bargains, using the big establishments with such a clever housewife's skill that she saved a heap of money; and lastly Henriette, who, very elegant, only procured certain articles there, such as gloves, hosiery and her coarser linen.[6]

While these changes were transforming the bourgeoise in Paris, in other capitalist cities—in New York, Chicago, London, Berlin—the department store was becoming a common temple of consumption, as Zola put it, a "cathédrale du commerce moderne."[7]

The novel addresses its readers as if they too were shoppers entering an illusory realm, desiring transubstantiation through purchase. Reading was a leisure activity conducted by women in the private sphere.[8] Zola's own prose descriptions function, as Kristin Ross has keenly noted, like Mouret's display strategy:

Readers are presented with a flux of rapidly described part objects: both goods and body parts . . . Zola's phrases and clauses crowd together, eclipsing the verb, creating the impression of syntactic blocks as movable or interchangeable as any of the counter displays in Mouret's store.[9]

Ross also describes the structural architecture of the novel's narrative matrix, which counterbalances the horizontal expansion of the store with the "vertical momentum" of Denise's career rise in store management.[10] The "Ladies Paradise" destroys family businesses and produces myriad collateral melodramas. As the magasin expands, colonizing adjacent small businesses, buying up property in the surrounding neighborhood, the store itself becomes a monstrous embodiment of Paris, then undergoing Haussmann's planification. Denise, whose uncle's business has been ruined by the store's commercial expansion, is caught in the tug of allegiances between the blood relatives who have coolly welcomed her and her brothers to Paris and the commercial organization that hires her into its paternalizing custody.

In *The Ladies' Paradise* there is one woman who frequents the store who is neither one of the many respectable married women—the *femme honnêtes*, Mademoiselle Marty, Mademoiselle de Boves, Mademoiselle Bourdelais—nor a prostitute, a *fille publique*. She is referred to only as *la jolie dame*,[11] and the shop clerks (both *vendeurs* and *vendeuses*) never know whether she is someone's wife or someone's mistress.

He knew the customer very well, an adorable blonde who often came to their department, and who the salesmen called among themselves "the pretty lady," knowing nothing of her, not even her name. She bought a great deal, had her purchases taken to her carriage, and immediately disappeared.[12]

The jolie dame—the shopper whose social relation to men is anonymous and irrelevant—is a paradigm flâneuse. Denise negotiates the narrow passage between all of these positions. She is not a buyer—neither a femme honnête nor a femme publique. She is a vendeuse, but is not herself for sale. Her sales skills attract Mouret, but she stubbornly refuses his advances. A novel that has traveled its narrative course with Denise as a woman of strident independence concludes with her consent to marry Mouret. With marriage as narrative closure, *The Ladies' Paradise* conforms to the conventions of gothic romance, where a woman of lowly class origins overcomes great odds and weds a man of higher social station. Zola's ending embraces this cliché of upward mobility and yet, if read in continuity with (not countervention of) Denise's stridence, suggests less that she has been "bought" than that she has risen to become Mouret's equal partner.

The masses of women who stoked the furnaces of this commercial machine became—to give Poe's "Man of the Crowd" female counterparts—*femmes de la foule*. But these hordes of female consumers, empowered with "mobility" in the public sphere, also form a prophetic indication of a organized "movement" of "New Women." As Williams's discussion of Consumer Leagues formed in France in the 1890s demonstrates, feminism and the consumer movement were considered "as natural allies."[13]

As if in distant reverberation of the darker consequences of this newfound consumer power, Dutch filmmaker Marleen Gorris's 1981 film, *A Question of Silence,* has its women shoppers bludgeoning a male store manager to death with hangers and shopping cart. A woman caught shoplifting in a shopping mall boutique is joined by two other women in an improvised collective lynching of the imperious store manager. In the subsequent trial, all of the other female customers remain silent, an act of subversive solidarity. In the courtroom, they begin to laugh as if the pleasurable extension of such consumer empowerment—the true "Ladies Paradise"—is the laughter of revolt against scopic regulation of their consumer autonomy.[14]

In private leisure, Zola's reader was provided a virtual transit in a fictional world, a textual "ladies paradise." But the department store offered a more public leisure to the flâneuse. Just as Benjamin will claim the film as an explosive that "burst" the nineteenth-century world "asunder," the flâneuse broke out of an equivalent "prison-world"—into the public spectacle of consumption.

Lumiere Freres, *Arrivée d'un train
en gare le Ciotat*, 1895. Courtesy
The Museum of Modern Art,
New York.

Our taverns and our metropolitan streets, our offices and
furnished rooms, our railroad stations and our factories
appeared to have us locked up hopelessly. Then came the
film and burst this prison-world asunder by the dynamite
of the tenth of a second, so that now, in the midst of its
far-flung ruins and debris, *we calmly and adventurously go
travelling.*

WALTER BENJAMIN, "The Work of Art in the
Age of Mechanical Reproduction" [1]

In this well-traveled passage from his now-canonical essay on modernity,
"The Work of Art in the Age of Mechanical Reproduction," Benjamin
offers a hyperbolic image of the changes wrought by the explosive advent
of "the film." With a weight of near-biblical drama, the film is poised to
release despondent captives from the "prison-world" of nineteenth-century
architectural space. For Benjamin, "the dynamite of the tenth of a second"
sent a temporal charge that tore at the spatial materials of modernity; its
brickworks, pavements, window glass, and iron girders were "burst asunder." The film was privileged as the agent of this rupture, an epistemological
TNT. And in its wake, the flâneur remained, left with a different yet "calm
and adventurous" way of "travelling."

The above "passage" is embedded in a discussion of the close-up, followed by the frequently cited maxim:

With the close-up, space expands; with slow motion, movement is extended.
The enlargement of a snapshot does not render more precise what in any case
was visible, though unclear: it reveals *entirely new formations of the subject.*[2]
(emphasis added)

Benjamin was attempting to assess the various cultural effects of photography and the cinema, of mechanical reproduction and the loss of aura, the impact of an "unconscious optics." Certainly other commentators on film had noted the formal significance of the cinematic transformations of magnification (the close-up) and temporal distention (slow motion). Jean Epstein, for example, anticipated Benjamin's rhetoric in his writings in the early 1920s. To Epstein, the close-up was "the soul of the cinema," an essential component of cinematic specificity, *photogenie*.[3] And to Epstein, slow motion brought a "new range to dramaturgy. Its power of laying bare the emotions of dramatic enlargement."[4] Béla Balázs found equally significant physiognomic revelations in the new cinematic trope of the close-up.[5] The writings and film practice of Epstein, Delluc, Dulac, Balázs, Vertov, and Clair both argued for and demonstrated the formal specificities of the cinematic medium.

But unlike these other theorists, Benjamin would note the more profound exponents of the alterations of space and time made possible by mechanical reproduction: the *social* changes produced by spatial proliferation and its metonymic aspect, repeatability over time. "Even the most perfect reproduction of a work of art," Benjamin would write in "Work of Art," "is lacking in one element: *its presence in time and space*, its unique existence at the *place* where it happens to be" (emphasis added).[6]

The absent "presence" of a mechanically-reproduced work of art was what Benjamin began to theorize as "aura," the mystified quality of authenticity of the original that was lost in the age of mechanical reproduction.[7] Benjamin was attentive to the spatial alterations produced by mechanical reproduction (in mass distribution and its flipside, mass reception),[8] but he also speculated on the reconfigured temporalities that mechanical reproduction allows.[9] To this we will return.

The "Work of Art" essay, perhaps the most celebrated of Benjamin's posthumous career, contains his most sustained discussion of film. Situated in the larger context of Benjamin's work (the essay was drafted in January and February of 1935), "Work of Art" was written while he was "in the midst of" his ambitious and never-to-be-completed utopian project to analyze the "far-flung ruins and debris" of the nineteenth century: the *Passagen-Werk*, a study of the Paris arcades.[10]

Benjamin took the "passages" as a succinct instantiation of the fragmentary nature of modernity—its hodgepodge accumulation, its uncanny juxtapositions, its "theater of purchases"—and, above all, its curious temporality. The passage (and here it is important to retain the word *passage*—not arcade) was an architectural monument to *time* and its passing. Benjamin was drawn to the remains of the nineteenth century as a collector, ragpicker, bricoleur of its rubble. ("the rags, the refuse: I will not describe but rather exhibit them."[11])

Adorno describes Benjamin's method:

His preference in the *Arcades* for small shabby objects like dust and plush is a complement of this technique, drawn as it is to *everything that has slipped through the conventional conceptual net* or to things which have been esteemed too trivial by the prevailing spirit for it to have left any traces other than those of hasty judgement.[12] (emphasis added)

And tells us:

he was drawn to the petrified, frozen or obsolete elements of civilization, to everything in it devoid of domestic vitality no less irresistibly than is the collector to fossils or to the plant in the herbarium. Small glass balls containing a landscape upon which snow fell when shook were among his favorite objects.[13]

The glass enclosed snow scene, a souvenir like the one Kane clutches on his deathbed at the beginning of *Citizen Kane,* serves as a symptomatic clue to Benjamin's unfinished project. "What was sold in the Passages were souvenirs [*Andenken*]," wrote Benjamin. "The [Andenken] was the form of the commodity in the Passage."[14] *Andenken* translates as souvenir, but also as memory; memory was the commodity-fetish retailed in the arcade, a "world in miniature."[15] The *Passagen-werk* was to be a compilation of such shards of memory, "a literary montage," an arrangement of texts that formed a monumental dialectic. As a piece of textual architecture like Kane's "never-finished, already decaying, pleasure-palace," the unassembled convoluts of the *Passagen-werk* formed a rambling Xanadu of monuments and ephemera.[16]

The passage was a fitting paradigm for all of modernity. A public space made possible by the recent advances of iron and glass architecture, the arcade was lined with luxury items produced in the economies of the newly industrialized textile trade. Hats, umbrellas, gloves, and cloth mantles were displayed in shop windows and vitrines as if they were antiquated objects in a natural history museum. The passage was not a museum or a warehouse, but a sales space where the purchase was a transaction endowed with near-philosophic significance. Commodities were transformed into souvenirs, memory-residue of the already passé.

The *Passagen-werk* occupied Benjamin until his death in 1940. Its traces left to posthumous speculation, its materials roughly assembled, its evidence scattered, the *Passagen-werk* makes us, as Susan Buck-Morss has written, "detectives against our will."[17]

For the structure of this massive work, Benjamin appealed to the concept of dialectics.[18] His method was to collect fragments, to construct dialectical images (*dialektische Bilder*) as a montage of opposites.[19] ("Dialektik im Stillstand—das ist die Quintessenz der Methode."[20])

> . . . to carry *the montage principle over into history.* That is, to build up the large structures out of the smallest precisely fashioned structural elements. Indeed, to detect the crystal of the total event in the analysis of the simple, individual moment.[21] (emphasis added)

Benjamin's method was almost cinematic, as if each quotation were a shot, "single in meaning and neutral in content," until it was placed in juxtaposition.[22] If thought of in this way, the *Passagen-werk* is like another *projét maudit* of the twentieth century, equal in its grandiose aspirations, destined conversely to remain incomplete. Eisenstein's plans for a film of *Capital*, sketched in notes from 1927 to 1928, contained, as Annette Michelson has argued, "the most radical of aesthetic syntheses": a film of Karl Marx's *Das Kapital* "with its formal side dedicated to Joyce."[23] Although Benjamin gives no avowed indication of familiarity with Eisenstein's "dialectic approach to film form,"[24] it is as if the *Passagen-werk* was an equally radical aesthetic synthesis: a text devoted to the commodity-fetish, with the "formal side" dedicated to the principles of Eisensteinian montage. Eisenstein's ambitions for "intellectual montage" were to produce films that "will have to do with philosophy" and whose "substance will be the screening of . . . a *Begriff* [concept, idea]."[25] Here it is tempting to consider a more portentous, and perhaps more accurate, analogy for the fragmentary remains of Benjamin's *Passagen-werk*—not a building left in ruins, but a film never completed.[26]

If seen through the lens of criticism of Adorno and the *Zeitschrift für Sozialforschung*, Benjamin was charged with the epithet of Marxist condemnation—being "undialectical." Criticizing Benjamin's assumption that culture simply "reflects" its economic base, Adorno wrote: "Your dialectic lacks one thing: mediation."[27] Although Adorno was critical of Benjamin during his life, in his introduction to the posthumously published *Schriften* in 1955, he wrote more sympathetically of Benjamin's intentions:

He correctly called the images of his philosophy dialectical: the plan for the book *Pariser Passagen* envisages as much a panorama of dialectical images as their theory. The concept of a dialectical image was meant objectively, not psychologically: the presentation of *the modern as at once the new, the already past and the ever-same* was to have been the work's central philosophical theme and central dialectical image.[28] (emphasis added)

The *Passagen-werk*'s "central dialectical image" was, as Adorno incisively diagnosed, modernity's unique superimposition of "the new and the already past and the ever-same." The passages instantiated this dialectic in metaphoric and literal terms. The simultaneity of this temporal triad—"the new, the already past and the ever-same"—will remain a key component of my description of postmodern temporality.

In May 1935, just as Benjamin finished the exposé "Paris—Die Hauptstadt des XIX Jahrhunderts," he described his plans for the "Arcades" book in a letter to his friend Gershom Scholem. The project would focus, he declared, on "the unfolding of a handed-down concept. . . . the fetish character of commodities."[29] Benjamin intended to read the commodity-objects on display in the faded arcades as substructural symptoms of the flaws of the superstructure. The commodities that appeared in the passages had a fortuitous and random arrangement, like the chance encounter of the umbrella and sewing machine which fueled Surrealism.[30] ("Der Vater des Surrealismus war Dada, seine Mutter war eine Passage. [The father of surrealism was Dada, the mother was a passage.]"[31]) Benjamin wanted to read these material fragments as a residue of a "dream world" readable not so much by the psychoanalyst, as the dialectician:

Passage des Panoramas, 1988.

Photograph © Anne Friedberg.

From this epoch spring *the arcades and the interiors, the exhibition halls and the dioramas. They are the residues of a dream world.* The utilization of dream-elements in waking is the textbook example of dialectical thought. Hence dialectical thought is the agent of historical awakening. Every epoch not only dreams the next, but while dreaming impels it toward wakefulness.[32] (emphasis added)

And, as Rolf Tiedemann writes:

Benjamin wanted to proceed similarly with the representation of history, by treating the nineteenth century world of objects as if it were a world of dreamed objects.[33]

In a complex calculus of analogies, Benjamin described the arcades as stocked with the dream residue of an epoch long in slumber. The commodity-fetish—umbrellas and dolls and millinery—were like museum relics that instantiated the dialectical image of the new and the "already past" and became, in convergent synthesis, the "ever-same."

THE COMMODITY-EXPERIENCE   Benjamin's plan to showcase the commodity-fetish was, of course, directly derived from the "mystical qualities" that Marx tries to describe in his section on "The Fetishism of the Commodity and Its Secret."[34]

The commodity is, first of all, an external object, a thing which through its qualities satisfies human needs of whatever kind. The nature of these needs, whether they arise, for example, *from the stomach or the imagination makes no difference.*[35] (emphasis added)

Marx began *Das Kapital* (1867) with an exacting description of the transformation of an object with use-value into its double, a "commodity" with an exchange-value. The commodity is a social construction, not found in nature, but an object invested with a special value derived, not from its "use" but from its relation to other objects in the marketplace.[36] Its "fetish-character" is based on an intangible attribute: the market-value of the desires it offers to satisfy.

Marx's descriptive and materialist account of the changes in the nine-teenth-century marketplace was also attuned to the subjective projections of need. The mystically enigmatic feature of the commodity was that it could replace need with desire. In *Theories of Surplus Value*, Marx wrote about the type of commodity that leaves "no tangible result" and answers an "aesthetic need":

> For example, the service rendered to me by a singer satisfies my *aesthetic need*; but what I enjoy exists only in an action inseparable from the singer himself; and as soon as his labour, the singing, comes to an end, my enjoyment is also over; I enjoy the activity itself—its reverberation on my ear. *These services, like the commodities which I buy, may be necessary or may only seem necessary . . . or they may be services which only yield enjoyment. But this makes no difference to their economic character.*[37] (emphasis added)

Here, Marx was describing the pleasures given by a service (such as a doctor or a lawyer) rather than a good. Yet the service described here is inseparable from the person delivering the service (in this case, the singer himself).

To restate this formulation in Benjaminian terms, as an effect of mechanical reproduction, the service becomes separable (*ablösbar*) from the person delivering the service; and the commodification of the service changes markedly. In "Work of Art," Benjamin discusses the film actor in precisely these terms. The separation of the actor from his or her "reflected image" (*das Spiegelbild*) is, according to Benjamin, responsible for the "cult of the movie star" which replaces the actor with the "phony spell of the commodity" (*fauligen Zauber ihres Warencharakters*):

> But now the reflected image has become separable, transportable. And where is it transported? Before the public. Never for a moment does the screen actor cease to be conscious of this fact. While facing the camera he knows that ultimately he will face the public, the consumers who constitute the market. . . . *The film responds to the shriveling of the aura with an artificial build-up of the "personality" outside the studio.* The cult of the movie star, fostered by the money of the film industry, preserves not the unique aura of the person but the "spell of the personality," the phony spell of a commodity.[38] (emphasis added)

In the example of Marx's singer, radio and recording techniques rendered the presence of the person providing the service unnecessary. Songs could be recorded and the recording could be broadcast: either way, the singer is absent as the service of singing is rendered. Hence, in the age of mechanical reproduction, *services replace goods as commodities*. And because such an aesthetic "service" can be rendered mechanically, the commodity—a recording, for example—returns to the status of a good, the product of an absent service. These goods, with the mysterious qualities of the commodity's "fetish-character," offer *commodity-experiences* that satisfy, as Marx would have it, the imagination, not the stomach.

Adorno would remark on these same features in his writing on the radio and the gramophone: "In the aesthetic form of technological reproduction, these objects no longer possess their traditional reality."[39] To Adorno, records—like photographs—become artifacts or, echoing his description of Benjamin's favored snow scene, "herbaria of artificial life." In an essay that prefigures Benjamin's discussion of "aura" in the "Work of Art" essay, Adorno writes:

Through the phonograph record, *time* gains a new approach to music. *It is not the time in which music happens, nor is it the time which music monumentalizes by means of its "style." It is time as evanescence,* enduring in mute music. . . . There is no doubt that, as music is removed by the phonograph record from the realm of live production and from the imperative of artistic activity and becomes petrified, it absorbs into itself, in this process of petrification, the very life that would otherwise vanish. The dead art rescues the ephemeral and perishing art as the only one alive. Therein may lie the phonograph record's most profound justification.[40] (emphasis added)

For Marx, the key aspects of modernity were the dramatic changes in consciousness brought about by industrialized space and time—the "annihilation of space by time" as he famously put it. The phonograph record, like other newly formed "commodity-experiences" facilitated a converse transformation: the annihilation of time. The range of visual phantasms offered by "show business" exhibitions—the phantasmagoria, diorama, panorama, even the legitimate theater—must be measured as early illustrations of commodity-experiences that the public would purchase.[41] These activities provided an intangible object—an *experience*—that only occasionally offered souvenirs.

In *Grundrisse,* Marx described how leisure time transforms subjectivity:

Free time—which includes leisure time as well as time for higher activities— naturally *transforms anyone who enjoys it into a different person,* and it is this different person who then enters the direct process of production.[42] (emphasis added)

In this regard, the effects of the commodification of leisure experience alters the process of production, producing workers who create a new market, desirous of leisure. That almost oxymoronic formulation, "entertainment industry" (or even "culture industry"), suggests a similar paradox of the "leisure-worker" whose labor produces nonproductive leisure experiences that deny work.[43]

Marx also described how transportation changed the perception of goods—transported food lost its regional association, its "aura."[44] Although Marx did not fully detail how the transformations produced by the changing modes of transportation and mechanical reproduction helped change the commodity-as-object into the commodity-as-experience, Schivelbusch has detailed these transformations in his consideration of the railway journey.[45] Train travel, Schivelbusch argues, turned humans into parcels who could ship themselves to a destination, reversing, in a sense, our perception of what the commodity is: *the traveler becomes the object* (the parcel). The experience of transit changes the traveler. Transportation alters the commodity, but it also becomes a commodity itself—the train ticket.

Marx and Benjamin wrote about the commodity in a marketplace that was coincident with the rise of industrialization and early capitalist economies, the height of "modernity." In a "post-industrial society,"[46] increasingly based on services rather than goods, the "labor theory of value" offers a decreasingly accurate explanation for the commodity.

Thorstein Veblen, author of *The Theory of the Leisure Class* (1899), expanded Marx's analysis of consumption and leisure, and added a gendered analysis of the role of "conspicuous"—*visually* evident—leisure and consumption. Veblen's model—which analyzed the consuming habits of the wealthy bourgeois—was, as Rosalind Williams has argued, "becoming obsolete at the moment he enunciated it."[47] To Veblen, "conspicuous leisure" was paired with "conspicuous consumption" as markers of a "leisure class." But Veblen's account assumed the social configuration of household comprised of man and wife, where the housewife engaged in "vicarious" leisure and "vicarious" consumption. The wife was the "ceremonial consumer of goods" and, to Veblen, "still quite unmistakably remains his [the husband's] chattel in theory; for the habitual rendering of vicarious leisure and consumption is the abiding mark of the unfree servant."[48] Leisured women who conspicuously spent their husband's money functioned only as a "chief ornament," whose consuming behaviors were only a further visible sign of a man's social power. Marx's model for the consumer was male; Veblen, even though he considered the female as consumer, saw in her only a sign of her husband's wealth. She remained a social hieroglyph— an ideogrammatic, almost pictographic character—a triangulated inscription like the commodity itself.

Although Veblen's model for consumption was quickly outmoded as women entered the work force, it gives testimony to the turn-of-the-century importance of women as consumers and suggests the grounding for the eventual shift from women buying for the household (as an indirect reflection of men's desires) to women buying for themselves. Consumption, which to Veblen appeared "vicarious," was a mode of social practice that enacted but could also transform social position. If the commodity was a social hieroglyph, shopping—as a selection of one object among others— also provided a new experience of social power. In addition, many of the changes in the nature of the commodity were the result of the changing positions of consumer desire.[49]

Shopping as Philosophical Speculation   The shopper enacts the social relations between things, and must read the social hieroglyphs of the commodity on display. "Marketing" means simply buying items in the marketplace, "stocking up." "Shopping," on the other hand, is a more leisurely examination of the goods; its behaviors are more directly determined by desire than need. To shop: as a verb, it implies choice, empowerment in the relation between looking and having, the act of buying as a willful choice. To shop is to muse in the contemplative mode, an activity that combines diversion, self-gratification, expertise, and physical activity.

Put in other terms, the speculative gaze of the shopper was an instrumentalization of the *mobilized* (but not *virtual*) gaze to a consumer end. The modes of distracted observation of the flâneur and flâneuse became the prototype for the shopper, a social character who was not afraid of the marketplace (agoraphobia), and who became agora*philic* instead.[50] Shopping must take place in a space that allows contemplation: the arcades and department stores that allowed "looking," without buying, were adequate to such a desire. The arcade was the "forerunner of the department store," as Benjamin continuously reminds us.[51] Until the arcade, shopping and leisurely inspection had been possible for food, but not for textile goods and luxury items. As Marx so extensively illustrated, the marketplace in capitalist countries went through dramatic changes in the nineteenth century. The mass production of goods and high volumes of consumers demanded new sales outlets and patterns of consumption changed in response to new retailing techniques. But the marketplace also changed because of the presence of the female consumer. Lower prices, fixed prices, entrée libre, and sales promotions produced new shopping behaviors and were part of the construction of new consumer desires. New commodities were created—household goods, fabrics, clothing, furniture, appliances— and they were marketed with a calculated visual appeal. As Dorothy Davis describes the consequences of such visualized speculation:

The sight of all sorts of other items, ornaments, pictures, mirrors, aspidistras, would suggest ideas they had never thought of, tempt them to a diversity of semi-luxuries, educate them in the pleasantest manner imaginable into wanting a higher standard of living.[52]

It was a newfound privilege for a woman to perform this calculation, if not a newfound power. Nowhere is the historical conflation of political independence and economic independence more emphatic—and ultimately more terrifying—than in Elizabeth Cady Stanton's 1854 rally cry for women's "right to buy," declaring and daring that women should "GO OUT AND BUY."[53] For Stanton, the liberation of women from their husbands' tyranny involved freeing their right to buy without his approval. The flâneuse-as-shopper may have had a new mobility in the public sphere and may have been enthralled with the illusion of power in consumer choice, but these freedoms were only possible at a price. Power was obtainable only through a triangulated relation with a commodity-"fetish."

Tourism: Packaging the "Mobilized" Gaze   Just as shopping was a contemplative experience that relied on a mobilized gaze, new forms of packaged travel were equally reliant on a mobilized gaze and marketed the traveling experience as a commodity. For Americans and Britains of a certain generation and class, the "Grand Tour" was considered a necessary part of one's education. All of Europe was a museum to be traversed with Baedekers, narrativized itineraries that organized experience. The concept of "grand tour" with its stayovers in Grand Hotels—each with their lifts, ballrooms, suites, and pools—offered the tourist a preplanned narrative of space. But just as patterns of consumption changed in the mid-nineteenth century and were no longer determined solely by class privilege, patterns of travel also changed markedly. While the "lady traveler" was an adventurous corollary of upper-class privilege, in the mid-nineteenth century the packaged tour began to offer the freedoms of travel to middle-class women.[54]

Thomas Cook, the first British entrepreneur of the packaged tour, became the master codesetter of middle-class tourism. (Cook, who began organizing tours in 1841, was active in the temperance movement—proposing the tour as a substitute for alcohol.[55]) The tourist industry successfully marketed an organized mobility, arrayed prearranged "sights" in narrative sequence. The guidebook served as textual captions to otherwise visual "sights." This commoditized combination of voyeurism (*sight*seeing) and narrative grew in parallel with the industries of telegraphy, photography, and the cinema.

The subjective effects on the tourist are not unlike those of the cinema spectator. Tourism produces an escape from boundaries, it legitimates the transgression of one's static, stable, or fixed location. The tourist simultaneously embodies both a position of presence and absence, of here and elsewhere, of avowing one's curiosity and disavowing one's daily life.[56]

Roland Barthes pinpointed these paradoxes of touristic experience. Dining on a train, Barthes contends in "Dining Car," imparts the philosophy "that the traveler should consume at the very heart of his journey everything constitutively opposed by the journey." Barthes is describing the paradoxical effect of a "transported immobility" where travel itself imparts a psychic stasis. In the railway dining car, Barthes describes how "each constraint seems to produce its contrary freedom, each gesture is a denial of its original limits."

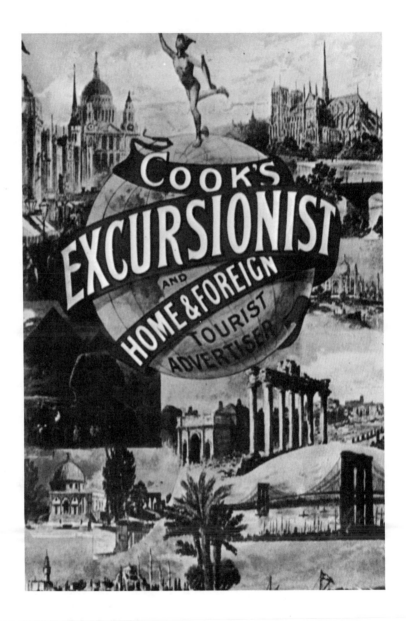

In 1851, Thomas Cook began *Cook's Excursionist* to advertise travel packages to the Great Exhibition in London.

Thus each time man constructs his displacement, it is to give it the superstructure of a house; each time he detaches himself from the ground, he requires its guarantee: all *arts of travel have for their goal the very illusion of immobility:* in the panic and pleasure of transplantation, Cook sells the spectacle of a stability.[57] (emphasis added)

And as Dean MacCannell effectively demonstrates in his *The Tourist: A New Theory of the Leisure Class,* touristic experiences were a "new species of commodities" designed to provide "staged authenticity."[58] The organized spectatorship of tourism—packaging this transported immobility in a narrative of "staged authenticity"—followed a historical development similar to that of the panorama, diorama and cinema where, as the gaze became more "virtually" *mobile,* the spectator became more physically *immobile.* Tourism relied on a more physically mobile subject, whose experiences were preplanned. But cultural activities that relied on such forms of organized spectatorship flourished interdependently of those reliant on the virtual gaze. As Altick describes in his remarkable history of nineteenth-century entertainments, *The Shows of London:*

Innovations as Thomas Cook's first guided tours of the continent in 1855, had markedly increased the desire to go abroad. For those who were able to do so, now that more of the nations's wealth was trickling down through the middle class, and cheap transport and modestly priced hotels were making continental touring for many a genuine possibility rather than a hopeless dream, *London's panoramas served as appetite-whetters* for the real thing.[59] (emphasis added)

RE: CONSTRUCTION—THE PUBLIC INTERIOR/THE PRIVATE EXTERIOR   "Construction," wrote Benjamin in "Paris—Capital of the Nineteenth Century," "occupies the role of the subconscious." As we now consider the activities that transformed the mobility of the gaze (activities such as shopping and tourism) in parallel with the development of architectural spaces that encouraged such mobility (the arcade, the department store, the exhibition hall) it will become readily apparent that iron and glass architecture was a primary factor in the alteration of nineteenth-century public life.[60]

Iron Construction In 1929 Benjamin wrote a small piece entitled "Der Saturnring oder Etwas von Eisenbau" ("The Saturnring or Something about Iron Construction").[61] Although the essay was scaled to the incidental form of the *feuilleton,* it contains a dramatic key to Benjamin's ideas on the impact of architecture on modern life.[62] To observe "something about iron construction," Benjamin muses upon an 1844 lithograph from Grandville's *Un Autre Monde:*

Instead of undertaking a historical development of these occurrences, we would like a loose consideration of a small vignette which comes from the middle of the century (like from the thick book in which it is found). If it is of a grotesque sort, it also signifies the unlimited possibilities that iron construction offered. The image comes from a work by Grandville from 1844 (*Un Autre Monde*)—which described the adventures of a fantastic little goblin who finds his way through interstellar space: "On a bridge, from which one cannot survey both ends at the same time, and the pillars of which are supported on the planets, one travels on wonderful paved asphalt from one planet to the other."[63]

The fantastic interplanetary stroll of the Grandville goblin on this iron bridge was made possible by iron construction. The *passerelle* (an aerial iron bridge) was used by architects of the Bibliotheque Nationale (1858) and the department store Bon Marché (Boileau and Eiffel, 1876) to connect a series of separate courts under a single glass skylight. Benjamin argues that iron construction (*Eisenbau*)

originated constructions which had no prototype in the past and served entirely new needs: market halls, train stations, and exhibition halls.[64]

Among these new structures—made possible for the first time by iron and glass construction—were the market hall of Paris, Les Halles (1853, Victor Baltard), London's Kings Cross Station (1851), and the Crystal Palace (1851, Joseph Paxton). Each of the these structures had no precedent, but used iron girders to vault massive interior spaces with transparent glass roofs. The Crystal Palace, built to house the London Great Exhibition of 1851, was prophetic. Its iron frame, columns, beams, and bracing rods held walls entirely of glass, a transparent case stretched over a high central vaulted

Ignace Isidore Gérard Grandville,

"Flâneur of the Universe," from

Un Autre Monde, 1844.

space, flanked by wings of various heights. The structure that Baltard built
for Les Grandes Halles in Paris (1853–1858) used iron and glass to vault an
interior that protected the stalls of food purveyors.[65] Zola dramatized Les
Halles as "the belly of Paris" in his novel *Le Ventre de Paris* (1873). Kings
Cross railway station in London provided a protected interior space for
arrivals and departures on a new machine of time travel—the locomotive.[66]

   Like the "winter-garden" these public buildings (the market hall, the
train station, the exhibition hall) offered to the visitor a *timeless* (or season-
less) public space. The winter-garden constructed a "theater of nature"
where nature itself became a commodity. Plants kept in these "hothouses"
required the maintenance of an artificially warm and humid climate.

Under the glass canopy of the winter garden were concentrated all the amusements that had been strung separately along a street or a boulevard: a concert hall, a music hall, a theater, a cafe, an art collection, billiards rooms, a restaurant, and dance and banquet halls. Embracing all this was a panorama of fountains, waterfalls, and galleries with cascades of plants.[67]

The desire to enclose the garden became a precedent for other forms of marketing artificial environments:

With the consciously pursued objective of bringing the public inside to view the plant kingdom, the winter garden was an early herald of the entertainment industry.[68]

Such atrium spaces, with vaulted glass roofs stretched over an iron skeleton, created a new form of *public interior,* dissolving the separations between private and public space. As described by architectural historian Anthony Vidler:

Between 1830 and 1848, in the Paris of Louis-Phillipe, the bourgeois monarch, *the interior developed its characteristic role in consumer society as the realm of private fantasy, private wish fulfillment, and private display of private taste.*[69] (emphasis added)

The once-private interior became a public realm, the once-public exterior became privatized ("The interior as street [luxury]; the street as interior [misery]."[70]) These reversals were produced by architectural innovations and the introduction of outdoor gas lighting.[71] The street, the site of exterior flânerie, was transformed. The flâneur reprivatized public space, turned the street into an interior.

Haussmann's redevelopment of Paris implemented a radical rupture of urban space and contributed to this privatization of public exteriors. The boulevards transformed the city:

In a space some thirty meters wide and up to two kilometers long, Haussmann concentrated the services and the circulation of the new commercial city. Paved with new macadam, lit with the latest design of gas light, carefully planned to separate pedestrian, stroller, loiterer, ambling service vehicle, and rushing carriage, planted with rows of trees to ensure shade in summer, provided with underground piping for rain, water, sewage, and gas. . . . In a very real sense the street had become an interior—gas lit and policed; the crowd felt a safety in a domain where buildings and light created an artificial sky at night.[72]

By 1924, Le Corbusier would describe the modern city as a machine. In *Urbanisme,* he writes, the street is a "traffic machine . . . a sort of factory for producing speed traffic."[73] The city itself was a machine for mobility, generating a newly mobilized gaze.

Glass: Walls, Mirrors, Windows

> The age of windows lasted four centuries.
>
> from the year 2049 in H. G. Wells's *The Shape of Things to Come*

Large sheets of cast glass, rolled and poured, were available as building or display material by the middle 1700s; by 1786, twelve-by-sixteen-inch panes were used as show windows.[74] By 1850 large sheets of glass could present "an uninterrupted mass of glass from the ceiling to the ground."[75]

Bentham's panopticon (1790) was dependent on sheet glass, the largest possible area of glass stretched over a slender iron structure. In the panopticon prison the transparency of glass was utilized for surveillance, while at the same time its solidity as a building material functioned to guarantee confinement.

But the predominant function of glass was its transparency. Glass shop windows served to bring light to the dank interior selling space of the store. By the middle of the eighteenth century, shopkeepers began to realize that the window might be a prime proscenium for commodity display. In *The Complete English Tradesman,* Daniel Defoe recorded the moment of transformation when, in London in 1762, there was an order to remove exterior shop signs and place a sign on or in the window. Objects placed behind glass were altered (and in some cases improved) in their appearance.

The shop window was the proscenium for visual intoxication, the site of seduction for consumer desire.[76] By the end of the nineteenth century, shop windows were well-established features of sales strategy. In 1900, the year that L. Frank Baum wrote *The Wizard of Oz*, he also published a treatise on window display entitled *The Art of Decorating Dry Goods Windows*.[77] In it, he describes a variety of techniques for catching the eyes of passing window-shoppers and turning them into absorbed spectators.

How can a window sell goods? *By placing them before the public in such a manner that the observer has a desire for them and enters the store to make the purchase.* Once in, the customer may see other things she wants, and no matter how much she purchases under these conditions *the credit of the sale belongs to the window.*[78] (emphasis added)

One of Baum's recommended techniques was what he called an "illusion window" that would be "sure to arouse the curiosity of the observer."[79] A window display called "the vanishing lady" used a live female model who, at intervals, would disappear into a drapery-covered pedestal and reappear with a new hat, gloves, or shawl. Female mannequins, posed in static seduction, were women made safe under glass, like animals in the zoo. The department store window

helped create the demands for which they catered with their everchanging windows and shop displays. . . . Long before the cinema or broadcasting existed, the department stores were helping to mould the tastes of the rising middle class.[80]

Baum's conception of the show window seems to bear a clear analogy to the cinema screen. A tableau is framed and as it is placed behind glass it is made inaccessible. From the middle of the nineteenth century, as if in a historical relay of looks, the shop window succeeded the mirror as a site of identity construction, and then—gradually—the shop window was displaced and incorporated by the cinema screen. Cinematic spectation, a further instrumentalization of this consumer gaze, produced paradoxical effects on the newfound social mobility of the flâneuse.

The analogy between the shop window and the cinema screen has been suggested by a range of film historians and theorists. Charles Eckert, Jeanne Allen, Mary Ann Doane, and Jane Gaines have all invoked "window-shopping" as an apt paradigm for film spectatorship.[81] "Window-shop-

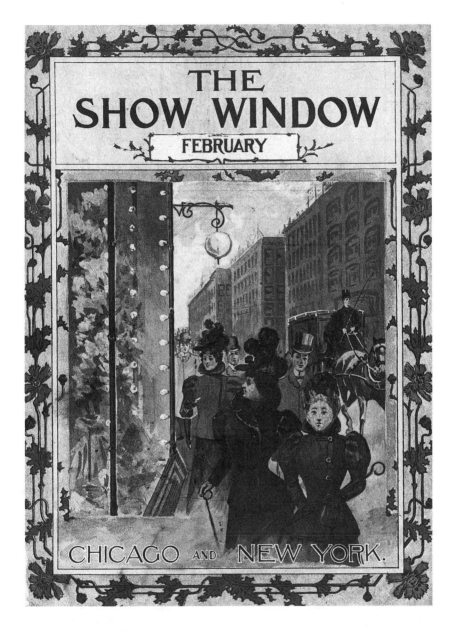

L. Frank Baum edited *The Show Window*, a
monthly journal of practical window
trimming, from 1897–1902.

ping" implies a mode of consumer contemplation; a speculative regard to the mise-en-scène of the display window without the commitment to enter the store or to make a purchase. Cinema spectatorship relies on an equally distanced contemplation: a tableau, framed and inaccessible, not behind glass, but on the screen. Seen in the context of the following architectural and social history, cinematic spectatorship can be described as emerging from the social and psychic transformations that the arcades—and the consequent mobility of flânerie—produced.

THE MOBILIZED GAZE: TOWARD THE VIRTUAL

The Arcade The arcades (or passages) reorganized public life in Paris between the revolution of 1789 and World War I. Unlike eighteenth-century London—a city that had the Pall Mall and the Strand as broad open-air shopping streets, streets where one could stroll and gaze into shops at a leisurely, undisturbed pace—walking in pre-Haussmann Paris was difficult due to narrow streets and the lack of sidewalks.[82] The arcade compensated for this lack: it provided a public interior for strolling.

In Paris, the Palais Royal was commercially developed in the 1780s into a covered arcade of shops (it was soon referred to as the Palais Marchand). The Palais was a public gathering place; the communards organized here and the foment of the Revolution began in the shelter of Paris's first arcade.

As a visitor to Paris in 1789 wrote:

One could spend an entire life, even the longest, in the Palais Royal, and as, in an enchanting dream, dying, say "I have seen and known all."[83]

When, in January 1790, utopianist Charles Fourier and his brother-in-law the gourmand, Brillat-Savarin, visited Paris they were struck by the Palais:

You think you are entering a fairy palace. You find everything you could wish for there—spectacles, majestic buildings, promenades, fashions.[84]

Balzac described an adjacent arcade, the Galerie d'Orleans in *Lost Illusions* (1839) as a "greenhouse without flowers," "a disreputable bazaar," and a "lewd hangar" containing a full spectrum from luxury to poverty, from dandies to thieves, ladies of fashion to prostitutes.[85]

The Théâtre Français and the Théâtre du Palais Royal were at either end of the Palais Royal. In addition to these human theaters, François Dominique Séraphin, a maker of automatons, opened a shadow theater in the Palais. Théâtre Séraphin displayed shadow plays activated by clockworks, not human hands. In 1786, a half-sunken "circus" was built in the middle of the garden with

an enormous colonnaded interior, lit from above by clerestory windows and a glazed roof, and terminated by apsidal arcades, it was used for spectacles and entertainment, balls and concerts.[86]

The arcade created an enclosed marketplace where consumption itself became the spectacle.[87]

Johann Friedrich Geist, in his definitive study, *The Arcade: History of a Building Type,* establishes a generic architectural form: a glass-covered passageway that connects two busy streets, lined on both sides with shops, closed stores with glass fronts. The arcade served as the organizing force of retail trade; it was a public space on private property.[88] The arcade eased traffic, protected the consumer from weather, and was accessible only to pedestrians. Geist lists seven characteristics of the arcade:

1. access to interior of a block
2. public space on private property
3. symmetrical street space
4. skylit space
5. system of access
6. form of organized retail trade
7. space of transition

This last characteristic, the space of transition, is what makes arcades, in a more philosophical sense, temporally-marked spaces—depots for arrival and departure. Geist places the arcade historically between the palace gallery and the railway station.[89]

Between 1800 and 1830, seventeen arcades opened in Paris. The arcade was a controlled world full of luxury goods, sheltering one from the miseries of the street, from images of urban poverty. And yet from their beginnings, the arcades contained other images, the commodities constructed and marketed to expand upon the mobilized gaze of the flâneur.

The major arcades of Paris, Passage des Panorama (1800), Galérie Vivienne (1826), Galérie Véro-Dodat (1826), Galérie Colbert (1826), Passage L'Opera (1821–1823), and Passage Choiseul (1825–1827) were complete by 1830; Passages Verdeau (1846) and Jouffroy (1847) followed. But the arcade form proliferated in other cities, as if it were the mark of capitalist commerce and trade. In London, the Burlington Arcade was built in 1819, the Royal Opera Arcade in 1818; in Brussels, Galéries Royale St. Hubert was built in 1847 and Galérie Bortier in 1848. In Milan, the grandiose Galleria Vittorio Emanuele II was built in 1865; the Kaisergalerie in Berlin was built in 1873. In the United States, the Cleveland Arcade rose in 1889. In Moscow, the New Trade Halls, GUM, was completed in 1893. Moreover as the nineteenth century ended, arcades were built in cities from Melbourne to Moscow, Athens to Zagreb, Johannesburg to Singapore.

Louis Aragon's 1926 novel, *Paris Peasant,* formed a vivid textual record of flânerie through the streets and arcades of Paris; his prose becomes a surrealist Baedeker to the marvelous, a disquisition on the found objects and sudden thoughts produced in the experience of the everyday. For Aragon, arcades ("which are rather disturbingly named *passages,* as though no one had the right to linger for more than an instant in those sunless corridors") are the "secret repositories of several modern myths . . . the true sanctuaries of the cult of the ephemeral." Aragon rued the "giant rodent" of Haussmannization which would "inexorably gash open the thicket whose twin arcades run through the Passage de l'Opera" producing a "complete upheaval of the established fashions of casual strolling and prostitution" and thus "modify the ways of thought of a whole district, perhaps of a whole world."[90]

Like Baudelaire, Aragon was transfixed by the presence of women in this public space:

In the changing light of the arcades, a light ranging from the brightness of the tomb to the shadow of sensual pleasure, delicious girls can be seen serving both cults with provocative movement of the hips and the sharp upward curl of a smile.

Passage Jouffroy (built 1845–47)

in 1988. Photograph © Anne

Friedberg.

In the passage:

so many female strollers of all kinds . . . varying ages and degrees of beauty,
often vulgar, and in a sense already depreciated, but women, truly women,
and palpably women, even at the expense of all the other qualities of their
bodies and souls; so many women, in league with these arcades they stroll
along.[91] (emphasis added)

These are prostitutes, whose "charming multiplicity of appearances and
provocations" and "infinite desire to please" were a fixture in the dank
heterosocial spaces of the passages. Aragon prefers these "streetwalkers" or
femme publiques to the more gentile femme honnêtes in Luxembourg
Gardens:

Ancient whores, set pieces, mechanical dummies, I am glad that you are so
much part of the scenery here: you are still vivid rays of light compared with
those matriarchs one encounters in the public parks.[92]

Aragon's novel offered a powerful example of the passage as a public interior
transformed into an imaginary realm. In front of a shop window, Aragon
has an oceanic vision:

I was astonished to see that its window was bathed in a greenish, almost
submarine light. . . . The whole ocean in the Passage de l'Opera. The canes
floated gently like seaweed. . . . I noticed a human form was swimming
among the various levels of the window display.[93]

The human form was, of course, female, a woman "who was naked down
to a very low waistline, consisted of a sheath of steel or scales or possibly
rose petals." The arcades were clearly spaces in which the flâneur flourished.
But for the male observer in these public spaces, the flâneuse was often no
more than a mannequin, a fixture in window display.

The Aragon novel gave Benjamin the "decisive impetus" for his project
on the Paris arcades. When Benjamin met Gershom Scholem in Paris in
1927, Scholem recalls:

Benjamin read those periodicals in which Aragon and Breton proclaimed
things that coincided somewhere with his own deepest experiences. . . .

Benjamin was not an ecstatic, but the ecstacies of revolutionary utopias and the surrealistic immersion in the unconscious were to him, so to speak, keys for opening of his own world, for which he was seeking altogether different, strict, and disciplined forms of expression. Louis Aragon's *Le Paysan de Paris* [*The Peasant of Paris*, 1926] gave him the decisive impetus for his projected study of the Paris Arcades from whose first drafts he read to me in those weeks.[94]

Benjamin was not the only cosmopolitan German to feel the lure of the arcade. For Franz Hessel and Siegfried Kracauer the passage was a determinant feature of modern urban life; its effects on subjectivity and experience were profound.

In Hessel's *Spazieren in Berlin* (1929)—a key text on urban strolling— the streets of Berlin provide mnemonic cues for Hessel to recall his childhood.[95] To Hessel, city streets, if used properly, could produce a traffic of memories. Hessel's prose on strolling (*Spazierengehen*) emphasizes the simple pleasures (*Genuß*) of flânerie rather than the analytical aspects that Benjamin would later champion as "the dialectic of flânerie." Hessel advocated strolling as a leisure activity, suggesting that the urbanite take "mini-vacations of the everyday" by walking short distances instead of waiting for a train or a tram.[96]

Hessel was Benjamin's guide to the streets of Paris when, in March 1926, Benjamin traveled to Paris to work with Hessel on a joint translation of Proust's *Remembrance of Things Past.* For two German writers in the French capital, the translation of the Proust text furnished a complex crucible for the textualization of memory. In their collaborative excursions, the Paris streets and arcades recalled the Berlin streets of their childhood, formed a telling translation of memory and the past. For Benjamin, the 1926 visit with Hessel was a madeleine to his first visit to Paris in 1913. Paris was the "Capital of the Nineteenth Century," and its streets were its time machines, transporting Benjamin back to his childhood in nostalgic flânerie for a Berlin experienced as a "theater of purchases" or a "cavern of commodities."[97] In her biographical remembrance of Benjamin, Hannah Arendt has described how, for Benjamin, the transit from Berlin to Paris was "tantamount to a trip in time—not from one country to another, but from the twentieth century back to the nineteenth."[98]

For both Benjamin and Hessel, city streets served as a mnemonic system, bringing images of the past into the present, what Benjamin dramatically pronounced as "telescoping the past into the present."[99] Hessel's effort to reclaim the lost "art of strolling" was presented as a resistance to the pace of modern urban life, a nostalgia for the unhurried past. When Benjamin reviewed Hessel's *Spazieren in Berlin* in 1929, his review essay, "Die Wiederkehr des Flaneurs" initiated a description of the public interiors inhabited by the flâneur.[100] Benjamin would repeat this description in each of his subsequent mentions of flânerie: "the newspaper kiosks his library, the benches his bedroom."[101] The flâneur was a "street person" at home in the public realm of urbanity. Unlike Hessel, Benjamin found, in the perceptive style of flânerie, an analytic and speculative gaze.

For Benjamin, the relation between the arcade and street was one of the relation between the interior and exterior. The arcade offered a sheltered retreat from the exterior chaos of the street and provided a public interior, a separate arena for public social life. Benjamin quoted an illustrated guide to Paris in each reworked version of his discussion of the arcades:

"The arcades, a rather recent invention of industrial luxury," so says an illustrated guide to Paris of 1852, "are glass-covered, marble paneled passageways through entire complexes of houses whose proprietors have combined for such speculations. Both sides of these passageways, which are lighted from above, are lined with the most elegant shops, so that such *an arcade is a city, even a world, in miniature.*"[102] (emphasis added)

The arcade presented this "world in miniature," a "grand poème de l'étalage,"[103] a spatial verse of visual display.

In Berlin, the Kaisergalerie (which opened in 1873 and was named after Kaiser Wilhelm I) marked the beginning of the "Gründerzeit" that ended at the end of the World War II. (The Kaisergalerie was destroyed by Allied bombing in 1944.) Modeled after the Galeries Royale St. Hubert (1847) in Brussels and the Galleria Vittorio Emanuele II (1867) in Milan, the Kaisergalerie marked Berlin as a capitalist city, and it exemplified imperial taste for foreign luxuries. In it, a Viennese-style cafe gave its patrons a taste for the Viennese combinations of coffee and cream. The first bar in Berlin, the Französische Bar, provided a public gathering spot for men of elegant means. Across from the cafe, a post office with writing rooms full of envelopes and stamps, provided (within the passage) a center for communication foreign and domestic.

In 1888, the World-Panoptikon opened in the Kaisergalerie. Described by Geist, the panopticon was a "hotch-potch of dioramas, panoramas, facsimiles, molded replicas of scenery, patriotic souvenirs, and all kinds of cinematographic attractions and apparatus."[104] By the end of the century, when the entertainment district—with its tourist shops and prostitutes—established itself along Friedrichstraße, the panopticon "tried to retain its clientele with films, stereoscopes, and amusement park rides" including an amusement, like Hale's Tours, in which a "passenger" sat in a simulated train compartment, with the noise and vibration of railway travel, and watched scenes of the Riviera pass by the window.[105]

Hessel described the "mild confusion" and "damp chill" he felt upon entering the Kaisergalerie, which by the 1920s had become a strangely empty museum of the past. ("So many store fronts, display windows, and so few people," writes Hessel.[106]) In a piece written for the feuilleton section of the *Frankfurter Zeitung,* "Abschied von der Lindenpassage," Kracauer described the "wilted extravagance" (*welken Bombast*) of the decaying Lindenpassage:

But now, under a new glass roof and decked out in marble, the former
passage reminds me of the vestibule of a department store. The shops still
exist, but picture postcards are the standard fare; the world Panorama has
been overtaken by the film and the Anatomical Museum has long ceased to be
a famed attraction.[107]

The arcade was a retreat from the public sphere which contained the flotsam of daily life and "sheltered the rejected and the refugees, a collection of things which were not suitable for dressing up the facade."[108] These transient discarded objects:

satisfy physical needs, the desire [*Gier*] for images, just as they appear in one's
daydreams. Both things, extreme closeness and great distance, give way before
the bourgeois public sphere which cannot tolerate them and retreat into the
secluded twilight of the passageway, where they flourish as in a swamp. *In
fact, as a passage, the thoroughfare is also the place where, as in no other, the
journey, the departure from the near into the distant, can be portrayed: body and
image become united.*[109] (emphasis added)

Kracauer contemplated this form of travel—the distant brought near—and found it a "clever coincidence that the entrance to the Linden arcade was flanked by two travel offices."[110] But the passage offered a different form of travel.

The trips to which ship models and advertisements call you have nothing in common anymore with the trips one used to take in the passage . . . bourgeois existence has taken over travel for its own purposes. . . . degrading them into amusements [*Zerstreuungen*].[111]

In the Kaisergalerie, the Welt-Panorama:

dangles that for which we long in front of us and quickly snatches away the familiar. . . . *The distance to the tangible body from the ephemeral distance is just a tiny leap.* Whenever I visited the world Panorama as a child . . . I felt myself *as if transported to a faraway place.*[112] (emphasis added)

For Kracauer, the passage "criticized the bourgeois world through the bourgeois world, a critique which beset every passerby" and was both "the product of a time and an intimation of its decline." Kracauer concludes his brief piece with the ringing question:

Was sollte noch eine Passage in einer Gesellschaft die selber nur eine Passage ist?
[What would be the meaning of a passage in a society which is itself no more than a passage?]

The passage, with its Welt-Panorama and travel agencies, negotiated transport, marketed ephemera, satisfied the desire for images, but also the desire for movement, transition. In the architectural passage, the mobilized gaze found its virtual analog.

The Department Store

Marshall Field's is an exposition in itself.

description of 1893 Chicago Exhibition

When you think about it, department stores are kind of like museums.

ANDY WARHOL

The department store as a building type emerged as a corollary to the dramatic changes in urban retailing between 1840 and 1870. As a consequence of the mass production of standardized goods, singly-owned, craft-oriented shops were displaced by *magasin de nouveautés*. When Aristide Boucicaut opened his Paris magasin Bon Marché in 1852, he made changes in merchandising which, in the competitive retail market, either put his competitors out of business or made them follow his lead. Boucicaut is credited with establishing fixed prices, marking the price directly on the item, and reducing prices because of the higher sales volume and rapid turnover of stock. The policy of entrée libre also encouraged entry without the obligation of purchase, and served to stimulate impulse sales. Due to his success, Boucicaut expanded his shop to a giant new building that was built between 1869 and 1887 (designed by the architects L. C. Boileau and Gustav Eiffel, the engineer). The new Bon Marché took a whole city block: its continuous exterior shop windows, interior light wells, galleries, and grand staircases were designed to encourage consumption.[113]

The department store was a multistory structure located in a central urban business district near public transport. The development of public transit (streetcars, buses, underground railways) assisted the mobilization of shoppers to these stores. Organized to carry a great variety of merchandise, a heterogenous assortment of products in separate "departments"—from ready-to-wear to home furnishings—the department store's single management provided centralized services for publicity, accounting, and delivery.

The department store posed a new design objective: the display and sale of a high volume of mass-produced goods to large numbers of consumers. As Siegfried Giedion points out:

To be fit for such a purpose, a department store—like a library stack room or market hall—must offer a clear view of the articles it contains, a maximum of light, and ample facilities for communication.[114]

Eugene Atget, "Mannequins, Avenue des Gobelins, Paris"
1910–1920. Courtesy International Museum of
Photography at George Eastman House.

Henri Labrouste's designs for the reading room of the Bibliotheque Nationale (1858–1868) used sixteen cast-iron pillars and provided a deep vaulted space, a double-naved reading room that was supported by the wrought-iron framework of the roof. The design of the Bibliotheque Nationale in Paris resembles the subsequent design for department stores: stack rooms (*magasin central*) and four stories with an atrium of grid walkways (*passerelles*), all under one glass roof. And it was under this vaulted sky of Paris, in the Bibliotheque Nationale, that Benjamin planned and worked on his *Passagen-Werk*:

For, looking down from the arcades in the reading room of the Paris National Library, the painted summer sky stretched over them its dreamy, lightless ceiling.[115]

The relation between the reading room and the library stack, which offers the reader a clear view of the articles in stock, became a spatial model for the department store, where the consumer also had a clear view of the commodities on display. The shopper, like the library reader, was on a mission for knowledge, computing the relations between the social hieroglyphs of goods on display.

Boileau and Eiffel's Bon Marché used passerelles, aerial iron bridges to connect the series of courts each covered with a glass skylight. The passerelles allowed the consumer an unique overview of goods on display. The glass roof illuminated the interior space, a winter-garden for commodities of all varieties.

In addition, the similarities between the museum and the department store were apparent to architects and consumers in the nineteenth century. The Magasin du Louvre (which opened in 1855) was a magasin de nouveautés with mass-produced objects for sale. Its namesake, the Museé du Louvre, displayed objects with "aura" which were not for anything but temporary experiential consumption.[116]

The department store differed from its market predecessor, the bazaar. The bazaar, a vaulted brick building, often with a dome, was a standard feature in the Islamic city. Structures like the warehouse and the greenhouse, which afforded storage and the possibility of display, provided architectural precedents for the department store.[117] In *Space, Time, and Archi-*

tecture, Giedion compares the department store with other large iron and glass structures:

> The department store has no equally large forerunner in the past. In this respect it is like the market halls, railway stations, and exhibition buildings of the nineteenth century, and the object it serves is the same: *the rapid handling of business activities involving huge crowds of pedestrians.*[118] (emphasis added)

Giedion found a national architectural difference between French and American department stores: the American store followed from the warehouse type, whereas the French store included a "perforated" interior space. In Philadelphia, a freight depot for the Pennsylvania Railroad—the Grand Depot (1876)—was a storage space until John ("The customer is always right") Wanamaker came up with the idea to transform the capacious space into a dry goods store. Wanamaker built a lifesize replica of Rue de la Paix in his store as "a consolation for Americans who could not go to Paris."[119] In Paris, the Boileau and Eiffel building's elegant iron and glass central atrium, with vertical proportions stretched toward a glass skylight, was the model for Zola's "cathedral of modern commerce."

While the flâneuse entered the grand magasins of the French capital, woman shoppers poured into "department stores" in New York (Macy's), Philadelphia (Wanamaker's), Chicago (Marshall Field's), and London (Selfridges, Harrods). In Germany, the combination of store design with enormous plate-glass windows, gaslighting, lifts, pneumatic tubes, and merchandising changes—national names, multiple shops, departments—transformed this "cathedral of modern commerce" into a transitional space for new modes of perception and experience.

With the department store came the need for moving shoppers through this commercial machine, drawing them to the merchandise beyond the first floor.[120] The store itself with its elevators, ventilating systems, electric lights, telephones, bathrooms, lounges, restaurants, post offices, and delivery services encouraged lingering in a public space, legitimized a new form of loitering through its association with consumption.[121] Zola's description of the store as "selling machine" captures the retailing tactic of this new kind of store: to move merchandise quickly, to increase stock turnover, to sell more. Elevators (and then escalators) moved customers to the upper selling floors and effectively mobilized the shopper's gaze through the commercial machine.[122]

Because the department store relied on its nonselling services (its restaurants, lounges, hairdressers, and so forth) to supply steady customers, the practice of *shopping* became more important than individual sales. As Susan Porter Benson describes the sheltered realms of consumption, buying was a "means of enhancing psychic well-being" and the department store was a "setting designed to break down her resistance to spending money."[123]

The department store was a semipublic space designed for the female consumer. The mobilized gaze was the mode of the shopper, whose distracted speculation measured desire against purchase. Kracauer used the "shopgirl" as an exemplum of the absorbed cinema spectator in his "Little Shopgirls Go to the Movies" ("Die kleinen Ladenmädchen gehen ins Kino" [1927]). For Kracauer, the movies offered the working class shop girl a new form of visual distraction.[124] The cinema theatre transformed the shopper's mobilized gaze to its virtual extension.

Shifts in urban population, the expansion of public transportation and new retailing techniques have been consistent socioeconomic determinants to cinema spectatorship. In the United States, as the population shifted to the suburbs after World War II, as the automobile displaced public transportation, and as suburban shopping malls replaced urban downtowns, patterns of film exhibition and reception also changed to follow suit.[125]

The World Exhibition

> World exhibitions were *places of pilgrimage to the fetish Commodity* . . . (they) glorified the exchange-value of commodities. They created a framework in which their use-value receded into the background. *They opened up a phantasmagoria into which people entered to be distracted.*
>
> WALTER BENJAMIN[126] (emphasis added)

Benjamin described the 1867 Paris Exhibition as a "phantasmagoria of capitalist culture." *Phantasmagoria* was an appropriate word: not only did it refer to the illusionistic screen entertainments that manufactured phantoms out of projected light, but it contains the root word *agoria* for the marketplace. The World Exhibition was a monumental site for the conflation of the *mobilized* gaze of shopping and tourism with the *virtual* gaze of the *faux*-real. As a witness to the 1931 and 1937 Paris expositions, Benjamin also diagnosed the twisted temporality of these exhibitions, vivid examples of "telescoping the past through the present."[127]

The "World Exhibition" imported an array of products from around the world, but conversely it also gave the visitor an opportunity to make a virtual tour of faraway countries. Full of colonial exhibits and industrial displays, the exhibition also provided an outstanding justification for new architecture. Even though display bazaars of nationally manufactured objects had become national pastimes (France sponsored such events in 1791, 1801, 1802, 1806, 1891, 1823, 1827, 1834, 1839, and 1844), the Great Exhibition of London in 1851 heralded the "Industry of All Nations," inviting competitor nations to display their wares. As the illustrated catalog to the exhibition asserted with a tone of imperialist pride:

Other nations have devised means for the display and encouragement of their own arts and manufactures; but it has been reserved for England to provide an arena for the exhibition of the industrial triumphs of the whole world. She has offered an hospitable invitation to surrounding nations to bring the choicest products of their industry to her capital, and there to enter into an amicable competition with each other and with herself.[128]

The list of exhibitions in the nineteenth century—London in 1851; Paris Expositions in 1855, 1867, 1878, 1889, and 1900; the World Columbian Exposition in Chicago in 1893; the Pan American Exposition in Buffalo in 1901—demonstrates that by the end of the century, it had become an established form of touristic display.

The exhibition also debuted devices and mechanical rides that uniquely "mobilized" the gaze: the (seven feet per second) elevator ascension of the Eiffel Tower in 1889, the "Ferris Wheel" and the *kinetoscope* in Chicago in 1893, the moving walkway (*trottoir roulant*) in the 1900 Paris Exposition.

Like the department store, exhibition architecture presented new design objectives and iron and glass architecture answered its needs. The 1889 Paris Exposition introduced two striking examples of engineering architecture:

The aerial view of Paris from the
Tour d'Eiffel offered a new vista
of urban space. Photograph by
Émile-Zola, 1900. © Massin and
Dr. Françoise Émile-Zola.

the Tour d' Eiffel (Eiffel and Boileau) and Galérie des Machines (Dutert).
Outrage over the raw iron scaffold and its offense to the Paris skyline
reached a flashpoint in the famed public petition—signed by writers including Guy de Maupassant and Alexandre Dumas—which declared the tower
a "disgrace. . . . an inkblot . . . the hateful shadow of that odious column
of riveted sheet metal."[129]

But even though the Eiffel Tower ruptured the Paris skies with this
wrought-iron spire, it offered its visitors a spectacular new vista of urban
space. The elevator ascension of the tower was one of the exposition's main
attractions; the gaze was mobilized to a new vantage. The aerial view of
Paris from the Tour d'Eiffel was previously available only to balloonists.
From this lofty *passerelle*, all of Paris unfolded like a grand magasin.[130]

The 1889 exposition contained a "Rue de Caire" and a Swiss village constructed in scenographic simulation. But in the 1900 exposition, there were more "attractions" that attempted to recreate geographical regions or historical periods, to bring both distant spaces and distant times to the center of Paris: a "Tour de Monde" recreated Africa, South America, and Asia with dioramas and plaster reproductions; a small Swiss village; a village in Andalusia (at the time of the Moors); and a proto-theme park of "Vieux Paris" which recreated medieval Paris, replete with strolling actors in costume. The "Quai des Nations"—a row of national pavilions of the most powerful nations—was designed with each building in indigenous style, lined up facing the Seine.[131] The visitor toured a virtual past and traveled to virtual distant locales.

The 1900 exposition also had a few more apparatical touring devices than previous exhibitions. One of the new features was a privately funded novelty, the trottoir roulant (a moving sidewalk with three speeds). On this sidewalk, 3.5 kilometers of moving track transported spectators through the exhibits and exhibition grounds as if they were goods on a conveyer belt. In the Russian exhibit, visitors could board seventy-foot-long train carriages—with dining room, smoking rooms, bedrooms—and take a "virtual" trip on the Trans-Siberian Railroad. Cosponsored by Compagnie Internationale des Wagon-Lits Cook, this "virtual" tour would condense the fourteen-day trip between Moscow and Peking into forty-five minutes. Scenes from Moscow Station, the Caucasus, and Siberia rolled past the windows on long canvases moving in one direction on an endless belt. In *Le globe celeste,* a seated visitor could voyage to outer space by watching rolling painted canvas. The Lumière Brothers presented the *maréorama.* Spectators sat on a platform shaped like a ship's hull, which simulated the rocking of the ocean as they viewed *cinématographe actualités* of a sea voyage to Nice, the Riviera, Naples, and Venice.

But perhaps the most dramatic mechanism to mobilize a virtual gaze was the *cinéorama.* A device engineered by Raoul Grimoin-Sanson, the cinéorama had spectators stand on an elevated platform made up like the basket of a balloon. This simulated vista provided a 360-degree panoramic view. With ten 70mm projectors in rough synchronization, the cinéorama displayed films taken from an airborne balloon. As Grimoin-Sanson recalls:

At the 1900 Paris Exposition, the moving sidewalk (*trottoir roulant*) transported

spectators through the exhibition grounds as if they were goods on a conveyer belt.

Photograph by Émile-Zola, 1900. © Massin and Dr. Françoise Émile-Zola.

With ten 70mm projectors displaying films taken from an airborne balloon, the

cinéorama simulated a 360-degree panoramic view. Raoul Grimoin-Sanson, *cinéorama*

at the Paris Exposition, 1900.

The sensation was extraordinary and many of the spectators experienced the same vertigo given by a real ascent. The animated view of Paris, between the flow of traffic and pedestrians who look up at the sky, constitutes a new sensation.[132]

The cinema projectors were put into reverse for the balloon descent. The cinéorama (and the later Hale's Tours) provided "virtual" travel without the danger or the expense.[133]

The 1900 exposition was in the center of Paris. A miniature world was constructed on 350 acres; from the entrance gate at Place de la Concorde to the Galerie des Machines—at the furthest end of Champs de Mars.[134] Not to miss the commercial opportunity, many of the Parisian department stores had pavilions. The department store was, after all, a singly-owned exposition. Whether or not this exposition was a success was debated for years.[135] But as the century ended, a new century began with other forms of mass entertainment. The mobilized gaze of the shopper, the tourist, the cinema-goer flourished in newfound virtual ways.

Many of these exhibitions remain etched in historical memory because of filmed "pan"-oramas of exhibition sights. Musser records that Edison executive James White visited the Paris Exposition in the summer of 1900 and, in addition to recording the event, he purchased a panning head for his camera tripod. On this trip White filmed *Panorama of Place de L'Opera, Panorama of Eiffel Tower,* and *Panorama of Paris Exposition, from the Seine.*[136]

Filmed "panoramas" produced a paradoxical effect. The moving camera encompassed a 180-degree to 360-degree circumference, expanding the confines of a theatrical proscenium. But at the same time this increased scope was reduced to the confines of a framed image. White's *Panorama of the Eiffel Tower* was a slow vertical pan, emphasizing the upward thrust of the iron spike. *Panorama of Place de L'Opera* returned to the site of Georges Méliès's apocryphal 1896 discovery of the substitution trick. As anecdote has it, Méliès was filming at the Place de L'Opera when his camera jammed. When he recommenced filming, an omnibus that had been in the earlier shot had driven on and a hearse had taken its place.[137] The historical significance of the Méliès incident has been magnified to signify the turn from verisimilitude in film history—Méliès as the "father" of cinematic trickery, using temporal ellipses to transform real time into a magical film time. Whereas Méliès's trick films relied on studio setting (Méliès reconstructed the floorplan of the Théâtre Robert-Houdin—complete with pulleys and trapdoors—in his studio in Montreuil), the panoramic film did not. Although it may have aimed for spatial verisimilitude, the panoramic film produced a mobilized panoramic gaze that was confined to the window frame of the film screen.

In 1901, Edwin S. Porter took the fluid-panning tripod to the Buffalo Exposition and filmed his remarkable *Circular Pan of Electric Tower* and *The Panorama of Esplanade at Night*. (The 1889 Paris Exposition was the first to use electricity, but there are no films of it.) In the daytime panorama *Circular Pan of Electric Tower* (filmed August 14, 1901), Porter made a 280-degree left-to-right pan of the exposition grounds. Like Zola's photographs of women on the trottoir roulant at the 1900 Paris Exposition, Porter's film provides remarkable documentation of the heterosocial flânerie of fairgoers. Men in boater hats stroll with other men, some arm-in-arm with women; women stroll arm-in-arm, and, at the very end of Porter's pan, we see a woman walking alone. The strollers either walk at cross-movement to the smooth panning of the camera, or a few remain stationary and look directly at the camera as it glides past. Nevertheless, women move as fluidly through this exposition space as men, and the supple camera pan increases the effect of a unfettered heterosocial space.

In *The Panorama of Esplanade at Night* (filmed on November 11, 1901), the camera is placed in a more distant position and as it pans (also left to right) across the esplanade, the buildings are seen only as outlines of glittering electric light. If there are men and women on a nocturnal stroll, it is too dark to see them. The camera traces a sight both eerie and beautiful and provides a remarkable record of the exhibition's transformation into a cinematic phantasmagoria.[138]

In Tom Gunning's terms, early filmmaking relied on this exhibitionist relation to the spectator; this "cinema of attractions" was closer to the bold visual display of the fairground attraction than it was to a storytelling form.[139]

The cinema of attractions directly solicits spectator attention, inciting visual curiosity, and supplying pleasure through an exciting spectacle—a unique event, whether fictional or documentary, that is of interest in itself.[140]

With his fluid panning tripod, Porter made a 280-degree pan
of the grounds at the Pan-American Exposition in Buffalo.
Frame stills from Edwin S. Porter, "Circular Panorama of
Electric Tower," 1901.

Gunning argues that this form of spectacle display did not disappear when narrative film became more dominant (around 1907), but "rather goes underground, both into certain avant-garde practices and as a component of narrative films" into a "Coney Island of the avant-garde, whose never dominant but always sensed current can be traced from Méliès through Keaton, through *Un Chien Andalou* and Jack Smith."[141] By emphasizing the fairground and exhibitionist roots of early cinema, Gunning challenges theories of spectatorship which rely instead on a more voyeuristic relation to an enclosed diegetic universe. Stressing that early cinema exhibition was itself an attraction, Gunning reads close-ups in early films such as *Photographing a Female Crook* (1904) not in a teleological history of conventions of narrative, but instead as "pure exhibitionism." Gunning's "cinema of attractions" is not quite coequal with the mobile virtual gaze that I am describing, but his reconceptualization of early cinema history further underlines the component pleasures of the cinema screen as a mobile display window.

The Amusement Park   Like the exhibition, the amusement park was a public site for distraction and entertainment, but it offered more participatory pleasures, bodily excitements. Its boardwalks, moving walkways, scenic railways, carousels, roller coasters, and Ferris wheels mobilized not just the gaze but the entire body.[142]

As Kathy Peiss has demonstrated in her study of working women and leisure in turn-of-the-century New York, the amusement park was also an unprecedented heterosocial space, allowing new public pleasures for working-class urban women. And these "amusements" were, above all, cheap.[143] For the price of admission there were unaccustomed extravagances, compensatory freedoms. Amusement parks offered a range of virtual mobilities: from the imaginary journeys that gave the thrill of the foreign to the reenactments (tenement fires, naval battles) which created the excitement of danger and the edification of a history lesson.

In Dreamland (which William H. Reynold opened in 1904 and which burned down in 1911), for example, one could visit Venice and Switzerland and witness the "Fall of Pompei" and "The Creation." The park had a 375-foot tower modeled after the Giralda tower in Seville.[144] In Luna Park, one could stroll through an Eskimo village, a German village, a Delhi marketplace, and then visit an imaginary location on "A Trip to the

Moon," or "A Trip to the North Pole." This meant that each "park" contained a pastiche of styles.[145]

The amusement park may have performed, as John Kasson argues, a parody of urban experience, turning the jumbled subjectivities of urban life into bodily enactments. Coney Island, writes Kasson, "appeared to have institutionalized the carnival spirit for a culture that lacked a carnival tradition."[146] And as popular attractions like the "Human Whirlpool" (at Steeplechase Park) and "The Tickler" (at Luna Park) demonstrated, one of the thrills of these rides was to literally throw the interaction between men and women off balance or to whirl gender roles into a centripetal frenzy. As Steeplechase Park's "Blow-Hole Theater" illustrated, in addition to bodily agitation, these attractions often turned the protocols of gender roles into a spectacle of parody and display.[147]

Thomas Edison's cameramen made early scenic records of Coney Island (*Shooting the Rapids in Luna Park* [1903], *Rattan Slide and General View of Luna Park* [1903] and in the same month, Porter integrated narrative comedy with Coney's scenic background in *Rube and Mandy at Coney Island.*[148] Films of amusement parks served the dual purpose of a virtual tour for those who could not visit them and as an advertisement for the latest rides and attractions for those who would.

Some historians have blamed the decline of the amusement park on the rise of the movies as a more successful illusion, a more virtual (less weather dependent) public entertainment: "Once upon a time Coney Island was the greatest amusement resort in the world. The radio and movies killed it. The movies killed illusion."[149] Certainly, the success of Disneyland, Disney World, the Universal Studio tours, and the MGM theme park is testimony to more than just the economic interdependence of the two experiences. When Disneyland opened in 1955, its "Trip to the Moon" was a cinematic evolution of the Coney Island attraction; "Tomorrowland" was a futurized elaboration on the "Vieux Paris" of the 1900 exhibition.[150]

FROM THE ARCADE TO THE CINEMA As argued in the last chapter, protocinematic illusions such as the panorama and the diorama introduced a virtual mobility that was both spatial—bringing the country to the town dweller—and temporal—transporting the past to the present. The virtual tours that these new devices presented were, in a sense, apparatical extensions of the spatial flânerie through the arcades. Not all of these "distractions" were located in

or near an arcade, but many of them were. In Paris, the Passage des Panoramas was, as we saw, lit by the same skylight that illuminated the panorama itself. The Théâtre Séraphin, site of marionette theater, shadow
plays, and phantasmagorias, was first located in the arcade of the Palais
Royal and moved, in 1858, to a location in the Passage Jouffroy. The Galerie
Vivienne—constructed in Paris in 1823—contained the *cosmorama,* an 1832
invention of Abbe Gazzara which reproduced landscapes in relief with mag-
nifying mirrors.[151] The Musée Grevin, the wax-figure museum modeled
after Madame Tussauds in London, opened in 1882 in the Passage Jouffroy.[152] The Musée Grevin was the site of the first Paris performances of
legerdemain by another soon-to-be-famed illusionist, Georges Méliès.

These architectural passages, as much sites for departure as destinations
themselves, became depots for the temporal tourism produced by a mobilized and virtual gaze. Benjamin's vision of modernity—the new, the
already obsolescent, the ever-same—found its metaphoric embodiment in
the passage and in these new apparatical exponents that produced a spatial
and temporal *passage.* Just as the department store followed the arcade, the
Passage des Panorama led to the Musée Grevin—and, eventually, to the
cinema.

In October 1895, months after reading H. G. Wells's utopian novel *The
Time Machine,* the British inventor R. W. Paul applied for a patent for a
"novel form of exhibition" in which "spectators have presented to their
view scenes which are supposed to occur in the future or past, while they
are given the sensation of voyaging upon a machine through time."[153]
Wells's science fantasy of time travel found literal embodiment in the
recently perfected machine of illusion—the cinematic apparatus.

Unlike earlier science fictions (in Louis-Sébastien Mercier's *Mémoires de
l'An 2440* [1770], a Parisian travels in a dream to 2440; in Washington
Irving's *Rip Van Winkle* [1820], the character sleeps for twenty years; in
Edward Bellamy's 1888 novel *Looking Backward,* his character Julian West
enters "mesmeric sleep" in a subterranean sleeping chamber and wakes up
in the year 2000)—in H. G. Wells's novel, the Time Traveller enters the
future on a *machine.*[154]

The Time Machine fictionalized an intricately crafted mechanism that
could transport its passenger into the future or the past at the rate of a
minute a year; the pull of the lever in one direction would "gain yesterdays,"
in the other one could "accumulate tomorrows":

"It is my plan for a machine to travel through time. . . . This lever, being pressed over, sends the machine gliding into the future and this other reverses the motion. This saddle represents the seat of a time traveller. . . . Upon that machine," said the Time Traveller, holding the lamp aloft, "I intend to explore time."[155]

Upon the "saddle" of this carriage wrought of nickel, brass, ivory, and rock crystal, Wells's unnamed narrator—the Time Traveller—sets out on a journey through time.

I drew a breath, set my teeth, gripped the starting lever with both hands, and went off with a thud. The laboratory got hazy and went dark. Mrs. Watchett came in and walked, apparently without seeing me, towards the garden door. *I suppose it took her a minute or so to traverse the place, but to me she seemed to shoot across the room like a rocket.* I pressed the lever over to its extreme position. The night came like the turning out of a lamp, and in another moment came to-morrow. The laboratory grew faint and hazy, then fainter and ever fainter. To-morrow night came black, then day again, night again, day again, faster and faster still.[156] (emphasis added)

As his motion through time accelerates, the Time Traveller compares the sensation to the bodily movement of an amusement park ride:

I'm afraid I cannot convey the peculiar sensations of time travelling. They are excessively unpleasant. *There is a feeling exactly like that one has upon a switchback—of a helpless headlong motion!*[157] (emphasis added)

He proceeds at "over a year a minute," in a "kind of hysterical exhilaration." The Time Traveller doesn't explain the mechanism of his Time Machine but instead regales his friend Filby and other doubtful cohorts—the Psychologist, the Provincial Mayor, the Medical Man, and the Very Young Man—with his adventures in "futurity." The bulk of Wells's novel is a description of the year 802701 where a gentle people, the Eloi, live in the apparent "ease and security" of a postconsumerist world where "the shop, the advertisement, traffic, all that commerce which constitutes the body of our world, was gone."[158] Following the mixed conventions of gothic romance and utopian novel, Wells's Time Traveller becomes enthralled with a childlike female who he must leave soon after he discovers the cannibalistic consequences of master and slave class differentiation between the Eloi and the Morlock. The time machine assures his return to his present. On this return, the perceptual sensations of time travel are reversed:

When I set out, before my velocity was very high, Mrs. Watchett had walked across the room, travelling, as it seemed to me, like a rocket. *As I returned, I passed again across that minute when she traversed the laboratory. But now her every motion appeared to be the exact inverse of her previous ones.*[159] (emphasis added)

In 1926, film historian Terry Ramsaye uses these two sections from the novel to draw the direct relation between Wells's conception of a "time machine" and the behavior of a film. (Ramsaye wrote to Wells to inquire about the "motion-picture root" for his time machine but Wells was "unable to remember the details."[160] The coincidence between Wells's novel (published in 1895) and Paul's patent application (October 24, 1895) causes Ramsaye to enthuse over the "Wells-Paul idea": "It sought to liberate the spectator from the instant of Now. . . . It was a plan to give the spectator possession, on equal terms, of Was and To Be along with Is."[161] Like the cinéorama and other devices that combined projection lanterns, scenic settings, and platform devices to simulate motion, the "mechanism" in the Paul patent was a platform on which spectators face an opening onto a screen. The platform was to be suspended by cranks, which provided a "general rocking motion." A current of air blown over the spectators was "intended to represent to spectators the means of propulsion." Paul's patent application described a mechanism that was arranged like the diorama, with spectators seated on a platform that would "create the impression of travelling":

After the starting of the mechanism, and a suitable period having elapsed, representing, say a certain number of centuries, during which the platforms may be in darkness, or in alternations of darkness and dim light, the mechanism may be slowed and a pause made at a given epoch, on which the scene upon the screen will come gradually into view of the spectators, increasing in size and distinctness from a small vista.

But unlike the diorama with its painted vistas, the views presented were cinematic. The "realistic effect" in this mechanism was composed of:

(1) A hypothetical landscape, containing also the representations of the inanimate objects in the scene.
(2) A slide, or slides, which may be traversed horizontally or vertically and contain representations of objects such as navigable balloon etc. which is required to traverse the scene.
(3) *Slides or films, representing in successive instantaneous photographs, after the manner of the Kinetoscope, the living persons or creatures in their natural motions. The films or slides are prepared with the aid of the kinetograph or special camera,* from made-up characters performing on the stage. (emphasis added)

Paul planned this "time machine" to be located in a context that simulated a historical "epoch"; spectators would "travel bodily forward through a short space" that reinforced the effect of temporal tourism:

In order to increase the *realistic effect* I may arrange that after a certain number of scenes from a hypothetical future have been presented to spectators, they may be allowed to step from the platforms, and *be conducted through grounds or buildings arranged to represent exactly one of the epochs through which the spectator is supposed to be traveling.*[162] (emphasis added)

In close coincidence with the Paul patent request in Britain, the French brothers, Louis and Auguste Lumière, had—on February 13, 1895—their first private projection of films recorded and projected on their patented device, the cinematograph. And on December 28, 1895, the first public projection of Lumière "actualités" took place in a *petite salle* in the basement of the Grand Café, Boulevard des Capucines. The cinematograph was a time machine that now brought time travel to the boulevard café.

The same impulses that sent flâneurs through the arcades, traversing the pavement and wearing thin their shoe leather, sent shoppers into the department stores, tourists to exhibitions, spectators into the panorama, diorama, wax museum, and cinema.[163]

Edwin S. Porter, *The European Rest Cure*, 1904.

A SHORT FILM IS MORE OF A "REST CURE"

The European Rest Cure (1904)

In Edwin S. Porter's half-reel comedy, *The European Rest Cure* (1904), the narrative makes a simple point: the "rest cure" of a European "grand tour" proves to be far from restful; the "foreign" is dangerous, the familiar benign. In addition to this narrative content, the form of the film illustrates the similarities between the narrative conventions of early cinema and tourist operations.[1]

The European Rest Cure is a thirteen-shot film that mixes actuality footage with acted fictional setups. It was a common trope for Porter to mix actuality footage with contrived narrative: of the film's thirteen shots, six are exterior (five introductory and one concluding shot), and seven are studio tableaux. The story is designed to dissuade the traveler from exotic locales; the natural beauty of home is presented in the photographic fluidity of the exterior shots of the harbor and pier.

The film opens with an exterior shot of an empty gangplank leading to a steamship. A steward enters the frame carrying a suitcase on his shoulders. He is followed by a man and two women. The camera pans slightly as they cross the gangplank to board the ship. The man kisses the two women in a gesture of farewell; his departure is drawn out as he waves a handkerchief and embraces the two women several times. As the women reluctantly walk away, the man runs after them for one last embrace. The shot ends with the man entering the ship and the title: ALL ABOARD. This opening shot establishes the narrative premise by emphasizing the man's difficult departure. Our tourist is a man who leaves his female relatives behind and he is homesick before he has left home.

In the next shot, the camera pans slowly left to right, past crowds of people on the pier. An ocean liner full of waving passengers pulls through the shot right to left. Like the first shot, this is also an exterior shot, but this one has no actors; rather it is actuality footage of a ship departure in New York harbor. The camera is mobile, panning slightly to the left as the ship leaves the frame. Men wearing boaters and women with parasols wave their handkerchiefs in farewell. The title is now a Frenchified good-bye: AU REVOIR.

For the next shot, the camera is placed on the ship as it tracks out past the New York skyline. The camera movement is expansive, mobile, and literally fluid. In this exterior shot, a man climbs down the side of the ship on a rope ladder. (The intertitle identifies the action: DROPPING THE PILOT.) The camera pans down to the water, following his descent to a boat that picks him up and pulls him off frame.

Title: THE STORM. After this title, the next shot is taken from a camera position at the bow of the ship as it pitches over rolling surf. As in the previous two shots, there is camera movement, panning, tilting, tracking. The frame-line is fluid and unbound. The storm-at-sea is the film's most mobile shot and it is followed in a nearly matched continuity cut without intertitle (the only shot in the film that is edited without an intertitle) by an interior studio tableau of a stateroom with canopy bed, dresser, and chair. The stateroom reels and rocks in a motion that matches the previous shot, but the illusion of a storm-tossed voyage is given by a contrived movement of the camera rocking on its tripod. A man sits in the chair center frame, grasping at his mouth, stomach, and head respectively, gesticulating wildly his dis-ease. As the camera continues to rock back and forth, he falls onto the bed, is tossed out of bed onto the floor, while water pours in through the porthole-shaped window.

Title: KISSING THE BLARNEY STONE.[2] This title signals the arrival in Europe, where the man's "tour" becomes a traversal of studio sets designed to be "foreign." The first of these tour stops is a static studio shot with painted clouds and faux stone walkway. The tourists—three men and two women—enter the frame and move laterally right to left. The tour is a heterosocial adventure and our man, now equipped with binoculars and a map, negotiates these foreign spaces with female tourists at his side. His fellow tourists dangle him over the stone wall, holding him by his feet so that he can kiss the Blarney stone, and he is unceremoniously dropped, falling off frame.

Title: DOING PARIS. In a painted trompe l'oeil of an arcade outdoor cafe (the Palais Royal?), there are two tables, one on each side of the frame. A man in a beret sits at one table and at the other table two women sit alone. Our man enters, sits with the man until the two women gesture toward him.

He gets up, crosses the frame, and joins the women. A waiter appears, takes their order, brings apertifs, and they toast and drink more. Very quickly, our man and the two *femmes publiques* stand up and dance wildly in a kick-line center frame. Three different women enter from the arcade and pull him away. By now, one of the first women is dancing on the table as the other kicks her legs in wild abandon. The man is hustled off frame. The film suggests that some women in public space are free spirits with regard to drink and dance, but the female tourists who accompany our man also monitor his opprobium.

Title: CLIMBING THE ALPS. There is no continuity between these disparate tour stops which follow each other in a sequence of painted tableaux. Against a backdrop of rocks and mountains, the tourists enter right to left and traverse the frame in a lateral movement, hiking with climbing sticks, escorted by a guard. Our man teeters nervously on the mountain path and, as he is helped up the mountain, he falls. His group throws him a rope and he is pulled back into the frame. The shot ends with the man on bended knee, praying.

Title: HOLD UP IN ITALY. Against a deChirico-like tableau of the Pompeii ruins in forced perspective, the tourists enter with a guide. Our man poses for a photo and the others toddle off, leaving him for a moment alone center frame reading his map. Three bandits (in sombreros) enter and rob him, emptying his pockets at gunpoint. They leave the frame and our man kneels in prayer as his fellow tourists return to the scene.

Title: CLIMBING THE PYRAMIDS OF EGYPT. Against a perspectival backdrop of the pyramids with the Sphinx in the distance, a guide and two half-dressed "natives" help the tourists climb a pyramid at the edge of the frame. Our man, now in a safari hat, is helped up the pyramid; he leaves the frame and the shot remains empty for a moment with only the painted desert and the angular shadow of a distant pyramid until our man falls off his pyramid, back into the frame. As his cohorts rescue him, the tour captain scolds the "natives."

Title: MUDBATHS OF GERMANY. In the center of this tableau two men in skivvies force our man into a round tub and cover him with mud. They then splash water on him while he shakes and quivers.

Title: HOME SWEET HOME. The film's final shot is an exterior; a porter enters the frame approaching a coach carrying a suitcase on shoulders. Following him is our man, a bit wobbly, a blanket wrapped around his shoulders. He is followed by the two women who were in the first shot. The title here is not ironic.

The tour itself is a series of claustrophobically circumscribed studio tableaux. Each shot is a stop on the "grand tour" (Kissing the Blarney Stone, Doing Paris, Climbing the Alps, Hold Up in Italy, Climbing the Pyramids of Egypt, The Mudbaths of Germany). The narrative is told as a series of "foreign" spaces, each made static and confined. The characters move left to right or right to left through interior spaces with painted backdrops. In each tableau, our tourist is thrown off balance, or falls off frame, or cowers at the center of the shot. For the spectator of this film, the foreign is presented in very clumsy faux-virtual landscapes, coded in a set of familiar xenophobic clichés. Paradoxically, "home" is represented with more realistic detail— actual footage of the harbor and port and with more camera mobility. As a film that professes an antitravel message, it asserts the beauty of cinematic spectatorship as a more spectacular and fluid form of virtual mobility.[3]

THE CINEMA AS TIME MACHINE

Paris Qui Dort (1923)/La Jetée (1962)/Alphaville (1965)

In Rene Clair's 1923 Paris Qui Dort (The Crazy Ray), a mad scientist manipulates the world with an invisible "crazy ray." (The X-ray was discovered in 1895 in a remarkable historical coincidence with emergence of the cinema.) The film makes no direct reference to the cinema camera as a machine with the capacity to stop, fast forward, and reverse motion, but Clair's "ray," the cinema's fictional equivalent, performs similar transformations on chronological narrative.

Like The European Rest Cure, Paris Qui Dort mixes actuality footage with a contrived narrative; here the streets and parks of Paris become the testing ground for Dr. Crase's experimental instrument. The film opens as Albert, the watchman at the Eiffel Tower, awakens to find that the city of Paris is "asleep." As he descends the elevator, the camera's mobilized gaze tracks a dramatic aerial vista of Paris through the iron latticework of the tower. Albert ventures into the streets and finds that automobiles are stopped midboulevard, people are "frozen" into statuesque poses, all of Paris is paralytically still.

The film narrativizes the animated transition between the mobility of the cinema camera and the immobility of the still photograph. As Michelson has

The cinema as time machine: In Rene Clair's *Paris Qui Dort*, a "crazy ray" had the capacity to stop, fast forward, and reverse motion. Frame stills from Rene Clair, *Paris Qui Dort*, 1923. Courtesy of the Museum of Modern Art, New York

shown, Clair's "frozen" Paris is remarkably reminiscent of the photographs of Eugene Atget. Benjamin wrote of Atget's haunting images of Paris: "It has quite justly been said of [Atget] that he photographed [the streets of Paris] like scenes of a crime."[4] In Clair's film, a would-be suicide on the edge of the Seine is frozen midjump, the note in his hand explaining that he can't take the pace of modern life; and a robber is frozen middash a few steps ahead of his police-pursuer.

Exploring the static streets, Albert meets a carload of five others who have just arrived in Paris by airplane—a woman of means, a man traveling to see his fiancée, a thief and his jailer, and the pilot. Together they discover that as motion is suspended in the city, so is the law: in a café they drink and eat without paying, they lift pearls from a woman's neck, take champagne and money from a waiter. *Paris Qui Dort* is a meditation on photography: the still images demonstrate the photograph's evidentiary potential (the fiancée is caught midseduction, with another lover) and its challenge to the aura of the original (the Mona Lisa, scavenged from the Louvre, hangs out the car window).

It doesn't take long for the characters to get bored with the world in its static state. When a wireless message is received in the tower, the group rushes to find the sender. They arrive at the laboratory of Dr. Crase, where his desperate daughter has radioed for help. The daughter explains her father's time experiment and takes them to see his crude, almost Expressionist machine with dials and a single lever. The group convinces Dr. Crase to return the world to movement; and as he pushes the lever forward, the film cuts to shots of the city as it begins to move. Michelson writes of this shift from paralysis to rescusitated motion:

A sort of electric charge or thrill is produced by the instants of freeze and of release. This of course is the aspect of filmic experience most characteristic of the moviola or editing machine experience of film.[5]

Paris Qui Dort is a narrative built around the shift from photography to film, exploiting the cinematic capacity of a time machine, an invisible but unacknowledged "crazy ray."

Chris Marker's 1962 film *La Jetée* uses Paris in an inverted formal strategy. In Marker's film, every image (with one notable exception) is a still photograph, and the formal tension between cinematic movement and photographic stasis is equally the subject of the film. The story—told in a narration over a series of still images linked by dissolves, fades, and cuts—is about a man who is obsessed by a single image from his childhood, a moment on the jetty at Orly airport before World War III. As the narrating voice tells us, after the war the man is selected to travel through time because of his particular "obsession with an image from the past." Like René Clair, Chris Marker uses Paris—the capital of the nineteenth century—as a site for this time travel. The film suggests that because the man is "given to strong mental images," he has an eidetic record of memory and a special access to the past. The images that we see, frozen in photographic stasis, suggest that the photograph is itself a time machine, a virtual passage to the past.[6]

Jean Luc Godard's *Alphaville* also uses Paris as a backdrop for experiments in time and, although its narrative does not claim that Lemmy Caution is traveling through time, *Alphaville* points to the complex temporality of cinema itself. Made in Paris in January and February of 1965, *Alphaville* selects "modern" buildings, night boulevards, and jukeboxes and uses them, without much disguise, as the Paris of the future. By adding sound effects, cigarette lighters become beepers and an electric fan with a blinking light behind it becomes the image of the computer, Alpha 60. Alphaville is a city in which memory is forbidden, words (conscience, tenderness) disappear, executions take place in a water ballet spectacle at an indoor swimming pool, and Alpha 60 recites the mantra of perpetual presence: "No one lived in the Past. No one lives in the Future." Both *La Jetée* and *Alphaville* are set in a dystopic future where nostalgia for the past is a pervasive affect. Viewed on videotape in southern California in 1992, *Paris Qui Dort* (filmed in Paris in 1923, set in a fictional Paris circa 1923), *La Jetée* (filmed in Paris in 1962, set in a fictional Paris after World War III), and *Alphaville* (filmed in Paris in 1965, set in a fictional Paris of the future) become vivid examples of how the cinematic apparatus conflates the time of production and the time of the fiction with the time of projection.

The cinema functions as a machine for virtual time travel in three ways: first, as a theatrical "set piece," set in a period in the past or in the future; second in its capacity, through montage, to elicit an elliptical temporality; and third, in its ability to be repeated, over time, imparting to each spectator a unique montage-consciousness.

The Time Machine (1960)

The 1960 film of the *The Time Machine,* made by special effects wizard George Pal,[7] makes numerous departures from the 1895 H. G. Wells novel. It is not surprising that a film adaptation of this novel would pay more attention to the visual mechanisms of time travel than did its written source material.

The film dramatizes Wells's turn-of-the-century excursion into the future by setting the narrative on the last day of 1899. The Time Machine is visualized as a Victorian sleigh with a plush red velvet seat, brass workings, levers, and flashing lights, with a spinning parabolic dish behind. It sits in the middle of a laboratory with glass beakers and other scientific instruments, facing the panes of a window. Before he climbs into the carriage, the Time Traveller (unnamed in Wells's novel) George (Rod Taylor) lights a candle and checks the clock. After he adjusts himself in the seat, he pushes the lever forward. The first countershot, demonstrating the machine's effect, shows a blur in focus. The subjective experience of time travel is clearly equated with a camera effect. The focus sharpens and George notes that the clock has advanced and the candle has burned down.

As George continues to push the lever forward, we see countershots of the (pixilated fast motion of the) candle burning down completely and the clock hands flipping around the dial. Flowers open and bloom, a snail races across the floor, hours speed across the face of the sundial. The motion of the time machine is now clearly that of the cinema camera; the fast motion acceleration is much like the nature films of Jean Painlevé from the Twenties.[8]

Out the window of his laboratory, George sees the shop window of a store across the way. He watches his housekeeper stop in front of the window. "Dear Mrs. Watchett," he narrates as she looks at the female mannequin on display, "always able to tell me what tie to wear but never able to decide to wear anything more stylish than the clothes she'd worn all these years." As George delivers this monologue, the medium-shot through the window cuts to a close-up of the mannequin in an ankle-length red velvet dress. George pushes the lever onward, and clouds and the sun streak in pixilated motion across the skylight. "I could stop for a day or an hour or even a second to observe." George stops the machine on June 10, 1900, and the mannequin in

The time machine as envisioned in
the 1960 film version of H. G.
Well's 1895 novel. *The Time
Machine.* Courtesy of the
Academy of Motion Picture Arts
and Sciences.

the window is now wearing a low-cut ankle-length green dress. "Thus I was able to see the changing world in a series of glimpses."

The shop window is his marker of temporality: the new, the already past, the ever-same. The mannequin and the shop window remain constant, the clothes and accessories are the new and the already past. On his next stop, the window mannequin is wearing a purple dress with a bustle. "Good Heavens! That's a dress!" exclaims George, "I wondered just how far women would permit it to go." Pixilated fast motion continues as a male window dresser pulls the clothes off the mannequin, we see her nude for a moment, and then he changes her to a red dress with fur cape. The pixilation continues without the male assistance, and the mannequin is undressed, attired in a short green bloomer dress, then undressed again, and changed into a white lace dress with parasol. "I began to grow very fond of that mannequin, maybe because like me, she didn't age."

Many of the alterations that the film makes in the 1895 Wells's story are made from the vantage of the year 1960. The time machine stops in 1917, the windows are boarded up, and the Time Traveller discovers the war with Germany; after a brief stop, George pulls down the boards, exposes his window again, and the window dressing moves onward in fast motion. "The years rolled by everything unfamiliar except for the smile of my never changing friend." He stops again in the 1940s during World War II and, in 1966, during an atomic emergency that sends people scurrying into shelters. From its 1960 perspective, the film rehearses the known past, and anticipates the atomic anxiety of the future.

Throughout film history, some cinematic narratives (from *Paris Qui Dort* to *La Jetée* to *The Time Machine*) have dealt with time travel in diegetic terms— but cinematic and televisual apparatuses do so *implicitly*. In this light, the proliferation of time-travel narratives in the 1980s (e.g., *Back to the Future 1, 2,* and *3, Peggy Sue Got Married* [1985], *Terminator 1* and *2* [1982, 1991], *Bill and Ted's Excellent Adventure* and *Bogus Journey* [1988, 1991],[9] *Time Riders, Late for Dinner* [1991]) seems symptomatic of anxiety about time and the loss of history.[10]

The feet of the *flâneur*. Les Halles,
Paris 1988. Photograph © Anne
Friedberg.

"I just arrived in this *stupid suburb*. I have no friends, no
money, no car, no license, and even if I did have a license
all I could do was drive out to some *stupid mall* and maybe
if I'm lucky play some fucking video games, smoke a joint
and get stupid.

You see there's nothing to do anymore. Everything
decent's been done. *All the great themes have been used up,
turned into theme parks.* So I don't really find it exactly
cheerful to be living in the middle of a totally like
exhausted decade where there is nothing to look forward to
and no one to look up to."

CHRISTIAN SLATER in the 1990 film, *Pump Up the Volume*[1]
(emphasis added)

Let us now shift from origins to exponents, from causes to effects—from
the beginnings of the rupture of modernity to its present-day remains. The
ultimate extension of nineteenth-century urban artificial environments—
parks, passageways, department stores, exhibition halls—is that contemporary urban "center," the shopping mall. If, for Benjamin, the arcade
instantiated all of modernity, the shopping mall is an equally pivotal site,
the key "topos," of postmodern urban space.

The nineteenth-century *passage* was readable to Benjamin while in its
decline (*Verfall*). Perhaps, equally, the contemporary shopping mall now
emerges as a comprehensible cultural space as it is threatened with its own
obsolescence. (Electronic technologies now bring information, entertainment, products, and services into the home, the privatized public space of
the shopping mall may soon be replaced by the "electronic mall" and the
"home shopping network."[2]) But whether or not life in the public realm

diminishes, electronic flânerie further turns spaces into their virtual replacements, "conduits" that supplant the need for physical mobility.[3] Just as the shift to a credit economy has relied on the virtual buying power of plastic, virtual realities, electronic "villages," and invisible "data highways" have become the new frontier. "Virtual" has entered the vernacular as the present predictive.[4]

And yet for the moment, the dystopic aspects of urban flânerie are all too apparent. As homelessness becomes an increasingly visible consequence of the economies of obsolescence, the fluid subjectivity of the flâneur takes on a direct, if deplorable, implication. The all-too-familiar "street person" with shopping cart conducts a dire parody of a consumer culture gone awry. As a grim reminder of the excessive valuation of the perceptual mode of shopping-flânerie, the flâneuse as "bag lady" can stroll the "aisles" of a derelict urbanity, where shopping can be done without money, the "shelves" stocked with refuse and recyclable debris.

In this chapter, I will discuss the shopping mall as an architectural and social space. As I have already demonstrated, the cinema developed as an apparatus that combined the mobile with the virtual gaze and turned it into a commodifiable experience. I now argue a further alignment of the seemingly separate activities of shopping and tourism with cinema and television spectatorship. The shopping mall developed as a site for combining the speculative activity of shopping with the mobilities of tourism; the shopping mall "multiplex" cinema epitomizes both in a virtual form. And, as a mobilized gaze becomes more and more virtual, the physical body becomes a more and more fluid site; in this "virtual mobility" the actual body—gender-bound, race-bound, ethnicity-bound—becomes a veritable depot for departure and return. Hence, the changes in reception produced by multiplex cinemas, cable television, and VCRs will force us to challenge previous theoretical accounts of spectatorship, the body, and temporality.

Although a discussion of how these changes relate to a "post" to modernity will be suspended until the next chapter, let us retain the above epigraph from the 1990 film *Pump Up the Volume* to set our introductory tone. Even the most banal rhetoric of the fin de siècle pleads a certain exhaustion: a foreclosed sense of the future, where the only imaginable option is a turning back onto the past.

THE MALL   The word *mall* is etymologically taken from *pall mall,* the protected grassy fairways for the eighteenth-century English sport called pall mall, a combination of golf and croquet. The game, one of many where a stick and a ball are exercised in the precision of eye-hand coordination, is played with a ball that is hit by a stick and aimed at a goal. But in the shopping mall the goal is less obvious. In the game of shopping mall consumerism, the ball is the consumer and the shop window the stick.[5]

As a commercial form, the shopping mall is a distinctive sign of the global dissemination of late capitalist economies; it originated in North America, spread to Europe, Australia, Japan, Central and South America, and the Middle East. The United States led other developed capitalist countries in this form of consumer marketing. In 1957 there were three thousand shopping centers in the United States; by the mid 1970s seventeen thousand; by 1986 over twenty-six thousand. (Australia is second to the United States in number of shopping centers—and, in 1973, it had fewer than one hundred.[6]) The "shopping *center*" was a commercial concomitant to the demographic shifts produced by post–World War II urban populations decentered to the suburbs, its location a consequence of the automobile and more efficient highway systems.

Like the arcade in the 1830s and 1840s, by the mid-1970s the shopping mall had become a generic building type. As an architectural space, the mall derives its form both from the vaulted interiors of the nineteenth-century arcade and from the multistoried central well of the department store; both structures were designed to maximize the commercial effectiveness of a public interior.

The first fully enclosed two-level shopping mall was built in Edina, Minnesota, in 1956. Designed by Viennese emigré architect Victor Gruen, it was the first shopping complex to turn the shops away from the parking lot and toward one another.[7] (In Minnesota, of course, the bitter cold winter climate made this a wise design decision.) In this environmentally-determined plan linking two "anchor" stores, Gruen's design for an indoor shopping center became a model for maximizing trading space via the multilevel enclosed mall. The "sales breed sales" logic of the department store was adapted to the shopping center where each store was still a separate (often competing) business.[8] In the United States, the energy crisis of 1973 added the natural-light atrium as a new design element to the enclosed mall. Atrium malls invoke a more direct architectural quotation of a capacious nineteenth-century public space, with vaulted clerestory roof, indoor plants, wrought-iron railings, and tiled floors.⁹ If the energy crisis produced a disturbing sense of scarcity for the American consumer, the bounteous emporiums of the shopping mall provided a reassuring salve.

The mall encourages the perceptual mode of flânerie while instrumentalizing it for consumer objectives. Jon Jerde, the architect of a paradigmatic Los Angeles shopping mall, the Westside Pavilion, describes his concept of the American variation on flânerie:

Urban and suburban Americans seldom stroll aimlessly, as Europeans do, to parade and rub shoulders in a crowd. We need a *destination, a sense of arrival* at a definite location. My aim, in developments such as Horton Plaza and the Westside Pavilion, *is to provide a destination that is also a public parade and a communal center.*¹⁰ (emphasis added)

For Jerde, the speculative gaze of the shopper provides the motor for such flânerie.

Like the nineteenth-century train station, the shopping mall provides the "sense of arrival" and of departure; the shopper strolls distractedly past an assortment of stores that promise consumerist digression. Zola described the department store as a "wonderful commercial machine"; the shopping mall is equally a selling machine designed to process shoppers through its cogs and pinions. Shopping mall planners employ a mechanist rhetoric to describe the circulation of consumers: magnet stores, generators, flow, pull. Escalators provide an illusion of travel, a mechanized mobility to the shopper's gaze in a serene glide through an entirely consumerist space.

Although architects and urban planners address the relation of the mall to its externals—its location in relation to the highway, the subdivision, the "metro-nucleation" of businesses clustered around the mall—the regional specificity of a shopping mall is not always considered. Many malls are planned as mini–theme parks—a mixed-use environment where the range of commodity-experiences "breeds sales." Such planning is a canny commercial synthesis of the activities of shopping and tourism, combining a wide variety of rationales for the mobile and virtual gaze of a shopper-spectator. Suburban mall planners rely on the logic of distraction to supply alternative vistas, a compensatory escape from drab suburbia and the imaginative parameters of its inhabitants. Enclosed malls that reclaim old market areas of cities (South Street Seaport in New York; Faneuil Hall in Boston; Ghiradelli Square in San Francisco) provide an equally canny combination of tourist destination with consumerist diversion.[11] As we will see, multiplex cinemas fit ideally into this commercial mix.

The "world's largest" shopping mall in Edmonton, Alberta (constructed from 1981 until 1986), provides a suitably hyperbolic example. The West Edmonton Mall is, in Jerde's sense, a destination. Consumers travel from all over Alberta on a pilgrimage to what the mall's publicists call the "Eighth Wonder of the World."[12] The West Edmonton Mall contains the world's largest indoor amusement park, a "wave pool" and five-acre waterpark with raging rapids, a fourteen-story-high triple-loop high-speed roller coaster, an ice rink, a saltwater dolphin tank, a full-size replica of the Columbus flagship *Santa Maria,* a fleet of submarines (larger than that of the Canadian Navy), a simulated "Europa" boulevard, a reconstituted "Bourbon Street," 110 eating establishments, and twenty-three cinemas. In addition, the attached Fantasyland Hotel has "fantasy rooms" that are thematic recreations of "ancient" Rome, a Hollywood nightclub, and a Polynesian catamaran. The West Edmonton Mall is a "world in miniature."

The mall is not a completely *public* place.[13] Like the arcade before it, the street is made safely distant inside the mall. Like the department store— with shared pedestrian areas between various departments—the mall becomes a realm for consumption, effectively exiling the realm of production from sight. Like the theme park, the mall is "imagineered" with maintenance and management techniques, keeping invisible the delivery bays or support systems, concealing the security guards and bouncers who control its entrances. The mall is a contemporary phantasmagoria, enforcing a blindness to a range of urban blights—the homeless, beggars, crime, traffic, even weather. And, while the temperature-controlled environment of the indoor mall defies seasons and regional environments, the presence of trees and large plants give the illusion of outdoors. The mall creates a nostalgic image of the town center as a clean, safe, and legible place, but a peculiarly timeless place.[14] As Barthes described the paradoxical "transported immobility" of tourism, the shopping mall imparts an inverse effect, a mobilized transportability: not psychic stasis, but psychic travel.[15]

""Europa Boulevard" in the West
Edmonton Mall, 1992. Photograph
© Anne Friedberg.

   At the same time that malls are mixed-use heterotopias, they are also
heterodystopias, the dialectical shadow of an Edenic ambulatory.[16] In a
marked discussion of the inner-city "Panopticon Mall," critic Mike Davis
has underlined the dystopic aspects of this consumerized "public" space.
Davis targets shopping mall developer Alexander Haagens who, borrowing
"brazenly" from Bentham's prison model, has developed more than forty
shopping centers (mostly in low-income neighborhoods) with closed-circuit
video surveillance. The Haagens-designed Martin Luther King Center in
Los Angeles is, for example, a fortress surrounded by eight-foot fences, with
video cameras and motion detectors at every entrance. Based on the same
"brutal dissymmetry" as the Bentham prison, this "security" system—

designed to protect owners and managers—turns the shopping mall into a "seeing machine" reproducing the scopic regimes of power and visuality that Foucault found basic to modernity. The shopper becomes a direct analog to the prisoner who internalizes the surveillant gaze; but here the consumerist exercise of power (through looking; where purchase—not theft—is the sanctioned way to "having") becomes the internalized mode.[17] In a further Orwellian direction, a Denver company now markets a security device—"Anne Droid"—a mannequin with a camera in her eye and a microphone in her nose. A female mannequin empowered with a surveillant gaze "returns the look" as a deceptive decoy against consumer theft.[18] Seen in this light, the shopper is dialectically both the observer and the observed, the transported and confined, the dioramic and the panoptic subject.

"Malling" as Cultural Activity

> Individuals no longer compete for the possession of goods they actualize themselves in consumption.
>
> JEAN BAUDRILLARD

> I've a mind to give up living and go shopping instead.
>
> PAUL BUTTERFIELD

In contemporary culture, the marketing of "commodity-experiences" has almost surpassed the marketing of goods. As *Fortune* magazine pronounced in 1986, there is "a new generation of consumers who crave experiences not goods. . . . in the metaphysics of the market, only those who buy and sell truly exist."[19] Or, in the hyperbolic phrasing of Baudrillard, "we have reached the point where 'consumption' has grasped the whole of life." In Baudrillard's description of the landscape of accumulation and profusion, consumption is synecdochal behavior, marking one's subjective interpellation into "consumer society":

Our markets, our shopping avenues and malls mimic a newfound nature of prodigious fecundity. Those are our Valleys of Canaan where flows, instead of milk and honey, streams of neon on ketchup and plastic—but no matter!

There exists an anxious anticipation, not that there may not be enough, but that there is too much, and too much for everyone: by purchasing a portion one in effect appropriates a whole crumbling pyramid of oysters, meats, pears or canned asparagus. *One purchases the part for the whole.*[20]

The overwhelmed consumer "purchases the part for the whole." As if to echo Benjamin's description of the passage as a "world in miniature," Baudrillard asserts "a drugstore can become a whole city."[21] The "drugstore"— the French version of a shopping mall—captures in a "kaleidoscopic mode" the profusion of merchandise in display. The consumer must compute the "calculus of objects":

The drugstore (or the new shopping malls) makes possible the synthesis of all consumer activities, not least of which are *shopping, flirting with objects, idle wandering, and all the permutations of these.*[22] (emphasis added)

William Kowinski's popular 1985 book, *The Malling of America,* provides a detailed descriptive account of "malling" as the "chief cultural activity in America." Kowinski is succinct in his claims for the shopping mall: "a new Main Street," "a virtual one-stop culture," "cathedrals of the postwar culture," "a utopia fashioned by the not-quite-invisible hand of merchandising."[23]

Despite the fact that the mall seems to embody the temperate and benign, it has figured as the site for a range of cultural extremes—from the dystopic locus of horror in films like George Romero's 1979 film *Dawn of the Dead* to the equally extreme claims of religious utopianists. In *Dawn of the Dead* zombie-shoppers ride the escalators in a lobotomized exaggeration of consumer robotics. In this film, the mall is a runaway machine; its escalators, fountains, videogames, and automated voice-announcements continue in endless repetition as the "back-from-the-dead" move with equally mechanical motions. "What are they doing? Where do they come from?" asks a terrorized shopper. Another shopper (as if recalling Benjamin's discussion of the passages as "residues of a dream world"[24]) provides an incisive reply: "Part instinct, part memory, what they used to do. This was an important place in their lives. . . . These creatures are . . . pure motorized instinct."

In *Dawn of the Dead* (George
Romero, 1979), zombie-shoppers
ride escalators in a lobotomized
exaggeration of consumer
robotics. Courtesy Museum of
Modern Art, New York.

At the other extreme, in *The New Religious Image of Urban America: The Shopping Mall as Ceremonial Center,* Ira Zepp describes the mall as a sacred ceremonial center where "people are meeting their needs for renewal and reconnection." Whereas the mall serves as a locus of alienation in Romero's film, Zepp claims, "the need we have for solidarity with one another is a religious expression" (emphasis added).[25] In this argument, shopping becomes a ritual rejoinder to spiritual impoverishment. The commercial basis of the shopping mall "community" provides a tangential secondary gain.

With a more ideological valence, Meaghan Morris's study of shopping centers in Australia initiates a "feminist study" of shopping practices which implies the potential for shopping as a form of critique. "Like effective shopping," Morris argues, "feminist criticism includes moments of sharpened focus, narrowed gaze—of skeptical, if not paranoid, assessment."[26] As we have seen, the historical relation between feminism and female consumerism supports this analogy (made emphatic in Stanton's rallying cry: "GO OUT AND BUY!"). A recently sighted bumper sticker—"A Woman's Place Is in the Mall"—confirms the demographics: as one study maintains, at the mall, 85 percent of the shoppers are women.[27]

In this light, the shopping mall appears to be a historical endpoint of increasing female empowerment, a "Ladies Paradise" for the contemporary flâneuse. And yet, to embrace the practice of shopping as a form of protofeminist subjectivity will risk overlooking some notable liabilities. The prerogatives of the female shopper may be endorsed in the market (as in "the customer is always right"), but the relation between *looking* and *buying* is not an unmediated one.

First, the relation of female "spending power" to female "earning power" is a critical equation in a consumer economy. Shopping is more than a perceptual mode involving the empowered choices of the consumer, it— quite simply, quite materially—requires money. A credit-card economy may encourage the fantasy of *virtual* "spending power," but this imaginary diversion has a price. Veblen read female consumption as a "vicarious" sign of a husband's or father's wealth. Today's female consumer may be enacting a postmodern version of an equally "vicarious" empowerment; instead of deferring payment to husband or father, she defers payment to the bank.[28]

And second, despite the illusion that shopping is about choice, the desires that activate these choices have been, in many cases, created by display techniques, advertising, and, often, by films themselves. It has been a staple

Car window tag. © 1987 H & L
Enterprises, El Cajon, California.

of studies of consumer culture to describe the ways in which commodity-
"fetishes" have been created and then displayed to prey upon a shopper's
psychic needs, where consumer "choice" is only a reaction to a constructed
desire.[29]

The public space of the market is a contemporary arena for symptomatic
pathologies. In this way, today's "compulsive shopper"—driven by an irre-
sistible urge to buy—becomes a fitting contemporary equivalent to the
nineteenth-century hysteric.[30] Following Elaine Showalter's question about
the relation of feminism to hysteria ("Was hysteria—the 'daughter's dis-
ease'—a mode of protest for women deprived of other social or intellectual
outlets or expressive options?"), one might ask: Is compulsive shopping a
mode of protest for the powerlessness felt in other social or intellectual
arenas?[31]

In a recent self-help book, *Women Who Shop Too Much,* Carolyn Wesson
offers an eleven-step recovery program for "shopaholics" and "addicted
shoppers" who seek to "escape other problems, relieve anxiety, and feel
alive."[32]

Initially this analogy between hysteria and compulsive shopping may seem to neglect sexual etiology, but a further comparison of the theorization of hysteria and the psychic life of the shopper might provide support for conclusions about the fluid subjectivity of the spectator-shopper. As Jane Gallop suggests about the hysteric:

> Feminists' attraction to the case of Dora may be an attraction to hysteria itself. Freud links hysteria to bisexuality; the hysteric identifies with members of both sexes, cannot choose one sexual identity. . . . If feminism is the calling into question of constraining sexual identities, then the hysteric may be a proto-feminist.[33]

Like the hysteric, the shopper may be calling into question constraining identities—sexual, racial, class—but, to act out anxieties about identity in the realm of the market, one must believe in the commodity's transformative power.[34]

The mall is open to anyone—of any race, class, or gender—no purchase required. If shopping activates the power of the consumer gaze, then the purchase asserts power over these objects. The shopper pays only a psychic penalty if nothing is purchased in the displeasure of unsated consumer desire. As a form of incorporation, shopping is not unlike identification: "I shop, therefore I am," but also "I am what I buy."[35]

The Shopping Mall as Cinematic Apparatus   We will shift here from our discussion of gender and the subjective experience of shopping, to a consideration of the temporal and spatial construction of consumerism. Like the department store, the shopping mall operates as a selling machine and, as I've suggested, the shopping mall "machine" also produces a sense of timelessness. To magnify this claim: the shopping mall propagates a form of subjectivity that is directly analogous to the subjectivity produced by cinematic spectatorship. And conversely, the cinematic apparatus, now arrayed in mall multiplexes (and at home in the VCR) is a machine that functions much like the consumer space of the shopping mall. The shopping mall has not replaced the movie theater: it has become its logical extension.

Kowinski asserts: "There are more shopping centers in the United States than movie theaters (and most movie theaters are now in shopping centers)."[36] Yet, in this piece of syllogistic accounting, Kowinski has not calculated the exact relation between the movie theater and the shopping center. He approaches an equatio⟩ between them in the following epiphanic passage:

I saw the white pools of light, the areas of relative darkness, the symmetrical aisles and gleaming escalator, the bracketed store facades, the sudden strangeness of live trees and plants indoorᵉ. It was as if I were standing on a balcony, looking down on a stage, waiting for the show to begin.
That was it. This theatrical space. The mall is a theater.

But to Kowinski, it is not a movie theater:

This sense of a special world—permits a kind of unity of experience within an effortless enclosure that is something like the classic theater's unities of time, place and action. It's all here, now. The mall concentrates drama, suspends disbelief.[37]

This grand equation "mall as theater" is suggestive, and Kowinski later asserts, "the mall always felt something like a movie," but he leaves the analogy undeveloped.[38] Unlike the theater, which still retains an "aura" of performance and the real, the technology of the cinema offers a less auratic, more uniformly repeatable experience.[39]

Yet theorizing the shopper's subjectivity presents many of the same difficulties as theorizing cinematic spectatorship. The fact of purchase (number of items sold) does not adequately measure the psychic pleasures or anxieties of consumption, any more than box office statistics and television ratings tell us about the spectator subjectivity. Sales statistics can only reveal a limited amount about a commodity's subjective effect.

Shopping mall cinemas demand an expenditure. They provide the pleasure of purchase without yielding a tangible product. Instead they supply a commodity-experience—as do the virtual mobilities of tourism. Like tourism, which is prepared by mass publicity and cliché, the film industry prepares the contemporary spectator with auxiliary discourses of publicity—print advertising, television spots, preview trailers. Licensed movie tie-ins are reinforced in displays in mall stores.[40]

The shopping mall—and its apparatical extension, the shopping mall cinema—offers a safe transit into other spaces, other times, other imaginaries. These "elsewheres" are available to the consumer in a theatrical space where psychic transubstantiation is possible through purchase. Douglas Gomery describes the strategy of multiplex exhibition:

If a shopping mall of the 1970s offered a vast array of merchandise in its stores, Cineplex Odeon presented the customer with many more than the usual number of choices for its movie shows. . . . If mallgoers loved to browse and make "impulse" purchases for items from shoes to records, why shouldn't they be able to do the same thing for movies?[41]

Thought of in this way, the spectator-shopper tries on different identities—with limited risk and a policy of easy return. The cinema spectator can engage in a kind of identity bulimia. Leaving the theater, one abandons the garment, and takes only the memory of having worn it for a few hours—or having been worn by it.[42]

We will return to these issues later when we examine the subjective consequences of contemporary spectatorship, but for now, let us underline shopping as a powerful metaphor for spectatorship. Like cinematic spectatorship, the mall relies on a perceptual displacement; it defers external realities, retailing instead a controlled, commodified, and pleasurable substitution.

The 1991 Paul Mazursky film, *Scenes from a Mall,* provides a pertinent illustration. The film uses the shopping mall as its central stage—a public space where intimacy is more possible than in the domestic sphere of home or bedroom. The mall is an appropriate contemporary site for crises of identity because it is also a space where identity can so easily be transformed. But more than using a mall for its narrative setting, *Scenes from a Mall* becomes a Chinese-box metaphor for spectatorship; the mall itself is an analogic arena for shifts in identity and temporality that take place during the virtual flânerie of cinema spectatorship.

Scenes from a Mall, set in a generic mall space, uses the mall as a familiar and local idiom, the epitome of the everyday of everywhere. The Los Angeles viewer recognizes the exterior of a familiar and local mall space: the Beverly Center. Architect Charles Moore has captured the sense of the Beverly Center as the "brown hole" of Beverly Hills, describing it as "the most negative neutral brown-gray that human color sense has yet devised."[43] Its exterior hulk has the soft curves of a fifties coffee table; its shaved-off corners give the sense of a mammoth asymmetrical hat-box

In *Scenes from a Mall* (Paul Mazursky, 1991),
shopping is not a form of erotic foreplay, sex is
foreplay to the more fulfilling pleasures of
shopping. Courtesy Academy of Motion Picture
Arts and Sciences.

stamped with the pastel signet THE BEVERLY CENTER and the white
letters of its anchor stores, BULLOCKS and THE BROADWAY.

After the characters Deborah Feingold-Fifer (Bette Midler) and her husband Nick Fifer (Woody Allen) drive their red Saab into the belly of this
massive brown whale, and survive the congested gridlock of its digestive
ramps, they abandon their automotive skin and enter the mall. With the
magic of creative geography, the mall they enter is not the actual interior
of the Beverly Center. They've crossed the continent and entered the inte-

rior of the Stamford, Connecticut, Town Center. It hardly matters: with so many national chains—such as The Limited and Sharper Image—the space of consumer culture is interchangeable.

The narrative of *Scenes* details the breakup and reunion of a marriage counselor and her sports lawyer husband. (The marriage counselor's self-help book, *I DO, I DO, I DO,* on reaffirming the marriage vow, is on display at the mall bookstore.) At the point when the couple's relationship is at its most anguished—Woody Allen is beginning to have a panic attack—the two enter a movie in the mall multiplex. It is here, in front of a screening of *Salaam Bombay,* that the couple's desire is rekindled. Inside the Beverly Center's bounteous theater of purchases, *Salaam Bombay*—a neorealist Indian film that details the unrelenting poverty of urban over-population on the streets of Bombay—becomes a twisted tourist escape, where the "life of the natives" serves only as an impoverished backdrop to excesses of passionate anniversary lovemaking. (We know from one of the jibes Midler delivers to Allen that, in their sixteen-year marriage, they have never made love without the TV being on. And we also know that Allen's favorite "program" is the home shopping channel.) In this film, shopping is not a form of erotic foreplay: sex is foreplay to the more fulfilling pleasures of shopping.

The mall serves as a regional center with a global cosmopolitan outreach. The couple can visit Mexico and drink margaritas, toast champagne in a faux France (the Maison de Caviar), and buy Italian clothes that turn the couple into movie quotations. (Allen, as Marcello Mastroianni in a white jacket and dark glasses, cruises up the escalator to Nino Rota music as Bette Midler, as Guilietta-of-the-spirits-Masina, glides down the escalator in pumpkin chiffon.)

What seems striking here is not so much that a contemporary film uses the mall as locus for drama, but rather that, as a self-reflexive statement about spectatorship, *Scenes from a Mall* uses the multiplex cinema as the climactic (in all senses) site for a character transformation. No amount of shopping accomplished this. Only after cinematic spectatorship are the couple truly inspired as consumers, their shopping disorders magically cured.

As Mazursky's film suggests, the shopping mall is paradigmatic of the ever-shifting temporality of virtual flânerie. As I will argue in the next section, commodity-experiences that offer such fantasies of transformation and displacement are now as much a part of the public sphere in the shopping mall as they are uniquely private at home with the television and the VCR. It is, I argue, the ubiquity of these simulated experiences that has fostered an increasingly derealized sense of presence and identity. At the same time, the mechanical (and now electronic) capacity to manipulate time and space, essential features of both cinematic and televisual apparatuses, has produced an increasingly detemporalized subjectivity. Film theory has traditionally examined the consequences of spatial displacement into an elsewhere, but it has paid scant attention to the subjective consequences of cinema's unique temporal displacement, the elsewhen.

TEMPORALITY AND CINEMA SPECTATORSHIP   One of the essential properties of cinematic spectatorship is the basic temporal displacement it offers the spectator: the time of a film's production, the time of its fiction and the time of its projection are all conflated into the same moment in viewing. Many theorists have described how cinematic conventions of narrative and illusionist construction work to conceal this conflation, but less attention has been paid to the psychological or subjective *durée* of viewing many films over time—repeatedly, in odd sequence or, more recently, with alternative playback features of slow motion, reverse motion, and freeze frame.

In this section, I will argue the need to expand our conception of postmodern temporality to include an account of the cumulative psychic effects of film-going and its cultural impact on our concept of time and the past. Some of the following territory will be familiar to film scholars, but it will be necessary to retrace it in order to argue how cinema spectatorship itself provides a paradigmatic model for postmodern subjectivity. In the next section, I will argue that the inherent temporal flânerie of cinematic spectatorship has been intensified in new forms of spectatorship produced by cable television, the multiplex cinema, and the VCR.

For much of film theory, time is discussed in analogy with spatial verisimilitude (i.e., real time versus film time). Many early film theorists were drawn to the unique formal capacities of the cinema to transform the temporal constraints of the real.[44] As an early theorist on the differences between real time and film time, Hugo Munsterberg described the cinema's capacity to overcome the Kantian categories of space, time, and causality. For the film spectator, Munsterberg wrote in his study of the photoplay in 1916, "the massive outer world has lost its weight, it has been freed from space, time and causality, and it has been clothed in the forms of our own consciousness."[45] Munsterberg described how the photoplay overcame this "outer world" by "adjusting the events to the forms of the inner world, namely, attention, memory, imagination and emotion."[46] The photoplay, Munsterberg realized, did not have the same temporal constraints as the theater, which was bound by the principle of real time even though "there may be twenty years between the third and fourth act."[47] The photoplay, quite simply "does not," according to Munsterberg, "respect this temporal structure of the physical universe":

With the full freedom of our fancy, with the whole mobility of our
association of ideas, pictures of the past flit through the scenes of the present.
Time is left behind.[48]

Munsterberg was describing the diegetic world of the film, where temporality had a more fluid set of principles than in the "outer world."

Like Munsterberg, Erwin Panofsky described the relation between a static spectator and a more spatially and temporally fluid diegetic world.

In a theater, space is static . . . the spatial relation of the beholder to the
spectacle is unalterably fixed. . . . With the movies this situation is reversed.
Here too, the spectator occupies a fixed seat, but only physically, not as the
subject of aesthetic experience. Aesthetically, he is in permanent motion as his
eye identifies itself with the lens of the camera, which permanently shifts in
direction and distance.[49]

Although he did not use these terms, Panofsky described the spectator as identifying with a mobile ("in permanent motion") and virtual gaze ("his eye identifies itself with the lens of the camera"). Yet this was the gaze *during* spectatorship. At the same time, Panofsky described the cinema's unique "dynamization of space" and the "spatialization of time," but did not elaborate on the subjective experience of temporality *after* the spectator left the film.

Panofsky borrowed these twin formulations ("dynamization of space" and the "spatialization of time") from the work of the philosopher Henri Bergson (1859–1941). Bergson's ideas about the metaphysics of memory and the subjective experience of time would have made important additions to Panofsky's discussion of the cinema. In his 1896 book, *Matter and Memory*, Bergson discussed a subjective time (*durée*) separate from agreed-upon standards of time and its measurement. Durée will emerge as a useful notion as we attempt to theorize the relation of cinema spectatorship to a "postmodern" temporality where external standards of time no longer apply and where "the past" is sold as a commodity-experience available *at any time.* Bergson uses the term *virtual* to describe the past and its relation to perception and memory:

We shall never reach the past unless we frankly place ourselves within it. *Essentially virtual* it cannot be known as something past unless we follow and adopt the movement by which it expands into a present image.[50] (emphasis added)

Despite his immense popularity as the winner of a Nobel prize in literature in 1927, Bergson remained out of intellectual fashion from World War II until Deleuze's recent reclamation of *Bergsonism*.[51] Deleuze provides a detailed exegesis of Bergson's description of duration in *Matter and Memory,* delineating memory as the "virtual coexistence" of the past in the present, and duration as the contemporaneity of the present and past:

While the past coexists with its own present, and while it coexists with itself on various levels of contraction, we must recognize that the present itself is only the most contracted level of the past.[52]

In this context, it is more striking that Bergson's speculations on time and memory have not been taken up further by film theorists. At the peak of his notoriety as a philosopher, Bergson invoked the fledgling "cinematograph" as a model for knowledge. In *Creative Evolution*—his most widely read, repeatedly translated book—Bergson dignified the cinematograph by suggesting that it was an apt representation of mental processes. ("The mechanism of our ordinary knowledge is of a cinematographical kind."[53]) This was in 1907, a moment otherwise marked by cultural disdain for the cinema, a form not yet sanctioned as an art or even as a legitimate form of entertainment.

In the culture that surrounded Bergson's writing about the subjective experience of time (*Matter and Memory* was published in 1896), there was a gradual switch to a universal agreed-upon "standard" time. The development of the railroad and wireless telegraphy were important determinants to the standardization of a "public time."[54] In a broad cultural history, *The Culture of Time and Space, 1880–1918*, Kern has detailed how the international movement toward a World Standard Time transformed modes of thinking about time and experience. Examining the coincident explorations of "private time" in visual and literary aesthetics, Kern situates the technology of the cinema—alongside the phonograph and electric light—as a challenge to "traditional" senses of time.[55] Like the electric light, the cinema produced a world made of artificial light, an unnatural reversal of nature's clock. (In the evening, the cinema can produce the brilliance of daylight; in the mid-afternoon, it can offer the gloom of night.) Like the phonograph and the photograph, cinema records the aural and visual traces of a past unhampered by the boundaries of life and death. Yet to early cinema spectators, this experience of "time-shifting" was the exception, not the rule. Although it is difficult to measure the impact on their subjective experience of time, early spectators had fewer time-shifted experiences in their lives than the contemporary spectator.

It is not until recently, in Deleuze's two-volume study of the cinema, *Cinema 1: The Movement-Image* and *Cinema 2: The Time-Image,* that we find Bergson invoked as an important philosophic precedent for a theoretical discussion of the cinema.[56] The second volume of Deleuze's foray into film theory promises to provide an account of temporality absent from much contemporary film theory. Although Deleuze's work has been marked by his tendency toward confrontational critique (see *Anti-Oedipus*), his writing on cinema does not directly engage (or acknowledge) previous film theoretical work. Instead of rebutting other contemporary theorists, Deleuze declares the importance of two theorists neglected in the formation of contemporary film theory: Bergson and C. S. Peirce. Deleuze avoids the language of much of poststructuralist film theory and supplies instead a full glossary of neologisms to describe the cinema's unique signification: chronosign, onirosign, lectosign, noosign, opsign, and mnenosign.

Deleuze argues that since World War II, *time* has come to dominate film. Even though this is a historical argument about cinematic style (he alleges a shift in the cinematic image since World War II: "the movement-image of the so-called classical cinema gave way, in the post-war period, to a direct time-image."[57]), Deleuze retreats from offering a historical explanation for these stylistic changes. The bulk of the book contains lengthy descriptions of the temporal structure in films by Welles, Resnais, Zanussi, Carne, Truffaut, Herzog, and Tarkovsky.

Deleuze's descriptions border on a theorization of where—*in time*—the spectator *is*, but his discussion of the "time-image" ultimately relies on a conception of diegetic film time, not the alterations in the spectator's relationship to temporality produced by film-going. For example, consider the following:

> *It is a mistake to think of the cinematographic image as being by nature in the present.* . . . And the first occasion on which *a direct time-image* was seen in the cinema was not in the (even implicit) mode of the present but, on the contrary, *in the form of sheets of past,* with Welles' *Citizen Kane.* Here time became out of joint and reversed its dependent relation to movement; temporality showed itself as it really was for the first time.[58]

A time-image here refers to the narrative structuring of temporality. Or, as is evident in his discussion of Resnais:

> In cinema, Resnais says, something ought to happen "around the image behind the image and even inside the image." This is *what happens when the image becomes time-image.* . . . *The screen itself is the cerebral membrane where immediate and direct confrontations take place between the past and the future,* the inside and the outside, at a distance impossible to determine, independent of any fixed point. . . . The image no longer has space and movement as its primary characteristics but topology and time.[59] (emphasis added)

In the most promising and yet undeveloped section of the book, "The crystals of time," Deleuze describes the "crystal-image" as having two sides, the actual (real-present) and the virtual (imaginary-past). The "actual image" is of "a present which passes," while the "virtual image" is of "a past which is preserved."[60] For my argument here about the mobilized and virtual gaze of spectatorship, Deleuze's work seems to provide theoretical reinforcement. And yet, even though he draws upon these Bergsonian theses of the past as virtual, Deleuze relies on descriptions of diegetically altered time and does not address the alterations in temporality produced by cumulative cinema viewing or the forms of playback viewing which can easily—with stop motion, reverse, and fast forward—turn a film's temporality, and the spectator's relationship to it, "out of joint."[61]

Unlike many film theorists who consider only the diegetic manipulations of time, André Bazin found that one of the values of the cinema's "integral realism" was its "*defense against the passage of time*" (emphasis added). In the "Ontology of the Photographic Image," Bazin explained this "preservation of life by a representation of life": "photography does not create eternity, as art does, it *embalms time*, rescuing it simply from its proper corruption" (emphasis added).[62] Bazin's valuation of this "embalmed time" was rooted in a commitment to the realist potentials of the cinematic medium's photographic base. To Bazin, the camera was an "impassive lens" with the "power to lay bare the realities."[63] In his famed 1946 essay, "The Myth of Total Cinema," Bazin asserted an historical teleology: that the cinema was the result of an *idée fixe,* a "guiding myth" that animated the search for complete and perfect illusion.[64] Because Bazin thought of the cinema camera as an unmediated instrument for capturing a "pro-filmic reality," and because he did not have a critique of its mediated illusionism, Bazinian "realism" has been a debate in film studies for more than two decades.[65] But for our purposes here, Bazin did speculate on the cinema's effect on the sense of the *passage of time* outside of the diegetic world of the film.

In the 1970s, the "apparatus theories" of Metz, Baudry, and others shifted the theoretical focus from the Bazinian and post-Bazinian debates about spatial and temporal verisimilitude, and from the then-current textual analyses that used narratological tools to describe the strategies for producing narrative space and temporality. Motivated by the desire to explain the psychic effects of cinematic spectatorship, and to describe how the filmic experience "produces" a subject, these theories argued that the cinematic "apparatus"[66] provides the illusion of a "present" but "absent" time. Even though Baudry and Metz provided a totalized description of the "cinematic apparatus" and its implied stylistic effects, this form of apparatus theory was based on the precepts of spectatorship of classical Hollywood films and disregarded oppositional or alternative strategies of style or exhibition. At the same time, apparatus theories provoked feminist correctives to such a generalized, ungendered account of subjectivity.

But apparatus theories—in their appeal to psychoanalytic theory to explain the psychic pleasures of cinema-going—supplied an account of the spectator's subjective temporality. In two essays, "Ideological Effects of the Basic Cinematographic Apparatus" (1970), and "The Apparatus: Metapsychological Approaches to the Impression of Reality in the Cinema" (1975), Baudry posited a general "effect" of the "apparatus" where the contents of the image or the forms of cinematic narrative are secondary or "of little importance."[67]

Baudry described the cinema as a "simulation machine" that induces a desired "artificial psychosis"—a mechanically reproducible representation of an elsewhere and an elsewhen:

It can be assumed that it is this wish which prepares the long history of cinema: the wish to construct a *simulation machine* capable of offering the subject perceptions which are really representations mistaken for perceptions.[68] (emphasis added)

Not far from the teleology of Bazin's "total cinema," Baudry posits a "wish" that generated the "long history of cinema." The wish is precisely, in Baudry's analysis, the pleasure found in a misrecognition (*méconnaissance*) where representations are *mistaken* for perceptions. (Or—to use different terms—where the "virtual" is confused with the "real.") The misrecognition of representations for perceptions is, as Baudry will argue, the locus of the apparatus's ideological power.[69]

To Baudry, the cinema's metapsychological effect induces a regression, a return to a phase of development when representation and perception were indistinguishable. This is stated in the following formulation:

It is indeed desire as such, i.e., *desire to desire, the nostalgia for a state in which* desire has been satisfied through *the transfer of a perception to a formation resembling hallucination,* which seems to be activated by the cinematographic apparatus.[70] (emphasis added)

The nostalgia that activates Baudry's spectator is a psychic regression. Cinephilia is, then, inextricably bound to the pleasures of this imaginary *temporal* return.

Baudry relies on two conditions present in Jacques Lacan's discussion of the mirror stage to describe cinematic spectation: the suspension of mobility (the spectator is seated), and the predominance of the visual function (in a darkened hall, in front of an illuminated screen).[71]

Metz also relies on a Lacanian model to describe the conditions of viewing—the darkened theater, the projector behind the spectator, the framed image. The cinema, to Metz, is a "technique of the imaginary" peculiar to the historical epoch of capitalism.[72] In Metz's prologue to *The Imaginary Signifier,* he identifies a general "wanting to go to the cinema" that is fueled by the spectator's metapsychological need for a "good object." Metz describes a cinematic institution that relies on a libidinal economy; the economic mechanisms of the film industry collude (in a "dual kinship") with the desire of the spectator. Both Metz and Baudry suggest that cinematic spectatorship *takes us back,* is regressive to some imaginary anterior moment; and that the pleasures of cinephilia are based on this imaginary return.[73]

Although Metz and Baudry do not assert it directly, their theories come close to describing cinematic spectatorship as a private temporality apart from public time or space. In this foreclosed psychic temporality, the past and the present converge.

As we turn to an examination of contemporary spectatorship, it will be important to retain the limitations in these theorizations of the cinema's relation to the past and the present and to build upon their contributions to the relationships between spectatorship, subjectivity, and time. The easy spatial and temporal flânerie of contemporary spectatorship recasts the "virtual" mobilized gaze into a more accessible and repeatable exponent—and this form of visuality, I will continue to argue, becomes paradigmatic of a postmodern subjectivity.

SPECTATORIAL FLÂNERIE

"No technology has affected Americans' time perception
more in the last four decades than television."

DON OLDENBURG, *Los Angeles Times,* September 24, 1987

Cinema spectatorship in the 1990s has been transformed by the time-shifting changes in spectatorship produced by the multiplex cinema and the VCR. Time-shifting removes the ontology of "live" television and aligns televisual reception with the elsewhere and elsewhen that has always characterized cinematic spectatorship. If we first examine the principles of "classical" cinema spectatorship, we will see how these precepts have met with various technological challenges; first by televisual spectation, and then more significantly, by developments in nonbroadcast cable television, VCRs, and the new interactive technologies.[74]

Principles of "Classical" Spectatorship In their massive and detailed 1985 book, *The Classical Hollywood Cinema: Film Style and Mode of Production to 1960,* David Bordwell, Janet Staiger, and Kristin Thompson describe the "Hollywood cinema" as a "distinct mode of film practice." Their study "attempt[s] to articulate a theoretical approach to film history," by examining the historical conditions that led to this "classical model," "integral system," and "totality." To do this, Bordwell, Staiger, and Thompson conduct a complex alternation between three distinct historical inquiries: modes of production, film style, and technological development. But as avowed in the preface, this slights a history of reception:

An adequate history of the reception of the classical Hollywood film would have to examine the changing theater situation, the history of publicity, and the role of social class, aesthetic tradition and ideology in constituting the audience. This history, as yet unwritten, would require another book, probably as long as this.[75]

Although the spectator is a component of most descriptions of classical film practice, spectatorship is usually described as a product of a specific film or genre. Or, as we have seen, the "apparatus" theories of the 1970s attempted to generalize the conditions of spectatorship.[76] In order to propose a theoretical account of the recent changes in spectatorship, it is important to specify the principles of classical spectatorship which no longer apply.

Here I will suggest six precepts of cinema spectatorship. Each of these has met with historical challenges; some have been challenged by televisual spectation, and yet all are more significantly challenged by developments in nonbroadcast cable television, VCRs, and new interactive technologies.

1. *Dark room with projected luminous images:* As we have seen, this was a form of "screen entertainment" from the mid-seventeenth century. As Musser illustrates, the magic lantern tradition was distinct from, but not unrelated to, "peep show" viewing practices of the stereoscope, phenakistoscope, mutoscope, and kinetoscope devices.

2. *Immobile spectator:* As everyone from Baudry (who compares cinematic spectation to the prisoners in Plato's cave) to Musser points out, the cinema relies on the immobility of the spectator, seated in an auditorium. In theories of classical spectatorship, the spectator's immobility is an essential condition of visual mobility.

3. *Single viewing:* As soon as the photographic negative made possible a standardized image, photography and then cinematography made possible the reseeing of *exactly* the same image(s) over time. Film experiences had an unprecedented repeatability—repeatable like books or revisitations to art works and architectural monuments, but with a more exacting verisimilitude. The *ciné-clubs* of Paris in the 1920s and the London Film Society (1925–1939) relied on the practice of reseeing films; films that were several years old would be reshown in repertory fashion. Although the Hollywood "mode of film practice" necessitated a distribution-exhibition mode based on novelty and obsolescence, requiring ever-new products to fill the cinemas, during the "classical" period, films were occasionally "rereleased."

Also, as Doane has noted, cinematic texts have subjective residues beyond the initial viewing. Doane cites a remarkable quote from a 1947 article on motion pictures as trade commodities:

The motion picture is one product which is never completely consumed for the very good reason that it is never entirely forgotten by those who see it. *It leaves behind a residue, or a deposit, of imagery and association,* and this fact makes it a product unique in our tremendous list of export items.[77] (emphasis added)

Psychoanalytic explanations of repetition compulsion (Metz) or regressive pleasure (Baudry) may aid in accounting for the repeatable aspects of cinephilia, but these theories do not offer an explanation of how a lifetime of film viewing alters our perception of time and the past.

4. *Noninteractive relation between viewer and image:* The relatively passive position of the spectator is a corollary to the spectator's immobility.

5. *Framed image:* In classical spectatorship, the scale of the framed image relied on a "larger than life" proportion. 70-mm, 35-mm, and Cinerama screen size followed the eighteenth-century "cult of immensity" of panoramic painting.

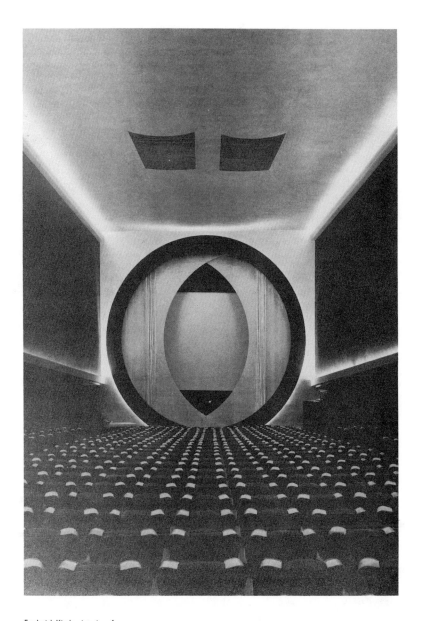

Frederick Kiesler, interior of
movie theater, 1928.

6. *Flat screen surface:* Despite early experimentation with stereopticons, classical cinema spectatorship of both cinema relied on a two-dimensional surface. With the exception of 3D exhibition in the early 1950s and occasional 3D productions, spectatorship has been marked by the two-dimensionality of the diegetic world.

As I will argue, these principles of spectatorship—and the theories necessary to explain them—rely on viewing contexts that have undergone radical changes.

Principles of Contemporary Spectatorship

> "The dissolution of TV into life, the dissolution of life into TV."
>
> JEAN BAUDRILLARD, *Simulations*[78]

Televisual spectatorship challenges these precepts of classical cinema spectatorship:

1) It does not rely on a dark room with projected luminous images; the TV is a light source, not a projection.

2) It allows for a modicum of mobility, complicating the bodily relation to the screened image. As a multi-use activity, the television spectator enacts the distracted gaze of the flâneur in new configurations; ironing, laundry, and childcare become rhythmic components of viewing.[79]

3) Television programming relies on scheduled reruns that give the viewer an opportunity to catch up with missed programs; with the time-shifting and movie rental capacity of the VCR, every household is a potential ciné-club.

4) If cinema spectatorship relied on the limits of what was programmed by the theater owner and the theater chain, the television viewer—although still constrained by the offerings of television programmers—has channel alternatives, synchronic choice. As cable television has expanded the synchronic alternatives to upward of fifty channels, the marketing of the remote control "wand" has accelerated viewer's choice.[80] The VCR also provides "viewer choice" along diachronic lines. VCRs allow for time-shifting and playback of rental tapes.

5) Image scale remains one of the most distinct differences between cinematic and televisual spectatorship. Television spectatorship conventionally

relied on a smaller, home-sized screen; but recent innovations like Sony's Jumbotron (an 82-foot-by-131-foot outdoor screen that televised the Expo 85 held near Tokyo) take image scale to its televisual extremes.

6) With the exception of some rare experimentation with 3D TV, televisual spectatorship has not challenged the two-dimensionality of the flat screen surface. Having outlined these differences between cinematic and televisual spectatorship, it will also be important to retain some of their similiarities.

E. Ann Kaplan has argued that television is uniquely "postmodern," and the cinema is a "modern" form. In her book on music television, *Rocking Around the Clock: Music Television, Postmodernism and Consumer Culture,* Kaplan asserts:

> For it is the televisual apparatus that is partly responsible for the kind of consciousness that no longer thinks in terms of an *historical* frame. That sort of "frame" involves precisely the kinds of boundaries and limited texts that television obliterates in its never-ending series.[81]

Although Kaplan considers television's impact on concepts of history, she does not credit the equally direct challenges to history and memory which were made by earlier forms of a mobilized virtual gaze.[82] Kaplan's argument about the postmodern specificity of the televisual apparatus hinges on an equation of "postmodernist" with "decenteredness."[83] For Kaplan, the televisual spectator is "decentered" in ways that the filmic spectator is not; she distinguishes the televisual from the filmic spectator by emphasizing the distinctions between the continuum of televisual "flow" and the discrete "fixed two-hour limit of the Hollywood movie":

> While the filmic spectator is drawn into the filmic world through structures that appear to satisfy the desire for plenitude and for the unification of split subjectivity, the TV spectator is drawn into the TV world through the mechanism of consumption (i.e., constant unsatisfied desire, the constant hope of a forthcoming but never realised plenitude). . . . For the subject is always a potential viewer at the flick of the switch, as is not the case for the film spectator who pays for and consumes a delimited "text" in a fixed space and amount of time. . . . The historical spectator is more inside the TV world than is the film spectator who knows that he is "dreaming."[84]

The differentiation here between filmic and televisual spectatorship implies that the filmic spectator is *not* drawn through what Kaplan calls "the mechanism of consumption"—an insatiable desire for plenitude—but rather, that the "delimited" cinematic experience supplies the spectator with "structures that appear to satisfy" this same desire. Kaplan also implies that the cinema spectator knows that this is only an effect.

Sean Cubitt has recently made a more convincing outline of these differences:

Film offers to take us *out of ourselves* and to provide us *with a new imaginary identity for the evening: television is constantly seducing us and rejecting us. . . .* TV, viewed with the kind of serious scrutiny which it rarely gets, would induce a kind of schizophrenia made up of constant transitions from one identity to another, its insanity redoubled by repetition. Luckily, distraction largely eliminates this frightening possibility.[85]

MTV provides, for Kaplan, an extreme of "aspects inherent in the televisual apparatus"—a continuous advertisement relying on a mode of address that promises plenitude. Kaplan also argues that, unlike the cinema, the male gaze is not monolithic on MTV:

The televisual apparatus enables *the production of a variety of different gazes* due to the arrangement of a series of short, constantly changing segments in place of the two-hour continuous film narrative, of the usually single book-length or theatrical narrative.[86] (emphasis added)

The assumption here is that a two-hour film narrative does not produce a "variety of different gazes" and relies, instead, on a single positioned gaze. Kaplan's model, based on segmentation and fragmentation of televisual programming, assumes that the context of cinematic spectatorship has no impact on the two-hour segment.[87]

Television's ideology of presence—what Raymond Williams called "flow" or what Stephen Heath and Gillian Skirrow referred to as "absolute presence"—has traditionally distinguished televisual spectatorship from its cinematic counterparts.[88] Williams's study, *Television: Technology and Cultural Form,* described the ways in which television altered social relationships, basic perceptions of reality, scale, and form of society, the central processes of family, cultural, and social life. Separating television and cinema technologies from earlier "public technology"—the railroad and city lighting—Williams described television as a technology that "served an at once mobile and home-centered way of living: a form of *mobile privatization*."[89] Television developed in a sociohistorical context, Williams argues, where the social need for mobility occurred at the same time as a trend toward self-sufficiency. Williams's term *mobile privatization* takes the same virtual mobility that I have been emphasizing and places it in the privatized space of the home (*Tele*[far]-*vision*: vision from elsewhere). The commodity-experience of early television spectatorship relied on the presence of the television set and the potential of live broadcasts in the living room.[90]

Using Williams's categories, the differences between the televisual and the cinematic become more distinct. To Williams, the technology of the televisual "broadcast" meant a centralized origin and an individual receiver. Cinematic technology offered a more diverse (Williams says "specific and discrete") set of origins and a collective system of reception. Whereas the telephone developed as a privatized system of individual-to-individual communication, the radio developed as a means to deliver words and music to a large audience at once.[91] Williams emphasizes the radio as a model for television broadcasting.

The spectatorial flâneries made possible by new technologies of reception invite revisions to previous conceptions of the differences between cinema and television. The advent of cable television and video rentals ("source shifting") has significantly challenged the radio model for televisual spectatorship and moves reception more toward comparisons with the telephone and film viewing.[92] Once we consider the contextual changes in spectatorship, the distinctions between televisual and cinematic reception begin to diminish.

For example, the recording capacities of the VCR have markedly altered television's "absolute presence."[93] The market of commodified video-movies available to the home viewer has meant that the "aura" of the original moment of cinema exhibition also disappears. The VCR metonymizes a cornucopia of images in temporal terms. It becomes a privatized museum of past moments, of different genres, different times all reduced to uniform, interchangeable, equally accessible units. The videocassette transforms the size and accessibility of film experience, markets it as a book-sized, readily available commodity. As a "commodity-experience," the vid-

"Time Shift Video," New York,
1988. Photograph © Anne
Friedberg.

eocassette proffers an exponent of the spatial loss (the loss of aura that, as Benjamin describes, is incurred by mechanical reproduction) and offers a loss of aura of the second order, a temporal loss (which the opportunities for repetition-replay produce). One can literally "rent" another space and time when one borrows a videotape to watch on a VCR.[94]

Or, as Virilio describes the temporal consequences of the VCR:

> The machine, the VCR, allows man to organize a time which is not his own, a *deferred time,* a time which is somewhere else—and to capture it. . . . The VCR . . . creates two days: a reserve day which can replace the ordinary day, the lived day.[95] (emphasis added)

The shopping mall multiplex cinema extends the spectatorial flânerie of the VCR along both spatial and temporal axes. The multiplex positions its cinema screens in the spatial metonymy of a chain of adjacent shop windows; the temporal metonymy of "show times" is arrayed as if the multiplex is a set of contiguous VCRs. To get to the screens of a shopping mall multiplex one must pass through a cornucopia of framed images—shop windows designed to perform a muted and static form of consumer address. When one reaches the cinema screen, the stillness of the shop mannequin is transformed into the live action of film performance, as if the itinerary through the mall has reenacted the historical impulse from photography to film. Multiplex, multiple screen cinemas become spatially contiguous VCRs, offering a readily attainable panoply of other temporal moments, the *not-now* in the guise of the *now.*[96]

Cinematic and televisual spectatorship has been conventionally differentiated: one goes *to* a specific film, but one watches (not a specific program but the apparatus) television. The staggering of screening times in a multiplex cinema turns cinema-going into an activity more like watching television, providing the cinematic spectator with the absolute presence of the (almost) always available.

And, if we assess the subjective impact produced by placing the time-shifting control with the viewer (taping broadcast or cable programs, renting videotapes or laser discs, the menu of choice at multiplex cinemas), the concept of a "public time" has dissolved into privately controlled time schedules. Time-shifting has placed the control of this time tourism in a remote-control magic wand. Each spectator has become the Docteur Crase of Clair's *Paris Qui Dort.*[97] The "zap" of remote channel-switching has

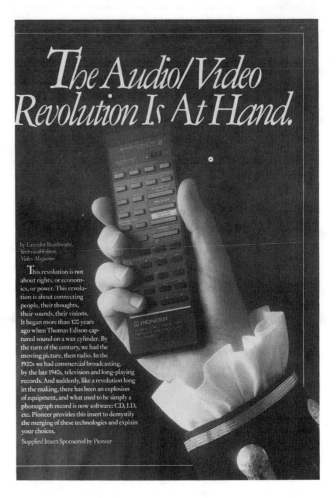

The Audio/Video
Revolution Is At Hand.

by Lancelot Braithwaite,
Technical Editor,
Video Magazine

This revolution is not about rights, or economics, or power. This revolution is about connecting people, their thoughts, their sounds, their visions. It began more than 100 years ago when Thomas Edison captured sound on a wax cylinder. By the turn of the century, we had the moving picture, then radio. In the 1920s we had commercial broadcasting, by the late 1940s, television and long-playing records. And suddenly, like a revolution long in the making, there has been an explosion of equipment, and what used to be simply a phonograph record is now software: CD, LD, etc. Pioneer provides this insert to demystify the merging of these technologies and explain your choices.

Supplied Insert Sponsored by Pioneer

Time tourism and "remote control."

changed the nature of montage; every viewer is a ready-made *montagiste,* cutting and pasting images from a wide repertoire of sources at the push of a button. Montage, once an analogy to dialectical thought or the shock value of the surreal, now also signifies a form of consumer choice with the controls in the hands of a new virtual shopper.

The cinema spectator (and the armchair analog, the VCR viewer) with fast forward, fast reverse, many speeds of slow motion, easily switching between channels and tape, always able to repeat, replay, return—is a spectator *lost in* but also *in control of* time. The "media" proliferating around us—invading the everyday with images produced, repeated, returned to, simultaneously preserved and instantly obsolete—has produced a shifting, mobile, fluid subjectivity. Cinematic and televisual spectatorship offered new freedoms over the body—the race-, gender-, age-, and class-bound body could be "implanted" with a constructed (albeit ideological) virtual gaze.

As we will see in the next section, virtual reality (VR) technologies further challenge the precepts of classical spectatorship. (The dark room, two-dimensional flat surface, and framed image are replaced with a full peripherally-constructed world; VR devices rely on interactive features that resist spectator immobility.) Although VR devices maintain a fiction of bodily absence, they combine fictive absence with the paradoxical presence of one's own bodily movement. VR devices that rely on apparatical protheses—goggles and gloves—produce an illusion of a participatory order. One's *actual body* remains in the real world while one's *phenomenal body* moves about in a "virtual environment." For the postmodern observer the body is a fiction, a site for departure and return.

CYBERTECHNOLOGY: FROM OBSERVER TO PARTICIPANT

To enter this artificial world, a person puts on special clothing that is wired to a computer. Gloves transmit and receive data, and goggles include two tiny video screens. The computer generates images, either of the real world or an imaginary one that appears to the viewer in three dimension. In a way, it's like watching television, but it's more lifelike because it allows for action. A user can be sitting in the cockpit of an airplane or swinging a club on a golf course.

" 'Virtual Reality' Takes Its Place in the Real World,"
New York Times, July 8, 1990

Descriptions of VR technologies recall Wordsworth's depiction of the panorama: "mimic sights that ape/ The absolute presence of reality." The histories of both cinema and television technology have been marked by attempts to expand the "reality" of the spectating experience—by increasing screen size (70mm, Cinemascope, Cinerama, large-screen video), improving sound quality (THX, stereo television), or embellishing the dimensionality (3D) of the viewed object. But both cinematic and televisual spectatorship relied on the relative immobility of the viewer—the spectator in the position of looking *into* a separate "window on the world." Virtual reality technologies attempt to expand the "reality effect" to more exacting extremes by switching the viewer from a passive position to a more interactive one, from an observer separate from the apparatus to a participant.

In the VR system described above, goggles containing two miniature color video monitors create a full analogue of depth perception, simulating stereoscopic vision by providing a slightly different perspective to each eye and also by permitting motion parallax, the shift that occurs when an observer changes position. With the use of a glove that translates hand movements into electric signals, the user can grasp and manipulate computer-generated "virtual objects," can point, talk, and gesture. Multiple users can enter the same virtual reality and play "virtual catch."

The applications for virtual reality technologies have not yet been determined (telerobotics, dildonics, and virtual travel are all in experimental stages), but as a form of "virtual transport" these systems demand a reconceptualization of the spectator. In a marked epistemological shift in the experiential position, an externally driven subjectivity is replaced by a more self-generated subjectivity.

Jaron Lanier, CEO of VPL, one of the pioneering virtual reality companies, predicts that virtual reality technology "is going to shut down television. . . . *Virtual Reality is not going to be the television of the future. It's going to be the telephone of the future*" (emphasis added).[98] Timothy Leary claims that "most Americans have been living in Virtual Reality since the proliferation of television. All cyberspace will do is make the experience interactive instead of passive."[99] Cyberjournalist John Perry Barlow describes the experience of virtual reality: "In this pulsating new landscape, I've been reduced to a point of view. . . . It's a Disneyland for epistemologists."[100]

Virtual reality is two-way, interactive. It allows for interspecial, cybernetic, intergendered interactions: you can be a Weimaraner, a vacuum cleaner, a trumpet, a table. Previous "identity-bound" positions of race, class, ethnicity, age, and gender can be technologically transmuted. In virtual reality, quadriplegics can have moving arms and legs, men can be women, women can be men, and so forth. (But because it is a visually reliant technology, the blind cannot have eyes.) Early prognosticators have speculated on the possibilities of substitute identities in this "non-existent space." "Virtual reality," reports the *New York Times*, "will let people transcend their identities. You could be Ronald Reagan, Elvis Presley or a bag lady."[101]

Still, the power resides with those who build the systems, design the software, and decide who is allowed to use it. The technology for cybernetic artificial "realities" has, so far, been the province of isolated inventors and government research teams, and a few small companies and interested corporations.

The high end of "virtual" research has been conducted by NASA and the air force, in an attempt to find military or research applications for these new technologies. In many cases, the technologies were pioneered because of a military or scientific need.[102] NASA has been researching technology that can project "telepresence"—robots in space would have the benefit of a thinking, managing, responding human "presence" of a human who wasn't actually there. The air force has been researching a technology that could separate bodies from combat for the video-game interaction and "looks that kill" possibilities.

The mass-market "low-end" uses of this technology are only beginning to become apparent. For the Christmas 1990 consumer market, Mattel Toys offered the "PowerGlove" accessory for the Nintendo game.[103] Flight simulators, golf instruction software, and surgical technique demonstrations suggest the pedagogic potential of this technology, but also remind us of its hidden ideological force.

Cybernetic Neologisms If—as the early Wittgenstein would have had it—the limits of our language are the limits of our world, these new technologies have expanded the ontological boundaries of our current language and a new lexicon is needed to describe the frontiers beyond.[104] Leep/Pop-Optix, a Massachusetts-based company that sells virtual reality systems, has patented some of its neologistic trademarks for their products or services. Leep published a lexicon of "cyberspeak" as an advertisement for their company. As the Leep lexicon defines it,

ARTIFICIAL REALITY: The oxymoron on the table. Stereoscopic, interactive, data-based worlds displayed with such a wide field of view that the actor is on the *inside looking out* as opposed to being on the *outside looking in*, as with conventional monitors, no matter how large the screen.[105] (emphasis added)

"Artificial reality"—indeed an oxymoron—offers a subjective change of position for the actor-participant.

At this point, it is too early to tell in what direction "virtual worlds" will be taken. *Cyberspace* is not based on mimetic spatial contiguity; *cybertime* is not based on concepts of real time. As Lanier asserts, virtual reality technology could produce profound effects on the subjective experience of time and memory:

The particular experiences that make up time can be decoupled from physical time. *You can play back your old experiences, you can go through them backwards or forwards, fast or slow.*[106] (emphasis added)

Hence, it can be imagined as a cyberrealm with new and different powers of moving through space (from microscopic to extraterrestial) and traveling through time (from decades past to millenniums future).

From Cinema to the Televisual to the Virtual At this early stage of technological development, virtual reality devices form a historical analogy to televisual technology in its early forms: an almost contentless means of communication, looking for a marketable purpose. As Williams wrote about radio and television:

Unlike all previous communications technologies, radio and television were systems *primarily devised for transmission and reception as abstract processes, with little or no definition of preceding content* . . . the means of communications preceded their content.[107]

As we have seen, there is always a complex interaction of new needs with new inventions; iron construction produced new public spaces for new needs; telegraphy was spurred by the development of the railroad; photography and motion picture were related to needs for sending pictures by

wire. VR technologies will follow the communication model of the telephone user—participatory and interactive—rather than the model of the
radio listener—passive and with limited choice. It will be important to
remember that the VR user has a proscribed choice, but the illusion of
power is more direct.

POSTMODERN FLÂNERIE: TO SPATIALIZE TEMPORALITY

> The American city seems to have stepped right out of the
> movies. To grasp its secret, *you should not then begin with
> the city and move inwards toward a screen; you should begin
> with the screen and move outwards toward the city.*

JEAN BAUDRILLARD, *America*[108] (emphasis added)

I have taken an elliptical route to the discussion of postmodernity. I
began with an examination of a commodified type of cultural experience
that evolved in the midst of the nineteenth century when the conditions
of modernity began to become manifest. With the growth of urbanism and
the metropolis, the commodity-experience became a more dominant feature. As visual experience became commodified in shop display, in tourist
experiences, and in cinema spectatorship, the fluidity of flânerie (once
offered predominately to men) was now offered as a pleasure to anyone—
of any race, ethnicity, or gender—who had the capacity to consume. Cinema spectatorship brought together the mobilized gaze of the shopper and
tourist into a "virtual mobility"; the spatially and temporally fluid subjectivity of this form of visuality is often at odds with bodily position. Yet,
despite this imaginary "mobility," women and ethnic and racial minorities
rudely discover the bodily truth in the differential between this virtual
position and the real.[109]

As this mobilized virtual gaze has become a fundamental feature of everyday life, experiences that produce such subjective fluidity are now as much
a part of the public sphere (in, for example, the shopping mall) as they are
a part of the private (at home, with the television and the VCR).

In modernity, as some commentators have described, pseudoevents dis-
solve the differences between hard and soft news, mix up the roles of actors
and audience, subjects and objects.[110] Already fragile in modernity, these
boundaries have been more fully eroded. With the "virtual" technologies
and computer-generated realities, the mimetic has entered into a hyper-

realm.[111] The simulated newscast, the simulcast, has become more "real" than documentary footage.[112]

In order to describe adequately the role of cinematic and televisual apparatuses in postmodernity, it will be necessary to exceed stylistic descriptions of film and televisual texts. As I've begun to indicate, both cinema and television's capacity for endless replay and repetition—the remarketing of the past—is more than the textual or thematic use of nostalgia, but becomes a commodity-form itself. To assess the politics of contemporary representation, we must continue to theorize these aspects of the everyday and their effect on the unconscious, our relation to time and to the "real."

The Bradbury Building, 1893.

Photograph © Julius Schulman.

ARCHITECTURE: LOOKING FORWARD, LOOKING BACKWARD

It was the first interior of a twentieth century public building that I had ever beheld and the spectacle naturally impressed me deeply. I was in a vast hall full of light, received not alone from the windows on all sides but from the dome, the point of which was a hundred feet above. Beneath it, in the centre of the hall, a magnificent fountain played, cooling the atmosphere to a delicious freshness with its spray. The walls and ceiling were frescoed in mellow tints, calculated to soften without absorbing the light which flooded the interior. Around the fountain was a space occupied with chairs and sofas, on which many persons were seated conversing. Legends on the walls all about the hall indicated to what classes of commodities the counters below were devoted.[1]

The above description was written in 1887, in Edward Bellamy's utopian projection of Boston in the year 2000, *Looking Backward*. But it could equally describe a "skylit commercial space" of the late 1980s. Bellamy's projection of the year 2000 was telescoped forward through the lens of 1887, and he fictionalized a world without airplanes, automobiles, or electricity but with women's rights, music in the home, and socialism.

Yet this 1887 science fiction did animate its immediate future. The Bradbury Building in downtown Los Angeles, built in 1893, was specifically inspired by Bellamy's time-travel novel.[2] Designed by George Wyman, the Bradbury Building is five stories high, with a full-width skylight raised on a clerestory, exposing the central atrium to full light. The interior iron and glass court with its open balconies, staircases, and elevators has been described hyperbolically by architect Charles Moore as "one of the most thrilling spaces on the North American continent."[3] We see this space in *Blade Runner*, the 1982 film that poses Los Angeles as the quintessential postmodern city—the capital of the twenty-first century in the same way that Paris was the capital of the nineteenth and New York was the capital of the twentieth. *Blade Runner* contains a pastiche of temporality in its architectural

referents including Frank Lloyd Wright's Mayan-style Ennis Brown house
(1924), the Million Dollar Theatre (1918), and Union Station (1939).

Bellamy's text also seems to describe the contemporary shopping mall.
(Or, to quote Baudrillard, "The Year 2000 has already happened.") Here, in
order to illustrate the place of the cinema in this architectural time machine,
I will compare a Los Angeles shopping mall, the Westside Pavilion, with
another site of cultural consumption, the Musée D'Orsay in Paris. The
Westside Pavilion displays wares and goods of consumer culture; the Musée
D'Orsay displays wares and goods of a culture to be consumed.

The Musée d'Orsay   The Gare d'Orsay, a train station in operation from
1900 to 1939, is now the site of the major museum of nineteenth-century
French art. Since the Musée d'Orsay opened in 1987, there has been much
ado about the revisionist subtexts of its curatorial and architectural decisions.
Marvin Trachtenberg muses on the ghostly presence of trains in this
revamped *gare*.[4] In the massive twin constructions lined up on either side of
the building's grand nave, he sees "lithic trains," frozen in monumental
stone and almost hidden by their obviousness. They are "waiting to carry the
museum visitor . . . back into the world of 19th century art."[5] But other
visitors may be struck by something else: the sense that the Musée d'Orsay is
indeed an elaborate waiting room, a station for departure and destination, but
that the awaited train is the long overdue twentieth century.

The museum's design prescribes an itinerary for the visit, a linear
progression that disallows random peripatetics. Those who follow this route
through the Musée d'Orsay's chronology of art history (roughly from 1848
through 1914), *are* led into the twentieth century. In the uppermost corner,
the last and most obscure part of the specified course, is an exhibit called *La
naissance du cinéma*.

Here, amid many protocinematic toys and devices (including Etienne-Jules
Marey's chrono-photogun) are selections from the program present at the
first public projection of films: the *actualités* shown by the Lumière brothers
in 1895. And here one witnesses the arrival of a train at the station endlessly
repeated in a loop of the Lumière's *L'arrivée du train en gare*. This seemingly
anticlimactic end to the museum visit is actually fitting, for the arrival of the
cinematic apparatus rather unceremoniously "burst asunder" the nineteenth
century, when as Benjamin declares, "our railways stations appeared to have
locked us up hopelessly."

Grand nave, Museé d'Orsay.

Photograph © Anne Friedberg.

Westside Pavilion, Los Angeles.

Photograph © Anne Friedberg.

The Westside Pavilion   The Westside Pavilion opened in West Los Angeles
in May 1985 with canonical mid-1980s mall attributes: skylit clerestory,
vaulted iron and glass roof, interior landscaping (ficus and palms), fountains,
park benches, neon signs, and a food court. Its architect, Jerde, used
European glazed street tile flooring and a mixture of Mediterranean and
stucco walls painted in Jerde signature colors—pale plum, salmon, aqua,
rose, and lime.

On the top floor of the Westside Pavilion, after one takes a full escalator
"tour" of the shop windows on two levels, is the multiplex cinema, the

four-screen Samuel Goldwyn Pavilion. Both the transformed train station—the Musée d'Orsay—and the Westside Pavilion are architectural spaces that necessitate a full tour of the wares on display before one can reach its uppermost corners, which house, either as an aside or as a central lure, the cinema.

It is here that the mall and the museum dramatically open venues onto other times, other spaces, other imaginaries. The traveler-tourist or shopper-browser need not travel further. The imaginary museum of the cinema satisfies the peripatetic urge, "mobilizes" a "virtual" gaze in static comfort.

Andy Warhol, "Where is Your
Rupture," 1960. © Andy Warhol
Foundation for the Visual Arts /
ARS, New York.

Post: the term itself demands a cultural seismology—an attempt to measure the magnitude and moment of rupture with the modern, and to appraise its effects.[2] But too frequently arguments about postmodern*ity* take positions on modern*ism,* but not modern*ity.* The murky quality of much of the debate about the postmodern would become more focused by a simple clarification: the use of separate terms for the social and philosophical dimension—modern*ity* and postmodern*ity*—and for its concurrent cultural movements—modern*isms* and postmodern*isms* (i.e., we live in postmodernity but the arts may exemplify modernism).[3]

In each of the various arts where postmodern*ism* has been debated—literature, art, architecture, music, dance, performance—modern*ism* itself has meant something different. The term, *post*modern*ism,* has been used in literature since the early 1960s,[4] since the middle 1970s in architecture,[5] since the late 1970s in dance and performance,[6] and applied to film and television only in the 1980s.[7] In film and television criticism, postmodernism has come to be used as a descriptive term for a genre or a period style but without an account of how the cultural configurations of postmodernity have themselves been profoundly altered by cinema and the television. As I have been suggesting, cinematic and televisual spectatorship has produced a new form of subjectivity; and this subjectivity is produced apparatically, whether or not the style per se is "postmodern."

In the following chapter, I will argue against the type of critical applicationism that adopts the adjective *postmodern* to describe contemporary cinematic styles. First, film theorists and film historians have yet to agree on what is "modern" in cinematic terms. Second, a description of the cinematic apparatus itself will demonstrate the further difficulty of defining what is "modern" or "postmodern" in cinematic terms. But first, since much of the debate about the postmodern (in both aesthetic style and social effect) has taken its terms and assumptions from the architectural model, it is first necessary to demonstrate how architectural postmodernism does not fit as an analogy for film stylistics.

THE ARCHITECTURAL MODEL   For architecture, the rupture between modern and postmodern is dramatically visible. Architectural historian Charles Jencks— the self-proclaimed definer and typologist of "postmodern architecture"— points to a precise moment when the modern ended and the postmodern began: the dramatic destruction of the Pruitt-Igoe housing project in St. Louis ("Modern Architecture died in St. Louis Missouri on July 15, 1972, at 3:32 P.M."[8]). The image of a dynamite explosion leveling these buildings provides an arresting visualization of the "end" of architectural modernism.

"Modern Architecture died in St. Louis, Missouri, on July 15, 1972, at 3:32 p.m." The dynamite destruction of the Pruitt-Igoe housing project, St. Louis, 1972. Courtesy *St. Louis Post Dispatch*.

In Jencks's description, "postmodern" style is marked by its departure from the aesthetic purity and streamlined functionalism of modernist International Style architects like Mies van der Rohe, Le Corbusier, or Walter Gropius. The postmodern reaction to these forms of architectual modernism relies instead on the pluralist combination of modern and premodern architectural styles. The hybrid buildings of Robert Venturi, Peter Eisenman, Michael Graves, James Stirling, Aldo Rossi, John Portman, and Arata Isozaki are models for Jencks's description of "Post-modern Architecture" as "half-Modern, half-conventional."[9] Graves's Portland Building (1982), for example, incorporates the boxy functionalism of modern architecture and the classical columns and ornamental motifs of premodern architecture. Monumental buildings such as Philip Johnson's AT&T Building in New York (1978–1982)—a modernist box with a Chippendale top—or Portman's Bonaventure Hotel in Los Angeles (1976)—a medieval fortress of mirrored glass—are vivid illustrations of this additive style.[10] In addition, vernacular architecture—condominium units, storefront design, shopping malls, and what in Los Angeles is called a "pod mall" or "mini-mall"—also provides examples of this combination of stylistic elements from High Modernism's nautical railings to portholes and glass surfaces, all decorated with the folly-esque colors of mint and salmon.[11]

Postmodern architecture, in Jencks's terms, reintroduced elements of style that modernism had purged—ornament, metaphor, historical allusion—and built spaces that were intended to be more popular, more human, and more individually oriented than the spartan Le Corbusier and Mies glass boxes of High Modernism. Although he partially attributes the stylistics of postmodern architecture to a reaction to the social failure of modern architecture, Jencks defines postmodernism most assertively in terms of style: a "double-coding" of the elite and the popular, the old and the new, a continuation of modernism and its transcendence.

Jencks makes many of his distinctions between "modern" and "post-modern" using analogies with other forms of visual art. Modernists, he claims, took the *process* of art as their subject, while postmodernists take the *history* of art as their subject. As a typologist, Jencks becomes very shrill about "category mistakes" in which Late Modernists are confused with Postmodernists. Late Modernists still rely on a concept of the "new," whereas Postmodernists have a new relation to the past.[12]

As we will see, it would be difficult to find an analogy in film history for the Pruitt-Igoe housing failure. Does one assume that the model of "modern" cinema was the "classical Hollywood film" with its economy of structure, its narrative continuities, its popular appeal, its reduction of metaphor—a sort of refined glass box, efficient in its production of narrative pleasure? If so, what moment or film would instantiate such a dramatic rupture? Did it occur with the narrative bricolage of Orson Welles's *Citizen Kane* in 1941? Or earlier—before the classical Hollywood "mode of practice" took hold—in the montage exercises of Eisenstein and Vertov in the 1920s?

Michael Graves, The Portland Public Services

Building, Portland, Oregon 1980–82. Courtesy

Michael Graves, Architect.

Jameson confounds this distinction by considering as "modern" a list of filmmakers including Fellini and Bergman—whose films have been thought of as a challenge to the Hollywood model—along with the films of Alfred Hitchcock, that master of "classical" editing. In a sentence that requires a good deal of parsing to detect its meaning, Jameson discusses symptoms of the "postmodernism" style in film:

> It can be witnessed in film, not merely between experimental and commercial production, but also within the former itself, where Godard's "break" with the classical filmic modernism of the great "auteurs" (Hitchcock, Bergman, Fellini, Kurosawa) generates a series of stylistic reactions against itself in the 1970's and is also accompanied by a rich new development of experimental video (a new medium inspired by but significantly and structurally distinct from experimental film).[13]

This sentence, a key sentence for Jameson's catalog of the postmodern changes in cinematic form, has an incredibly tangled sense of where the actual "breaks" are. We are left with a series of unanswered questions: Is the break between modern and postmodern the same as the break between commercial and experimental? Are Hitchcock, Bergman, Fellini—the "auteurs"— exemplars of cinematic modernism while Godard is postmodern? If Bergman and Fellini are modernists, does this make the classical Hollywood cinema premodernist? And what does that say about earlier cinematic forms, before the codes of cinematic narrative were well established? What do we say about conventions of narrative construction that evolved in other national cinemas? How do they relate to "postmodernism"? Certainly, the "classical model"—a model deemed in retrospect— was challenged in its own day by a variety of avant-gardes that were otherwise involved in all that modern came to mean in the other arts.[14]

All of these questions form fault lines underneath the surface application of *modern* and *postmodern* as stylistic terms. As I will continue to argue, the very apparatus of the cinema makes the stylistic categories of modernism and postmodernism inappropriate.

THE CINEMA AND MODERNITY/MODERNISM: THE "AVANT-GARDE" AS A TROUBLING THIRD TERM   Because the invention of the cinema was coincident with the urban and cultural changes that marked moder*nity,* the cinema has been commonly thought of as a "modern" apparatus. And yet most work on cinema and modern*ism* retreats from theorizing modernity itself, leaving the relation between modernity and cinematic modernism ambiguous at best. Cinematic modern*ism* has been most frequently described in analogy to the aesthetic challenges to the mimetic mandate of representation in painterly modernism or literary modernism.[15]

To complicate matters, in historical accounts of cinema, as in the other arts, there remains a profound and lasting conflation of what is considered "modernism" and what is considered the "avant-garde."[16] While the warring definitions of cinematic modernism and the cinematic avant-garde are largely a historiographical debate, to examine cinematic modernism one cannot avoid a discussion of the history of the cinematic "avant-garde."[17] Hence, even to approach a discussion of the cinema in postmodernity, one wades further into a nominalist quagmire.

Cinema and the "Avant-Garde" Both Peter Bürger (*Theory of the Avant-Garde*) and Andreas Huyssen (*After the Great Divide*) have attempted to correct an assumed coextensivity between the avant-garde and modernism, a conflation assumed by critics as diverse as Renato Poggioli, Irving Howe, and Jürgen Habermas.[18] But if this correction has had any impact on our current concept of a cultural avant-garde, it has largely been to exile it to a fixed historical period (now referred to as "the historical avant-gardes") rather than address it as an ongoing front.[19] In *Theory of the Avant-Garde*, Bürger makes the distinction between modernism, which attacks the conventions of language, and the avant-garde, which attacks the institutions of art.

The history of the French cinema, a key battleground for these semantic disputes, will provide us with an illustrative case of how Bürger's distinctions do not fit cinema history. One of the implicit agendas of both the "first" and "second" French "avant-gardes" was to have the cinematic medium taken seriously as an art form. Much of this campaign took place as a discursive struggle in the French journals, such as *Le Film, Le Journal du Ciné-Club, Cinéa, Cinéa-Ciné-pour-tous,* and later, in international journals, such as *Close-Up* and *Experimental Film.*[20] The language of these critics, many of whom became filmmakers, was to announce the cinema as a "new art."[21] Filmmakers and their discursive supporters wished for the incorporation of the cinema into the institutions of high art, preferring to build cathedrals for their art than to challenge the idea of its institutionalization.

Filmmakers Marcel L'Herbier and Louis Delluc, for example, employed the terms *impressionist* and *impressionism* as self-descriptive labels, drawing the parallels between their cinematic visuality and painterly or musical impressionism.[22] In this case *impressionism* was used contemporaneously, not just in historical retrospect. Richard Abel has attempted to clarify the various labels used in French film histories (impressionism, avant-garde, modernism). Abel is dubious of terms that narrowly define modernism as anti-illusionist and antinarrative and wants to open modernism to include the "narrative avant-garde."[23] Abel appeals to the historical distinction between the "First Avant-garde," which included feature-length narrative filmmakers (Delluc, Germaine Dulac, Jean Epstein, L'Herbier, and Abel Gance) between 1919 and 1924, and the "Second Avant-garde," composed of abstract or non-narrative films from 1924 to 1929. In these distinctions, the avant-garde includes narrative and non-narrative films. Rather than make an exact distinction between modernism and the avant-garde, Abel combines them.

The film experiments of this avant-garde were not confined to a single national cinema and also attempted to cross another borderline, that between cinema and the other arts—literature, painting, sculpture, music. Films such as painters Viking Eggeling and Hans Richter's *Rhythmus 21* (1921) and *Symphonie Diagonale* (1922); photographer Man Ray's *Le retour a la raison* (1923); cubist painter Ferdinand Leger's *Ballet mecanique* (1924); Luis Bunuel and Salvador Dali's *Un Chien Andalou* (1929) were received in the realms of high art, exhibited in galleries or ciné-clubs, separate from the venues of the burgeoning new "mass cultural" popular cinema.

The above experimental films were part of a campaign to challenge the assumptions that cinema was a (lowly) form of mass entertainment and was, instead, worthy of inclusion in the academies of high art. Hence the cinema has its own convoluted history of allegiance to the principles of the "avant-garde," and does not neatly fit into Bürger's assumptions about the avant-garde attacking the institutions of art. In addition, Bürger defines the techniques of crosscutting and montage as essentially avant-garde. This would make every film from *Birth of a Nation* to *Potemkin* to *Psycho* an avant-garde film.

Cinema and Modernism The cinema also has a paradoxical place in critical discourse about modernism. The narratological and mimetic conventions that developed as the cinema became a popular mass cultural form are precisely the conventions of representation that modernisms were challenging. The cinema can be seen as a "modern" form embodying distinctly *anti*-modern narratological conventions (closure, mimesis, realism) disguised in "modern" technological attire.

A useful approach to such a terminological impasse about cinematic "modernism" is offered by Huyssen's formulation of the "divide" between modernism and mass culture. Modernism, Huyssen maintains, was constituted "through a conscious strategy of exclusion, an anxiety of contamination by its other: an increasingly consuming and engulfing mass culture."[24] In this context, Huyssen also examines the rhetorical treatment of "Mass Culture as Woman," a discursively debased partner in a long-standing and bitter cultural divorce.[25]

But Huyssen's effort to locate the chasm on a discursive plane—placing a "great divide" between mass culture and modernism—makes it somewhat easier to chart a rupture or break between the modern and the *post*modern.[26] The concept of a great divide forces the seismological cleavage, the *division,* onto a cultural rather than temporal model. Attempts to simply periodize the modern and the postmodern thus become misplaced road signs supported by a misleading *post.*

If the "divide" between mass culture and modernism is properly understood, Huyssen posits, then the postmodern can be welcomed for its potential to reconcile, to fuse these disjunctures. In all of this, the avant-garde (a "hidden dialectic") asserts itself as a historical paradigm that rejected the "divide" from mass culture, and offers a heritage that Huyssen wishes to resurrect. The "historical avant-garde" (which includes Russian constructivism, Berlin Dada, and French surrealism) would be Huyssen's chosen genealogical forebear for the postmodern.

Once one endorses the concept of such a divide, it is no longer useful to trace a singular history of high art; one must, instead, examine the bifurcated lineage of art and its relation to mass culture. Even though the boundary between what has been considered the "avant-garde" and what has been considered "modernism" may be very fluid, Huyssen maintains that the distinction rests in their respective attitudes toward mass culture. And because the conflation of modernism with the avant-garde only occurs later within art critical discourse, Huyssen wants to point out that the avant-garde, unlike modernism, always rejected the separation from mass culture. Huyssen uses the "historical avant-gardes" as a wedgelike presence, to sharpen modernism's relationship between high art and mass culture, but the cinematic avant-gardes fall into a tricky terrain. The avant-garde film is generally defined in distinction from the mass cultural entertainment film, placing its experiments on the modernist side of the divide. Perhaps because of the conflation with modernism(s), these cinematic "avant-gardes" have been defined in strict separation from mass culture.

Postmodern art, Huyssen wants us to note, follows the lineage of the historical avant-garde, in that it has been driven to cross boundaries, to force intersections between the spheres of high and low, or public and private, which modernism wished to keep separate. In these terms, post-modern art exists in new configurations with modernism, with mass culture, and with the avant-garde. In Huyssen's view, the "postmodern condition" in literature and the arts is one where the distinctions between high art and mass culture have become quite blurred. Huyssen's "divide" between mass culture and modernism—and its undercurrent, the avant-garde—suggests that the cinema is, unlike all other art forms, uniquely poised to be "postmodern."

As if following this lead, J. Hoberman has attempted to rehistoricize the American avant-garde and to apply the (early eighties) debates about *post-modernism* to a historical account of the cinematic "avant-garde."[27] In an essay entitled "After Avant-Garde Film," Hoberman provides a historical survey of the range of manifestations of "avant-garde" filmmaking, and adds the strategies often equated with postmodernism—appropriation, quotation, pastiche—to his description of the resurgence of "fringe" film-making in New York in the late 1970s. The films of Beth and Scott B., Vivienne Dick, Becky Johnston, James Nares, Eric Mitchell, Charlie Ahearn, and others, Hoberman asserts, were a "postmodernist repetition" of the New York underground of the mid-1960s. Postmodernist because the repetition was "second generation," sometimes parodic, sometimes homagistic allusions to Warhol, Fellini, and Antonioni. Although Hoberman doesn't claim this explicitly, he is also calling this work "postmodern-ist" because these filmmakers were positioned against what had become an "avant-garde ghetto"—the institutionalized empires of the Museum of Modern Art, Anthology Film Archives, and their academic alliances. These filmmakers were challenging what Bürger would call "the institutions of art." It is as if the cinema only became "avant-garde" *after* modernism.

Hoberman also offers a polemical rereading of Peter Wollen's earlier polemic, "The Two Avant-Gardes" (1975), which traced the historical bifurcation between an avant-garde that followed the formalism of cubist cinema and an avant-garde that followed the political concerns of the Soviets.[28] Hoberman argues that Wollen was describing a subtextual conflict between two "postmodernisms"—"the genuinely populist, Sixties postmodernism of Pop Art and underground movies *versus* the mandarin Seventies postmodernism of continental theory."[29] Although the ramifications of these two postmodernisms—the populist and the mandarin—aren't fully elaborated, Hoberman has begun to hint at a cinematic instance of what Huyssen described as the "great divide." At the time Hoberman was writing, this divide split between films that were aligned with mass culture— (DePalma's wanton appropriation of Hitchcock and Antonioni)—and films that were aligned with the poststructuralist avant-garde (Yvonne Rainer, and what Hoberman and others called "the New Talkies"). Hoberman concluded with a hint that video art might offer "the perpetuation of a postmodern avant-garde." In this sense, Hoberman positioned what might be deemed "avant-garde" aesthetic practice in an otherwise foreclosed terrain of the televisual.

Hoberman's piece seems marked now as one written from the vantage of the mid-1980s. Are there two postmodernisms? In contemporary film culture, does this split between stylistic and political art practices still pertain? Is there a formal cinematic postmodernism as opposed to a political cinematic postmodernism? If the distinctions between high art and mass culture have become ever more blurred, how can we discuss postmodern film in terms of style and neglect its place in the larger cultural apparatus?

Certainly the dissolution of an "avant-garde" into the totality of consumer culture was a cultural deficit of the socioeconomic configurations of the Reagan 1980s. When, in 1987, Hoberman turned his review of the Whitney Biennial into a bleak prophecy, a distressed obituary for the cinematic avant-garde ("Individuals persevere, but the movement seems moribund. . . . the real irony is that a major reason for the marginalization of the avant-garde is precisely the absence of a commodity to exploit."[30]), he was criticized for his aging standards and his own dismissals. As a letter to the editor complained:

It would never have occurred to him during the heyday of '6os underground film to allow an institution like the Whitney Museum to define what was innovative and compelling in filmmaking.[31]

Hoberman described that year's Whitney Biennial as "the most dismal selection of avant-garde films since the Biennial began including the form in 1979." And yet, like modernism's inclusion in the institutions of academy, the institutionalization and academicization of the cinematic avant-garde has had its critical effects.

As if to seal the fate of the avant-garde film, two years later, *New York Times* critic Caryn James, reviewing the next Whitney Biennial, queried: "How can avant-garde filmmaking survive in a consumer culture so pervasive that it seems to absorb its own critics?"[32]

JAMESON AND THE CINEMATIC "POSTMODERN"   To date, Jameson has provided the most detailed account of the role of cinema in postmodernity. In two essays, "Postmodernism, or the Cultural Logic of Late Capitalism," and "Postmodernism and Consumer Society," Jameson directly addresses the symptomatic aesthetics of postmodern*ism* and film.[33] In these essays, and in his other discussions of postmodernism, Jameson has deftly peeled away the first layers of postmodernism's mirrored skin. His descriptions, as we will see, offer the depth of cultural insight that is only available to a theorist who takes the risk of evaluating a range of aesthetic products—from architecture to music to the visual arts. Jameson provides a detailed diagnosis of postmodern cultural practice, covering a wide range of symptomatic cases with a thin sheen of analytic brilliance. Jameson locates his analysis of film and the postmodern in a discussion of the "nostalgia film."[34] The "nostalgia film" may indeed be an indication of a key aesthetic symptom, a cinematic version of postmodern style, but, as we will see, the phenomenon of nostalgia extends well beyond this one genre or period style; it is an inherent feature of the photographic and cinematic apparatus itself.

Although Jameson doesn't perform an exact taxonomy, his descriptions divide the "nostalgia film" into: 1) films that are about the past and set in the past (*Chinatown, American Graffiti*); 2) films that "reinvent" the past (*Star Wars, Raiders of the Lost Ark*); and 3) films that are set in the present but invoke the past (*Body Heat;* we could add *Miami Vice, Moonlighting, Batman*). The "nostalgia film" is described in stylistic terms—cases where a film's narrative and its art direction confuse its sense of temporality. Films such as *Chinatown* and *The Conformist* take place in "some eternal Thirties; beyond historical time."[35]

But if we extend this analysis of diegetic temporality to include the apparatus's inherent capacity to alter the spectator's relation to temporality, then *every* film has the jumbled relation to the historical referent that Jameson finds exclusively in the "nostalgia film." As I began to illustrate in the last chapter, all films—now in the age of easily replayable, accessible time-shifting—provide a temporal mobility for the spectator as "time-tourist."

Perhaps because Jameson is one of the few theorists in the postmodern debate who has attempted to account for the role of cinema and the televisual, his work has become the cornerstone of most subsequent discussions. But it will be necessary to take his analysis a few steps further to theorize the institution of the cinema and its larger cultural role in the contemporary figuration deemed *post*modernity.

When Jameson first began writing on postmodernism in the early 1980s, he began by remarking on the "inverted millennarism" implicit in discourses that proclaimed an "end" of ideology, an "end" of history, an "end" of modernism.[36] Jameson wanted to posit a *coupure* and to theorize the historiographical problems involved in demarcating a rupture between the modern and the postmodern.

One of Jameson's key contributions as theorist of the postmodern has been his assertion that the emergence of postmodern*ism* is directly connected to ("late") consumer capitalism and the "postindustrial"[37] society that matured after World War II.[38] In the essay, "Postmodernism, or the Cultural Logic of Late Capitalism," Jameson asserts this relation:

Postmodern culture is the internal and superstructural expression of a whole new wave of American military and economic domination throughout the world.[39]

Both internal and superstructural: Jameson argues that the cultural effects of American military and economic domination have produced a particular aesthetic form, a superstructural detritus, "postmodern culture." This is a reflection theory, where the schizophrenic, decentered, panicked subjectivity produced by late capitalism produces, in turn, cultural products that are embodiments of such fragmentation.

At the core of Jameson's discussion of the postmodern is a shift in cultural groundworks which, Jameson claims, gives a different signification and valence to aesthetic strategies. Here, the separate terms of modernity and modernism might sharpen Jameson's argument. When, for example, he describes postmodern*ism* as a new social formation, not simply an extension of modernism, he is describing postmodern*ity,* where modern*isms* have been canonized into the academy and are no longer shocking. The stylistic similarities between modernist art and what is called "postmodernist" art have to be read, he would argue, in terms of the major differences in the socioeconomic context in which they are received. (In short, "modern*ism*(s)" read differently in "postmodern*ity*.")

In a slightly earlier essay, "Postmodernism and Consumer Society" (1983), Jameson first proposed the idea of a cultural "dominant":

Radical breaks between periods do not generally involve complete changes of content but rather the restructuration of a certain number of elements already given: features that in an earlier period or system were subordinate now become dominant.[40]

By shifting away from a purely stylistic description, Jameson describes how modern*isms*, once oppositional arts, had, in their day, a different social function than contemporary arts, which "may have all the same formal features of the older modernism" but have shifted their cultural position and lost some of their oppositional force.

In the later essay, "Postmodernism, or the Cultural Logic of Late Capitalism" (1984), Jameson elaborates the concept of a "dominant." He questions his own "empirical, chaotic and heterogenous" list of postmodernist texts and offers a "periodizing hypothesis,"[41] which, instead of simply supplying a roster of stylistic innovation, asserts that postmodernism is not a style but a "cultural dominant"[42] or a "force-field."[43] The term *cultural dominant*, then, supplies a more historiographically rigorous explanation of the continuity and discontinuity between the modern and the postmodern; it allows for the coexistence of the features of both. The idea of a "cultural dominant" requires a dialectical imagination of history, where the coupure is not temporal but discursive and epistemological.[44] My discussion of postmodernity parallels Jameson's theorization of a "cultural dominant." Rather than proclaiming a temporal moment of rupture, I have traced the subtle transformation produced by the increasing cultural centrality of the image producing and reproducing apparatuses.

Warhol's Multiple: An Aesthetic Symptom   If we digress briefly to examine Jameson's analysis of the work of Warhol, it will illustrate some of the limitations in Jameson's initial conceptualization of the cinema and the postmodern. Jameson's consideration of Warhol's work will provide us with an insight as to why his account of film in postmodernity slights the multiple metonmyic distribution of cinema over time.

Jameson uses the aesthetic product—a symbolic document of its time such as Van Gogh's *Peasant Shoes* or Munch's *The Scream*—as an indication of a shift in the "dynamics of cultural pathology" from modernity to postmodernity. He maintains that the twin symptoms of modernity—anxiety and alienation—have given way to a new cultural pathology of fragmentation. Jameson finds symptoms of this fragmentation in the work of Warhol, whose *Marilyn* series (1962) and *Shoes* (done with diamond dust, 1980) are, to him, symptomatic documents of postmodernity. In these works, as in many of Warhol's silkscreen multiples, the pieces are produced by repeating a single, celebrated photographic image. Jameson asserts that it is the "black and white substratum of the photographic negative" that brought Warhol into the "age of mechanical reproduction."[45]

But it was not just that Warhol was using the photographic negative in his silkscreened works which brought Warhol into a new configuration with reproduction and distribution. A key element of Warhol's work was the metonymic display of the *multiple:* identical images repeated (like unchanging film frames) in serial—but not sequential—repetition.

Grounded in rubber stamp multiples, a staple of the commercial art illustration world when Warhol entered it in the late 1940s, the multiple became a central strategy in Warhol's work.[46] Not only were works produced in silkscreen series, they were exhibited in multiple serialized display (*Eighty-Two Dollar Bills* [1962]; *Marilyn x 100* [1962]; *Thirty Are Better Than One* [1963]; *Dollar Signs* [1981]). The subject here was fragmented by its identical reproducibility.[47] In this way, Warhol used mechanical reproduction both diachronically and synchronically—spatially and temporally. In a sense, even before Warhol began making "movies," his silkscreen work followed the historical trajectory from photography to film. As he spatially reproduced his close-up "part objects" (Marilyn's lips, Coke bottles) they became temporalized into a series of repeated "part objects" that produce an image of timelessness.[48] (In fact, Warhol's film work frequently employed a static camera, producing an almost unchanging series of images frame to frame; when his film work is reproduced in still illustration it is done in the form of a film strip in order to illustrate the frame arrangement. Each frame appears as an image in multiple.[49])

As Warhol retrospectives cover the globe (the Museum of Modern Art retrospective travels to the Georges Pompidou in Paris then on to Prague,

Andy Warhol, "Thirty Are Better Than One," 1963.

© Andy Warhol Foundation for the Visual Arts /

ARS, New York.

Hungary, Yugoslavia, and Warsaw. Will Moscow be far behind?), the poly-valent slippages of context—of political context and the passage of time—force us to rethink these silk-screen images. Hailing so blatantly from the United States as if in colorful multiples, they unfurl the flag of American-based consumer culture. What do these images do, if not celebrate a culture of abundance and multiplication? Warhol's work provides an aesthetic sanction to these proliferations of spectacle—billboards, supermarkets, advertisements. Or, if not condoning commercialism, his work provided a lesson of adjustment. We live among all of these images, equal under the sign of signage: the hammer and sickle is equal to Marilyn or Mao or Reagan-for-Van Heusen shirts. Warhol's work makes natural what—in the 1960s and 1970s and even in the waning utopian hopes of the 1980s—we hoped it might critique. His work had an aesthetic of rebellion that became an aesthetic of sanction, an acceptance of the values of the culture of consumption that it first intended to critique. The work was forged not out of the conviction to relinquish the pleasures of ownership but to celebrate it, not an abstraction of commercial signage but instead its prophetic land-scape.

Jameson, unlike many theorists of the postmodern, has forced a political analysis of positions in the debate ("every position on postmodernism in culture . . . is necessarily an implicitly or explicitly political stance on the nature of multi-national capitalism today"[50]).

By 1987, when Jameson wrote "Postmodernism and Utopia," he had a manifest nostalgia for the dialectic, detecting the faint echoes of a "Utopian vocation" of "collective cultural fantasies" in the work of contemporary artists Salle, Haacke, and Wasow.[51] In this essay, Jameson has a more affirmed sense of modernity's passage, a more digested sense of postmod-ernism's effects. (Phrases such as "the sharp pang of death of the modern" and "the modern is sealed for good" assure us of this.[52]) And, as he rethinks modernity and postmodernity in terms of time and space, Jameson makes a distinction between modernism's experience of existential time and deep memory and postmodernism's discontinuous spatial experience.[53] Jameson suggests a " 'great transformation'—the displacement of time, the spatial-ization of the temporal"[54]—which separates the postmodern and its "new spatial aesthetic" where "older form[s] of place" have disappeared, replaced by the "Disneyland simulacra of themselves."[55]

These more recent descriptions of postmodern temporality suggest a productive route for an adequate consideration of cinematic and televisual forms.

CINEMA AND POSTMODERNITY Despite these semantic battles, the term *postmodern* has entered into the critical vocabulary of film style. If, as James recently asserted in the *New York Times,* "post-modern films rejuvenate old genres—westerns, adventure serials and musicals—by being them and mocking them at the same time,"[56] how do we find a coupure, a historical or stylistic moment that separates the categories modern and postmodern?[57]

In a more sophisticated version of the same definition, Linda Hutcheon suggests, if not a manifest break between the modern and the postmodern, a more nuanced relationship, one of metareferentiality. What happens, Hutcheon asks, when a film like *Stardust Memories* parodies a "modernist" film like *8½*?:

> What happens, I think, is something we could label as "postmodernist," something that has the same relation to its modernist cinematic past as can be seen in postmodern architecture today—*both a respectful awareness* of cultural continuity and a need to adapt to changing formal demands *and* social conditions through *an ironic challenging* of the authority of that same continuity.[58] (emphasis added)

For Hutcheon, whose work on postmodernism has consistently defended the critical potentials of parody and dialogism, double-voiced ironic parody becomes a corrective antidote to that other form of recalling the past, nostalgia.

This assumption, that postmodern style involves citation, the invisible quotation marks of parody ("being them and mocking them at the same time") has come to be an agreed-upon currency of its critical usage. In James's definition, the "old genre" is made the object of representation, not necessarily as parodic travesty—for humor or critique—but also with the possible intention of endorsing, repeating, underlining the earlier form—recapitalizing, in a sense, on a past success.

But before we assume that the "post" implies a referentiality back to an earlier instance of representation, it seems imperative that we again consider the apparatus of the cinema itself. Certainly the cinema is not the first story-telling medium where the same stories are consistently retold.[59] From its beginning, the cinema has rejuvenated and replayed its own genres and narratives. The cinematic apparatus is unique in its facility to replay and repeat its own exact form—the identical replication made possible by its photographic base allows the same film to be reprojected at a variety of points in time. Hence one cannot say that only postmodern cinema (as distinct from modern cinema) takes its own history, its own form, as a subject.[60]

To investigate this assertion, let us briefly consider a particularly cinematic form: the remake. From the very beginning of film production, films were remade.[61] Once one begins to examine the abundance of historical examples of this form, it seems necessary to attempt a taxonomy to distinguish how such intertextual referentiality might operate between the "original" and the remake. The remake itself can produce a *mise en âbyme* of references, an "original" that is ever-receding:

1) *Films based on stage or literary properties:* Dashiell Hammett's *Maltese Falcon* was made three times in ten years; first in 1931 directed by Roy del Ruth with Bebe Daniels and Ricardo Cortez; then as *Satan Met a Lady* (1936) directed by William Dieterle with Bette Davis and Warren William; in 1941 as *Maltese Falcon,* directed by John Houston with Humphrey Bogart, Mary Astor, and Peter Lorre. In these examples, the referent—the source for the remake—is literary rather than cinematic.

2) *Films that are remakes of earlier films:* D. W. Griffith remade his 1911 one-reeler *The Lonedale Operator* with Blanche Sweet as *The Girl and Her Trust* with Dorothy Bernard one year later, in January 1912. In these examples, the referent is cinematic not literary.

3) *Films that are remade as technology improves:* Films that were made in the silent era and later remade as sound films; or films made in black and white remade in color. Fannie Hurst's novel, *Back Street,* was made in 1932 (directed by John Stahl with Irene Dunne and John Boles; by Robert Stevenson in 1941 with Margaret Sullavan and Charles Boyer, and then [in color] in 1961 by David Miller with Susan Hayward and John Gavin).

4) *Films that are remade to update or change historical details: Four Horsemen of the Apocalypse,* made first in 1921 (Rex Ingram) as a World War I story with Rudolph Valentino and then remade in 1961 (Vincente Minelli) with Glenn Ford as a World War II story.

The intertextual referentiality between a remake and its "original" is largely extratextual, outside the film text itself in the historical or discursive context of the film's production or reception. Parodic remakes may have a more directly intertextual referentiality.

Remakes may or may not refer back to the earlier version, but sequels always do. Given the recent seasonal dependence on the sequel, it may appear that the sequel itself is a postmodern form. (The summer and fall releases of 1990—*Die Harder, Two Jakes, Robocop II, Young Guns II, Godfather III*—illustrate that the sequel is a reigning conception of successful industrial film production.)

But there are historical precedents for this rash of sequels. Series filmmaking—capitalizing on a known, market-tested good—was an early staple of film production. Serial films—different from series films that were complete in each installment—were another successful marketing strategy as the film industry began to experiment with longer narratives. The serial was a transitional form in the market war between the standardized one-reel format of the Motion Picture Patents Trust companies and the renegade "independents" who attempted films of a "feature" length.[62] Based on the pulp pop-cultural format of the serialized western, comic book, or melodrama, the serial connected otherwise complete narratives by frustrating their narrative closure. Louis Feuillade's serial detective, *Fantomas* (Gaumont, 1913–1914), based on the serial novel by Pierre Souvestre and Marcel Allain, was such a successful cinematic venture that it spawned imitations. The Pathé serial, *Perils of Pauline* (1914), produced in the United States with the American actress Pearl White, was the first American serial.[63] (The serial was a form that was also present in other national cinemas: Germany's *Homunculus,* Italy's *Tigris.*)

By 1916, the serial film was already parodying itself. As Abel records, the French film *La Pied qui etrient* (1916) parodies the first *Perils of Pauline, The Clutching Hand,* and the then newly renowned Charlie Chaplin. Epstein's *Les Aventures de Robert Macaire* (1925) was a parody of Henri Fescourt's *Mandarin* (1924).[64]

The genre film, itself a safe staple of the industry, has offered a solace of familiarity in its iconography and narrative concerns. Some would assert that a melange of genres or period styles—from forties *noir* to nineties *sci-fi*—becomes a particularly "postmodern" pastiche of past forms. If this is the case, it is unclear where one draws the stylistic line: is postmodernist style the additive quality of pastiche or is it the stylistic "literalization" of broader cultural symptoms?[65]

Film production has always teetered on this precipice between originality and repetition. The cinema has repeated and remade the same stories, from myths and fables to plays and novels that are endlessly returned to for source material. But more than this form of repetition, where the textual reference is reencoded in a new text, the cinema has a metonymic capacity of repeating the exact same film over time: reissuing it, redistributing it, reseeing it. At its very base, then, the cinematic apparatus has the capacity to replay itself ("being them and mocking them at the same time"). The repeatability of cinema products means that the apparatus can exactly quote itself, repeat its earlier form, if not its earlier context.

Consider, for example, a Victor Fleming film produced in 1939, set in 1863, but shown in 1992 (*Gone with the Wind*). Or a film produced in 1968, set in 2001, but shown in 1992 (*2001: A Space Odyssey*). Or more exactly, a film made in the city of Paris in 1964, set in a future world, but seen in 1992 in the city of Los Angeles (*Alphaville*), or a film made in Los Angeles in 1982, set in Los Angeles 2019 (*Blade Runner*), but seen in Los Angeles in 1992. The exact temporal referent of each of these films is quite slippery. As work on the genre of the historical film has shown, the particular moment of production will determine its view of the past.[66] And as work on exhibition has shown, the particular moment of exhibition will determine the audience's reception of the past.[67]

In Benjaminian terms, the "aura" of the event has already disappeared in the mechanical reproduction itself, but the aura of the original moment of exhibition also disappeared. Whereas cinematic spectation is most frequently discussed in spatial terms—the elsewhere produced in the cinematic effect—it is equally important to interrogate the elsewhen.

Jameson has dramatized the schizophrenia of the postmodern subject because "the ideal schizophrenic's experience is still one of time, albeit of the eternal Nietzschean present."[68] It is this subjective *timelessness* that provides an implicit parallel between the "postmodern condition" and cinematic and televisual spectatorship. But this subjective timelessness is not just a factor of diegetic temporality, it is a condition of the mobilized virtual gaze of spectatorship itself.

POSTMODERNITY WITHOUT THE WORD   A range of cultural diagnosticians have assessed related social and cultural effects of the technologies of the mechanical reproduction without relying on the terms *modern* and *postmodern*.

How, for example, is postmodernity different from what the frequently dismissed sociologist Daniel Boorstin called the "Graphic Revolution"? In his 1961 book *The Image: A Guide to Pseudo-Events in America,* Boorstin assessed the impact of making, preserving, transmitting, and disseminating "images."[69] Although Boorstin does mention Benjamin, whose "The Work of Art in the Age of Mechanical Reproduction" would seem to be the Ur-text for such assessments, he nevertheless described a familiar loss of aura of the original. The Grand Canyon, Boorstin proclaimed, has become only a faint reproduction of the Kodachrome original. While not using semiotic terms, Boorstin posits the ascendance of a Kodachrome signifier, the inversion of the established sign-signifier relation, as a symptom of modernity. As an illustration of the reversed priority of the image, Boorstin coined the term *pseudo-event* for the photo-opportunity staging of image-determined "events."

Debord also diagnosed a similar impact of representation on culture without invoking the terms modernity or postmodernity. In his aphoristic *Society of the Spectacle,* Debord pronounces, "everything that was directly lived has moved away into a representation," and he describes the effects that this has on our concept of history and memory. In a section called "Spectacular Time," Debord describes the spectacle as:

the present social organization of the paralysis of history and memory. . . . the abandonment of history built on the foundation of historical time, is the *false consciousness of time.*[70]

A "false consciousness of time" still implies that there is a "true" one, and that the mystifications of the society of the spectacle are a veil that can be somehow lifted. Debord and other Situationists elevated their own form of appropriation, *detournement,* as one of the ultimate counterstrategies.

Baudrillard takes this same phenomenon—representation of the thing replacing the thing—and extends it into a mise en âbyme of a "hyperreal" where signs refer only to signs. Hyperreality is not just an inverted relation of sign and signifier, but one of receding reference, a deterence operation in the signifying chain. "Body, landscape, time," writes Baudrillard in "The Ecstasy of Communication," "all progressively disappear as scenes."[71] Committing his own détournement, Baudrillard does not mention Debord or any of the Situationists whose ideas he roundly appropriates. Baudrillardian theory abandons ideological analysis in its move toward the hyperreal. In each stage of détournement, the loss of the referent seems to coincide with a waning of the political. Simply put, the representation of politics has been displaced by the politics of representation.

Another media theorist, Joshua Meyrowitz, describes related cultural features. In his book *No Sense of Place: The Impact of Electronic Media on Social Behavior,* he claims:

> The evolution of the media had decreased the significance of physical presence in the experience of people and events. One can now be an audience to a social performance without being physically present; one can communicate "directly" with others without meeting in the same place.[72]

In this passage, Meyrowitz is outlining the effect that television has had on the "situational geography of social life."[73] Meyrowitz describes how electronic media reorganize social space, breaking down the boundaries between here and there, live and mediated, personal and public. To describe the social impact of these changes, Meyrowitz uses the word "homogenized," a concept that implies a classless, genderless world where home, office, slum, and government building all have the same access to the world through the media. He maintains that the electronic media have not only reshaped our sense of "place," but have also blurred the boundaries between childhood and adulthood, and masculinity and femininity.

In all of these cases, the media technologies dematerialize, deindividualize, decenter the subject. Without the word *postmodern* there is no need for periodization, a marked break dramatizing these changes. Yet without the word, these theorists are less concerned with the stylistic variances in cultural products than with the totality of cultural impact, the mode of reception determined entirely by the mode of production.[74]

Having examined the subjective changes produced by industrialized space and time—when the social configurations of the modern began—and by the types of experiences that were first commodified in the middle of the nineteenth century, the subjectivity of the "postmodern condition" appears to be a product of the instrumentalized acceleration of these spatial and temporal fluidities. Postmodernity is marked by the increasing centralization of features implicit (from the start) in cinema spectatorship: the production of a virtual elsewhere and elsewhen, and the commodification of a gaze that is mobilized in both time and space.

Shop window, New York, 1988.

Photograph © Anne Friedberg.

Imagine a public library of the near future, for instance.
There will be long rows of boxes or pillars, properly
classified and indexed of course. *At each box a push button
and before each box a seat.* Suppose you wish to "read up"
on a certain episode in Napoleon's life. Instead of
consulting all the authorities, wading through a host of
books, and ending bewildered without a clear idea of
exactly what did happen, you will merely seat yourself at a
properly adjusted window in a scientifically prepared room,
press the button, and actually see what happened. . . .
There will be no opinions expressed. You will merely be
present at the making of history.

D. W. GRIFFITH[1]

The above vision of the "near future" belonged to D. W. Griffith in 1915.
Griffith's imagined "library" was a future exponent of an apparatus
equipped with the apocryphal power to "writ(e) history with lightning."
His "properly adjusted window" was the cinema screen. Griffith's fantasy
of a cinema with "no opinions expressed" was clearly an idealist one, effac-
ing all consequences of the interventions of representation, cinematic or
otherwise. He imagined the cinema not as an agent of memory, but as a
means of presenting history itself.

"At each box a push button and before each box a seat": Griffith's
prediction is partially realized in today's Vidéothèque de Paris. Located in
the Forum des Halles, an underground shopping mall beneath the former
Les Halles market, the Vidéothèque houses a collection of filmed docu-

ments on the city of Paris. Municipally funded, the archive includes Lumière Brothers' *actualités,* Gaumont and Pathé newsreels, and thousands of fictional films. In addition to two ample screening *salles* that exhibit regular repertory series organized by theme (such as Paris by Automobile, Paris by Arrondissement, Paris During the Occupation), the Vidéothèque has a facility for *consultation individualle.* This high-tech "scientifically prepared room" is equipped with forty individual video monitors each with a *minitel* keyboard. The user sits in a comfortable chair in front of a video monitor and keyboard, and types in films by title, by subject, or by filmmaker. (The computer will list the holdings.) On a recent search, for example, in response to the inquiry "passage couvert," a list of every film in the collection containing images of a Parisian *passage* appeared on the computer's video screen. With the push of a button, these images can be "called up." As if in a scene from *Alphaville,* a robot arm in the mezzanine "library" searches, finds, and pulls the requested title from a shelf, inserts it mechanically into a VCR that is, in turn, connected to the individual monitor. Once the film appears on the video screen, it can be played at various speeds of playback, freeze frame, or reverse. At the push of a button you are not "present at the making of history," but you have, instead, the history of cinema at your fingertips.

As we saw, Baudelaire's discomfort with photography was rooted in his suspicion that in the guise of presenting the past it would obscure it—that photography was not an agent of memory but an agent of forgetting. Jameson restates Baudelaire's warning in a contemporary mode: "The informational function of the media," writes Jameson, "would thus be to help us forget, to serve as the very agents and mechanisms for our historical amnesia."[2]

I would further argue that this loss of memory is a gradual product of the detemporalized, derealized subjectivity produced by cinematic and televisual spectatorship. In a "society of the spectacle" where all social relations are mediated through images, and where shop windows, billboards, and video screens surround us with their heteroglossic surfaces, a spatially and temporally fluid visuality has come to be the dominant mode.

The Mobilized Virtual Gaze   The history of modes of looking, based on mobility rather than confinement, traces an instrumentalization of visuality

"At each box a push button and
before each box a seat." Video
monitor and keyboard at
Vidéothèque de Paris. Photograph
© Anne Friedberg.

different from the panoptic model. Flânerie follows this mode of visuality and hence does not rely on the one-way power of gendered looking often linked with panopticism. Although flânerie began as a predominantly male perceptual mode it was, by the mid-nineteenth century, available to women—first as shoppers, then, as tourists and cinema-goers.

For Benjamin, the flâneur's ambulatory and distracted gaze found its most commanding outlet in the passage. Benjamin was attracted by the arcade's curious temporality, its embrace of "the new, the already past, the ever-same."[3] Like the arcade, the cinema embodies this conflated temporality. In Benjamin's liberating rhetoric ("the dynamite of a tenth of a second"), the film provides an explosive charge to burst asunder the "prison world" of nineteenth-century temporality.[4] As arcades have become shopping malls, and as dioramas and panoramas have evolved into multiplex cinemas and Videotheques, this new temporality has become a key component of postmodern subjectivity.

Phantasmagorias, panoramas, and dioramas relied on physical immobility as well as the painterly illusion of virtual presence. The virtual gaze of photography supplanted, in Barthes's terms, the "here-now" with the "having-been-there." For Barthes, who distinguished between the photograph's essential *pastness* and the film's essential *presentness,* the film fused the spatial immediacy of a virtual gaze with temporal *presentness* (a "being-there").[5] And, as I've argued, the mobilized gaze of shopping and tourism was combined with the virtual gaze of photography to produce a new form: the mobilized and virtual gaze of the cinema.

In the mid-nineteenth century, women were given entre libre to the public space of the department store. But, like the arcade, this public space was also a privatized interior (Rosalind Williams deemed it a "dream world"). The newly-conjoined *mobilized and virtual* gaze of the cinema answered not only the desire for temporal and spatial mobility, but for gender mobility as well. As I've begun to demonstrate, the spectator-shopper—trying on identities—engages in these pleasures of a temporally- and spatially-fluid subjectivity.

Here, theories of spectatorship which imply a one-to-one correspondence between the spectator position and gender, race, or sexual identity—as if identity were a constant, consistent continuum, unchallenged by the borrowed subjectivity of spectatorship—do not consider the pleasures of escaping this physically-bound subjectivity. Isn't cinema spectatorship pleasurable precisely because new identities can be "worn" and discarded? This question appeals to a much larger debate about identification and spectator effect, but it is one that *explores* gender, race, and sexual mobility, rather than one that fixes identity in spectator address.[6]

Temporality and Virtual Mobility   As we have seen, theories of cinematic and televisual spectatorship easily slide into debates about the metaphysics of presence. Jacques Derrida's consideration of the metaphysics of presence in language and representation is at the core of his critique of Western logocentrism. Spivak eloquently restates Derrida's concept of the jumbled temporality of the written trace: "the mark of the absence of a presence, an *always already absent present*" (emphasis added).[7] This description of the written trace (*grapheme*) nearly matches Barthes's assessment of the pastness of the photograph's "having-been-there." In these metaphysical terms, the temporality of the film reinstates the presence of speech; for the cinema spectator, the past is presented as *always already present* (Barthes's "*being-there* of the thing") yet this present is in virtual form.[8] Bergson's description of the "virtual coexistence" of the past and the present is useful here.[9] For the cinema spectator, the historical past is not experienced as if it had already happened, but rather as something more akin to Griffith's assertion that "you will merely be present at the making of history." In the pure metaphysics of cinema spectatorship, the past is unhinged from its foundations and becomes a component of the present. In addition, reseeing films outside of their historical context further separates the film from the context of a past.[10] Here, the symptomatology of postmodern amnesia—the loss of the capacity to retain the past—meets the detemporalized, derealized spectator.

Time Travel and Nostalgia   Deleuze adopts Bergson's spatialized conception of time in his phrase "regions of the past." This spatial model finds a fitting illustration in David McDermott's and Peter McGough's 1986 oil painting, *Twentieth Century Time Map 1972*. The "time map" has sections plotted out as if marking geographic or political boundaries. But each "country" has, rather than a name, a date or a decade attached; hence the land of 1945 to 1955 is to be found beneath that of 1935 to 1945. If one imagines traveling through this landscape, crossing the border between 1904 and 1998 or (with less dramatic transition) from 1903 back into the country

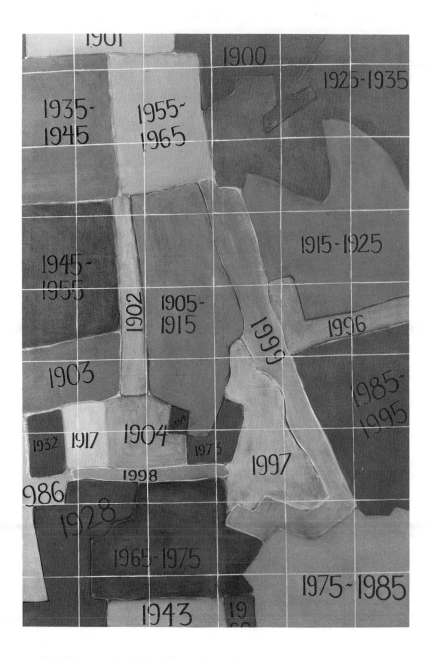

David McDermott and Peter McGough, "Twentieth Century Time Map—1972,"

1986. Courtesy Sperone Westwater Gallery, New York.

of 1902, it would not be unlike the temporal transit of the spectator at the Vidéothèque or in front of a home video monitor hooked to a VCR and the multiplicity of cable channels. This spectator could easily travel from 1945 to 1955 (a film noir or Italian neorealist film) to 1902 (Porter's *Romance of the Rail* or Méliès's *Voyage de la lune*). For McDermott, years and decades are ahistorical, presented in a selective topographic jumble (1968, for example, does not figure on McDermott's map).

This image of a time map is not unlike a wax museum where Joseph Stalin stands between Paul McCartney and Jeannette MacDonald. Annette Michelson invokes the Musée Grevin (the wax museum in the Passage Jouffroy) as a precursor to the cinema:

It struck me, as we went slowly through the long, dark, labyrinthine corridors, punctuated by the rather grand tableaux that chronicle the whole of French history, from the early Gauls until the Gaullist regime, that the wax museum, in its very special, hallucinatory darkness, its spatial ambiguity, its forcing of movement upon the spectator, its mixture of diversion and didacticism, is a kind of protocinema.[11]

Like the wax museum, the cinema serves up the past as present and virtual. In addition to scenes from French history from Charlemagne to Napoleon III, today's Musée Grevin contains a section, "l'aventure au cinéma," where Charlie Chaplin stands next to Larry Hagman, Jack Nicholson next to Boris Karloff, Barbra Streisand next to Shirley Temple. Otto Friedrich describes this creative historiography in the wax museum in Hollywood:

No city west of Boston has a more intensely commercial sense of its own past, and yet that sense keeps becoming blurred and distorted in Hollywood. Not only do decades vaguely intermingle, so that Harold Lloyd dissolves into the young Woody Allen, but the various forms of entertainment also merge. . . . It is possible to smile at the juxtaposition of Charlton Heston bearing the sacred tablets down from Sinai and a panoramic re-creation of Da Vinci's *Last Supper,* but why is Anthony Quinn standing next to Charles de Gaulle? And why, in this central group, which is dominated by the Beatles but also includes Sophia Loren, Amelia Earhart, and Thomas Alva Edison—why should the figure between Paul McCartney and Jeanette MacDonald be that of Joseph Stalin?[12]

The VCR brings the creative geography and jumbled historiography of the wax museum into a new aspect. The VCR converts the already temporally-mobile form of the cinema to a new degree of accessibility. With the VCR, the cinema is more directly a "memory implant," a component module of memory that can be added, removed, replaced.[13] With the videotape as uniform commodity, the VCR is a technological analogue to a prosthetic "implant." David Cronenberg's *Videodrome* makes viscerally literal the implanting or impregnating of consciousness; "videodrome" is a dangerous signal that produces an addiction to video-hallucination and transforms the body into a receptacle for a videocassette; hence, the implant carries violent ideological messages.[14]

One of the by-products of such temporal mobility may be a postmodern *nostomania* (excessive nostalgia) for the past. *Nostalgia* (from Greek, *nostos* = a return; *algos* = painful) means a painful return, a longing for something far away or long ago, separated by distance and time. An etymological history of the word *nostalgia* demonstrates that its first usage in the late seventeenth century was to describe the longing for a space, a technical term for "homesickness." By the late nineteenth century, as the discourses of history produced a concomitant idealization of the past, nostalgia also came to mean a longing for a time past. Late nineteenth-century revival styles and museology encouraged a return to the past, as if to compensate for the threat of the "modern" and the shock of the new. Nostalgia can hide the discontinuities between the present and the past; it falsifies, turning the past into a safe, familiar place.

Jameson diagnosed the "nostalgia" film as a sign of postmodern cultural malaise. ("The formal apparatus of nostalgia films has trained us to consume the past in the form of glossy images."[15]) But to take this further, cinema spectatorship and related cinephilia is itself based in nostalgic desire—a desire deferred in endless secondariness, nostalgia for nostalgia, in an endless return to selective, but secondary, representations.

As if hyperexponents of Jameson's "nostalgia film," the endless supply of cinematic sequels (*Godfather I–III, Chinatown/Two Jakes, Die Hard/Die Harder, Star Wars/Empire Strikes Back, Back to the Future 1–3, Rambo 1–3, Halloween 1–5, Terminator 1–2*) are all of them pieces of nostalgia for the earlier film, for the earlier commodity-experience, as if self-referentiaity were guarantee of profit. Yet these films are also an exponent of an even earlier originary piece of nostalgia—the "nostalgia" of film itself.

Nostalgia is an *algia,* a painful return, but it also offers up pleasures, albeit bittersweet ones. The compulsion to repeat is based in the desire to return. As Janice Doane and Devon Hedges have explored in their book, *Nostalgia and Sexual Difference,* some recent nostalgic strains of American politics and mass culture contain notable antifeminist impulses, as if fulfilling a cultural agenda of returning to a prefeminist moment when women were "in their place" as loyal subordinates.[16] Nostalgia can also take a utopian turn. Nostalgias for the 1960s, for example, often recall a radical period of experimentation, growth, and political engagement. For feminists, nostalgia seems to be a two-edged cultural sword: it can return to outworn values, erasing the effect of all intervening history; and yet nostalgia has the potential to reinvent the past, to contrast its values in a critical combination with the present. Vintage clothes, vintage cars, and old movies are recycled in a new relation to the past.[17]

To conclude, I would like to cite two quite separate but equally bold interventions on science and knowledge, each written from a distinct vantage: Max Horkheimer and T. W. Adorno's *The Dialectic of Enlightenment* (1944) and Lyotard's *The Postmodern Condition* (1979). When Horkheimer and Adorno wrote *The Dialectic of Enlightenment* in Los Angeles in 1944, it was a text produced at a striking historical moment—the peak of Hollywood productivity coincided with the ideologies of fascism and anti-Semitism sweeping through Europe. The "culture industry" circa 1944, with its few production centers (Hollywood) and large number of consumption centers (worldwide) could be seen as an illustration of the bleak switch from dialogic communication to a monologic authoritarian voice. Horkheimer and Adorno could read the cultural symptoms of a retreat into mythology and could witness the Hollywood activity of thoughts being sold off as commodities. The very structure of the "culture industry" in 1944 seemed to embody the end of the Enlightenment.[18] Today the culture industry takes on different forms. Domestic electronics (fax, modems, cable television) follow the interactive model of dialogic telephone communications. The personal computer turns the home user into a desktop publisher, the microwave turns every cook into an instant gourmet, the Walkman transforms each listener into a radio programmer. Both production and reception have been individualized; the culture industry no longer speaks in a univocal monolithic voice.[19]

Yet Lyotard's address on the state of culture in *The Postmodern Condition* has a tone of despair equal to that of *The Dialectic of Enlightenment.* Lyotard's assessment of the totalizing "computerization" of contemporary society leaves few cracks for alternative cultures, short of computer viruses and terrorist attempts, to challenge such a totality.[20] The illusion of choice that the new technologies imply is, in Lyotard's analysis, only an illusion.

As a fitting endpoint, a fin de siècle assessment, I invoke the lyrics from a 1979 Gang of Four song. Originally on the album *Entertainment!,* this recording is now anthologized on a compact disc aptly titled *Brief History of the Twentieth Century:*

At home he feels like a tourist
He fills his head with culture
He gives himself an ulcer

The song concludes with a subtle shift in its pronoun:

At home she feels like a tourist
She fills her head with culture
She gives herself an ulcer

Equally, the flâneuse has earned this power, this curse.

Barbara Kruger, "Untitled," 1987.

Courtesy Barbara Kruger.

WARNINGS AT THE POST

> Defining our world today as Postmodern is rather like
> defining women as "non-men." It doesn't tell us very
> much either flattering or predictive.[1]

So begins Charles Jencks's architectural study, *Postmodern Architecture*. Is it surprising that the critical debate over the cultural usefulness and political valences of the postmodern seems to send critics, notably male critics, into the parallel universe of discourse about another uncharted terrain, "dark continent,"[2] or "remarkable oversight"[3]—that of the feminine? The above equation between the postmodern and woman suggests quite clearly that the need to define postmodernism has sent theorists into the metaphorical pockets of familiar discourses. In the late 1980s the enigma "What is postmodernism?" (itself the title of a brief essay, a "svelte appendix," Lyotard's now canonical volume, *The Postmodern Condition*)[4] had become a riddle almost as taxing as Freud's question "Was will das Weib?"

The debates about the "postmodern" offer a pronounced example of how theoretical neologisms produce semantic fads, easy new packaging for tired intellectual goods. The introduction of new critical terms can also generate a sort of intellectual three-card monte, a strategy of distraction where the speed and heat of dealing out new rhetorical catchwords takes the focus away from otherwise important debates. For feminists, it has seemed urgent to consider the cultural discourse *about* postmodernity because this discursive activity has quickly displaced other quite crucial terms in ideological debate. If we examine the way in which debates about the "P" word have functioned in cultural discourse, it becomes apparent that the force of the debates about the postmodern has, in too many cases, rapidly displaced the concerns that feminist critique held foremost.[5]

Jencks may be an easy target, but the above epigraph provides us with a distinct example of how the categories of modern and postmodern have become sites for acting out anxieties about *other* differences. In *The Language of Postmodern Architecture,* Jencks takes issue with a list of sculptors who the art critic Rosalind Krauss defines as "postmodernists." Krauss's list includes Robert Morris, Robert Smithson, Michael Heizer, Richard Serra, Walter de Maria, Robert Irwin, Sol LeWitt, and Bruce Nauman. Jencks complains, "All things in a room that are not men are not necessarily women."[6] Of course, Jencks does not interrogate this analogy too deeply. The artists on Krauss's list are all men. And all things in a room being equal, he seems to insist that the difference between what he terms "Late Modernism" and what he terms "Postmodernism" are categories that should be as discernible as sexual difference. In this instance, the postmodernists are "not men" but "not women" either, a sort of new "third sex," leaving one to assume that, in this analogy and in Krauss's list, "la femme n'existe pas." Clearly, neither Jencks nor Krauss is interested here in the relation of gender or sexual identity to postmodern aesthetic practice or to the social configuration of postmodernity.[7]

POSTFEMINISM?   As the first bibliographies on modernism indicated, the debate was—until recently—a male province. Not only were most of the first critics engaged in the postmodern debate male critics (from Howe to Hassan to Habermas to Lyotard), but their concerns were distinctly separate from feminist ones. As Craig Owens, one of the few (male) critics to notice or mind the absence of feminist engagement in the debate, indicated in 1983: the discourse about postmodernism was "scandalously indifferent" to feminism.[8] At first one also assumed a reciprocal relation—that feminism had avoided taking up its differences with postmodernism. But as the 1980s drew to a close, this indifference was rapidly redressed. Books by Linda Hutcheon (*The Politics of Postmodernism*), Linda Nicholson (*Feminism/Postmodernism*), and Jane Flax (*Thinking Fragments*) were indications of the feminist endeavor to correct the imbalance created by such uneven development.[9]

The border skirmishes between the discourses of feminism and postmodernism have been partially mediated, redressed in a manner that has become a staple of feminist critique—oversights corrected, theoretical bases interrogated. Unfortunately, feminist scholarship often finds itself in this reactive position, engaged in a sort of intellectual cleanup operation, repairing the mess of misconceptions produced in theories that refuse to address the question of gender.

In surveying American feminist criticism in 1988, Toril Moi deemed feminism and postmodernism "strange bedfellows."[10] Although Moi did not pursue this figurative image, she did note that both *feminist post*modernism and *post*modern *feminism* are configured in the term *postfeminism*. If she carried her bedroom image further, "postfeminism" would be the copulative discursive product of the two intertwined theoretical "bodies." Moi's definition of "postfeminism" is supplied in her account of Gallop's book *Reading Lacan*, which she describes "as postfeminist precisely because it *seeks to replace feminist politics with feminine stylistics*" (emphasis added).[11] Moi's main complaint about postfeminism is that "it avoids taking sides,"[12] and abstains from taking an explicitly antipatriarchal stance. I won't pursue Moi's critique of Gallop's work here, but it is worth drawing out her assessment of the "postfeminist" condition.

To Moi, the "post" to feminism means an avoidance of taking sides, masquerading as femin*ine* while sidestepping the challenge to the patriarchal she sees as crucial to femin*ism*. If debates about the postmodern have displaced the authority of feminist critique, leaving us in the terminological mire of "postfeminism," are we content to let this periodization signify the renunciation of the political?

The discursive substitution of debates about postmodernism for the debates central to feminism is a prime example of a form of "cultural displacement." The discursive substitution of "post" words (*postmodern* and *postfeminist*) for feminist agendas should prompt a continued interrogation of the politics of theoretical language in order to sustain the goals that feminist critique has initiated.

In the largest sense, I would like to suggest a cultural critique that examines the "displacements" and "disavowals" conducted in the realm of popular culture. To read culture in this general way is to follow a Marcusan reading of political processes as inherently psychological.[13] In Freudian theory, displacement is a metonymic operation, where an idea is separated from its affect and displaced onto an associated idea, what Laplanche and

Pontalis describe as "the transposition of psychical energy from one idea to another."[14] If read to the letter of Freudian disavowal, rooted in a scenario of the visual—the sight of the female genitalia and the reaction to the absence of a penis—"cultural disavowal" would entail the cultural reactions to the anxiety of sexual difference, an anxiety that feminism is intent on reminding us of. "Cultural disavowal" has become a pronounced symptom of *post*feminist culture because the power structure where men retain their cultural priority has not significantly been altered. Ultimately, if we could abandon the compulsion to invoke debates about the "post" and shed the theoretical cloaks of metadiscursivity, we might be able to perform a more precise ideological analysis of contemporary culture and its subjects.

One way of illustrating this displacement of feminist critique by the discourse of postmodernism is to conduct the type of substitution tests that sociologists use to measure cultural specificity. In how many texts could we substitute the word "feminism" for the word "postmodernism" and realize that the meaning is interchangeable? To begin with only one example: If one simply substitutes the term *feminist* for the word *postmodern* in some of Lyotard's work, consider the following quote:

A [feminist] postmodern artist or writer is in the position of a philosopher: the text [she] he writes, the work [she] he produces are not in principle governed by preestablished rules, and they cannot be judged according to a determining judgement, by applying familiar categories to the text or to the work.[15]

And now compare Lyotard's text with Silvia Bovenschen's 1977 essay "Is There a Feminine Aesthetic?" in which she began to formulate the question of what a uniquely feminine aesthetic would be:

I believe that [postmodern] feminine artistic production takes place by means of a complicated process involving conquering and reclaiming, appropriating and formulating, as well as forgetting and subverting. In the works of those female artists who are concerned with the women's movement, one finds artistic tradition as well as the break with it. It is good—in two respects—that no formal criteria for [postmodernist] "feminist art" can be definitively laid down. It enables us to reject categorically the notion of artistic norms, and it presents renewal of the calcified aesthetic debate, this time under the guise of the [postmodernist] feminist "approach."[16]

If a "feminist aesthetic" is one that maintains it is not governed by pre-existing rules, cannot be judged by preexisting judgments, or by applying familiar categories, then the coextensivity between feminist and postmodernist aesthetics would seem quite convincing.

Certainly much of the rhetoric around postmodernity evoked the sense of an unmappable "dark continent" that (like "femininity") needed to be charted, put into the coordinates of Western metanarratives themselves. This paradoxical topomania for conquering the underbrush of the unknown is present in Lyotard's by-now-canonical, frequently quoted definition of the postmodern aesthetic:

> The postmodern would be that which, in the modern, puts forward the
> unpresentable in presentation itself. . . . that which searches for new
> presentations, not in order to enjoy them but in order to impart a stronger
> sense of the unpresentable.[17]

Lyotard's work provides only one example of the implicit figuration of (what could be considered) a feminist agenda in the new discourse about the postmodern. In *The Postmodern Condition,* Lyotard describes a crisis in the status of knowledge in which the grand narratives of Western culture have lost their meaning. The Enlightenment, which Lyotard and others have cast as foreclosed in postmodernity, was a major source of many of the values—truth, equality, freedom—which have been central to feminist thought from Mary Wollstonecraft onward. In this dim light, Lyotard must also see feminism as a metanarrative made obsolete in the postmodern.

Although Lyotard does not explicitly cite the femin*ist* or feminine in the above aesthetic formulation (*the unpresentable in presentation itself*), many contemporary French theorists are more direct. Alice Jardine has neologized this rhetorical operation of "putting into discourse of 'woman' " as "gynesis."[18] Jardine finds a "positive gynesis"—a valorization of repressed femininity—in the work of (male and French) theorists Lacan, Derrida, and Deleuze. Rather than simply repress the feminine, Jardine describes how "woman" or the "feminine"—the semiosis of woman as a signifier—has been used by these male theorists as a metaphor for reading and as a topography for writing that has the potential to disrupt symbolic structures. This "reading effect" (neologized by Jardine as *gynema*) is "never stable and has no identity," and produces, as Jardine claims, "a state of uncertainty and sometimes of distrust."[19]

To Jardine, "modernity" in French thought is the same as what in the United States is "more problematically" called "postmodernity."[20] It remains unclear whether it is simply that the French word *modernité* is used to refer to the same thing that the word postmodernity is used for in the United States. To Jardine, the word *postmodern* designates a "particular attitude, a certain posture toward thinking about the human and speaking subject, signification, language, writing, etc." Jardine's insistence that the words *modernity* and *postmodernity* are synonymous sidesteps the problem of periodization.

But even "positive gynesis," which valorizes femininity and may share some of the goals of feminism, is not exactly coextensive with it.[21] As an unfortunate side effect, a secondary loss, "gynesis" ultimately disempowers women as speakers. "Gynesis" may be the ultimate appropriation, a deeper philosophical transvestism. Indeed, gynesis as a discursive process may be responsible for one of the most striking features of postmodern discourse: the appearance of "male feminism" in which men are, like the title character of *Tootsie* (in which a man—Dustin Hoffman—plays a woman with more success than a woman), is able to have it both ways—retaining their cultural priority over women and poaching on the meager terrain of authority that women have seized. And the term *gynesis* may be an early symptom of the theoretical moment periodized as "postfeminist," when feminist critique (practiced by women) has lost its authority.

BEYOND INDIFFERENCE

> Any discourse which fails to take account of the problem of
> sexual difference in its own enunciation and address will
> be, within a patriarchal order, precisely indifferent, a
> reflection of male domination.[22]

STEPHEN HEATH, *"Difference"*

Stephen Heath's admonition can be used to screen the discourse of post-modernism for its own enunciation and address. Only a few male critics invested in the debate—Huyssen, Owens, Victor Burgin[23]—noted the initial feminist silence in the cacophony of the postmodern debate. First (and again) Owens:

The absence of discussion of sexual difference in writings about postmodernism as well as the fact that few women have engaged in the modernism/postmodernism debate, suggest that *postmodernism may be another masculine invention engineered to exclude women.*[24] (emphasis added)

And Huyssen in 1984:

It is somewhat baffling that feminist criticism has so far largely stayed away from *the postmodernism debate which is considered not to be pertinent to feminist concerns.* The fact that to date only male critics have addressed the problem of modernity/postmodernity, however, does not mean that it does not concern women.[25] (emphasis added)

Citing male critics who demarcate feminist concern introduces a common but paradoxical use of male authority, what Showalter has described as "critical cross-dressing,"[26] a triangulation of power whereby women empower themselves by aligning with men who align themselves with feminist priorities—a receding referent, a *mise en abîme* of feminist critique. Owens, sensitive to these difficulties, quite carefully positions himself as the matchmaker ("to introduce the issue of sexual difference into the postmodernism debate") not the referee ("My intention is not to posit an identity between these two critiques: nor is it to place them in a relation of antagonism or opposition"[27]).

Why should feminists address themselves to the philosophical, social, or aesthetic debates of postmodernism? Surely, feminists have had a large stake in the heart of Western philosophy, in performing a piercing critique and in proposing new paradigms.[28] But as a practical or theoretical project, feminism is not a singular discourse that posits fixed identity. Using topographical language to describe its conflicting claims, de Lauretis has recently written:

Feminism itself . . . is not a secure or stable ground but a highly permeable terrain infiltrated by subterranean waterways that cause it to shift under our feet and sometimes turn into a swamp.[29]

Feminism contains its own litany of debates, not the least of which is the essentialism-antiessentialism warfare that causes the incendiary epithet "essentialist" to be flung in all directions, most frequently as a gesture of dismissal.

In descriptions of the feminine, the salient metaphorical structures of topography, sight, and sound posit a descriptive spectrum between the unmapped, obscured, and silent *and* the positioned, visible, and voiced. The discourse of feminism has attempted to make the very unchartedness/masking/silence of the feminine into a positioned/visible/significant voice.

Owens, Burgin, and Huyssen, the only critics who seemed to notice or mind the absence of feminist engagement, were also the most enthusiastic about the potentials of postmodern aesthetic activity. Huyssen optimistically, but perhaps a bit voluntaristically, tries to chart the impact of feminism on his map of the postmodern:

It was especially the art, writing, filmmaking and criticism of women and minority artists with their recuperation of buried and mutilated traditions, their emphasis on exploring forms of gender- and race-based subjectivity in aesthetic productions and experiences, and their refusal to be limited to standard canonizations, which added a whole new dimension to the critique of high modernism and to the emergence of alternative forms of culture.[30]

Owens, perhaps a bit more tempered in his assessment, claims:

Still, if one of the most salient aspects of our postmodern culture is the presence of an insistent feminist voice (and I use the terms presence and voice advisedly), theories of postmodernism have tended to either neglect or repress that voice.[31]

However muted, Owens seems to hear that voice, find its presence in a long list of women artists—Barbara Kruger, Cindy Sherman, Mary Kelly,

Sherrie Levine, Martha Rosler—whose work constitutes a critique of male systems of representations, and of the problematization of image, language, and power in the art world. (One might add Lynne Tillman, Yvonne Rainer, Barbara Bloom, Nancy Barton, and Aimee Rankin.) From their work, Owens generalizes a destabilizing power:

> As recent analyses of the "enunciative apparatuses" of visual representation—its poles of emission and reception—confirm, the representational systems of the West admit only one vision—the constitutive male subject—or rather they posit the subject of representation as absolutely centered, unitary, masculine. . . . the postmodernist work attempts to upset the re-assuring stability of that mastering position.[32]

With such potential for postmodernism, feminism should enter the fray. If feminisms have had as one of their prime agendas the reordering of relations of power and difference, then appropriation and its aesthetic underbelly, nostalgia, must be interrogated for the ways in which these strategies in representation DO reorder relations of power and difference. But equally important here is the realization that postmodern aesthetic practice does not always undermine that authority, it can reassert it. The split between negation and affirmation of the past (whether it be the past of the modern or the premodern), the nature of one's dependence on that which one criticizes, becomes the central question for postmodern feminists.

NEITHER OR BOTH: AN EPILOGUE TO THE PERIOD OF THE PLURAL   And, of course, the superlatives of pluralism are not new. Recall 1859, when Dickens published *A Tale of Two Cities,* which opened with "Chapter 1: The Period." ("It was the year of our Lord one thousand seven hundred and seventy five.") Already he was describing a period almost a century prior.

> It was the best of times, it was the worst of times, it was the age of wisdom, it was the age of foolishness, it was the epoch of belief, it was the epoch of incredulity, it was the season of Light, it was the season of Darkness, it was the spring of hope, it was the winter of despair, we had everything before us, we had nothing before us, we were all going direct to Heaven, we were all

going direct the other way—in short, the period was so far like the present period, that some of its noisiest authorities insisted on its being received, for good or for evil, in the superlative degree of comparison only.[33]

And about the *post* of *modernism*: It was conservative politics, it was subversive politics, it was the return of tradition, it was the final revolt of tradition, it was the unmooring of patriarchy, it was the reassertion of patriarchy . . . and so on.

Can we say only, in this waning and brightening light, that the postman always rings twice; first time as tragedy, second as farce, and yet, the third time, is there a separate order beyond the simulacra of the referent? And has the postwoman yet rung?

PREFACE

1. As Reyner Banham notes at the beginning of his now-classic "reading" of Los
    Angeles:

    So, like earlier generations of English intellectuals who taught themselves Italian
    in order to read Dante in the original, I learned to drive in order to read Los
    Angeles in the original.

    From *Los Angeles: The Architecture of Four Ecologies* (London: Penguin Press, 1971),
    23.
        Paul Virilio has made the more direct equation between the automobile and the
    audiovisual: "What goes on in the windshield is cinema in the strict sense." ("The
    Third Window," translation of an interview in *Cahiers du Cinema* [April 1981],
    published in *Global Television,* edited by Cynthia Schneider and Brian Wallis [Cam-
    bridge, Mass.: MIT Press], 1988.)
        Jean Baudrillard has also suggested a related equation in his description of the
    "private telematics" of driving: "The vehicle now becomes a kind of capsule, its
    dashboard the brain, the surrounding landscape unfolding like a televised screen."
    ("The Ecstasy of Communication," translated by John Johnston, in *The Anti-
    Aesthetic,* edited by Hal Foster [Port Townsend, Wash.: Bay Press, 1983], 127.)

INTRODUCTION

1. The "postmodern condition" has become a diagnostic catchphrase taken from, but
    not exclusively referring to, Jean-François Lyotard's *The Postmodern Condition: A
    Report on Knowledge* (Minneapolis: University of Minnesota Press, 1984). In the
    United States, Lyotard's name is synonymous with the word *postmodernism* and the
    theoretical issues that characterize his previous and subsequent work have unfor-
    tunately been overshadowed.
2. "Postmodernism and Consumer Society," in *Anti-Aesthetic,* 125.

3. Charles Baudelaire, "The Salon of 1859," in *Art in Paris 1845–1862: Salons and Other Exhibitions,* translated and edited by Jonathan Mayne (Oxford: Phaidon Press, 1965), 153.

4. Ibid.

5. Roland Barthes follows some of the same ambivalences as Baudelaire in his discussion of photography as "counter-memory":

   A paradox: the same century invented History and Photography. But History is
   a memory fabricated according to positive formulas, a pure intellectual discourse
   which abolishes mythic Time and the Photograph is a certain but fugitive
   testimony.

   From *Camera Lucida,* translated by Richard Howard (New York: Hill and Wang, 1981): 93.

6. See Jürgen Habermas, "Modernity's Consciousness of Time and Its Need for Self-Reassurance," in *The Philosophical Discourse on Modernity: Twelve Lectures,* translated by Frederick Lawrence (Cambridge, Mass.: MIT Press, 1987).

7. See Daniel Bell, *The Coming of Post-Industrial Society* (New York: Basic Books, 1973); Fredric Jameson, "Postmodernism, or the Cultural Logic of Late Capitalism," in *New Left Review* 146 (July–August 1984): 53–92, and "Postmodernism and Consumer Society"; Guy Debord, *La Société du spectacle* (Paris: Editions Buchet-Chastel, 1967), translated as *The Society of the Spectacle* (Detroit: Red and Black, 1977); Gayatri Chakravorty Spivak, *In Other Worlds: Essays in Cultural Politics* (New York: Routledge, 1988).

8. The concept of the *virtual* provides a crucial ontological distinction here; from the Latin *virtus,* for strength or virtue, virtual is defined as "of, relating to, or possessing a power of acting without the agency of matter; being functionally or effectively but not formally of its kind" (*Webster's Third New International Dictionary*). In the physics of optics, a mirror provides a virtual image formed of "virtual foci." The term *virtual reality* has come to signify any illusionistic reproduction that is functionally or effectively convincing as real, and yet is constructed in simulation.

   I've chosen the word *virtual* here and not *simulation* to avoid the Baudrillardian connotations of a simulacrum unhinged from its referent. Henri Bergson uses the term *virtual* in *Matter and Memory* (1896) to distinguish between perception and the "virtual sensation" of memory. Gilles Deleuze takes up the term to describe the two sides ("actual" and "virtual") of what he deems the cinema's "crystal-image." See Gilles Deleuze, *Cinema 2: The Time-Image,* translated by Hugh Tomlinson and Robert Galeta (Minneapolis: University of Minnesota Press, 1989).

9. Film theories that attempt to describe the apparatical effects of the cinema have emphasized the spectatorial confusion between perception and representation. See Jean Louis Baudry, "Ideological Effects of the Basic Cinematographic Apparatus"

and "The Apparatus: Metapsychological Approaches to the Impression of Reality in Cinema," in *Narrative, Apparatus, Ideology,* edited by Phil Rosen (New York: Columbia University Press, 1986) and Christian Metz, *The Imaginary Signifier: Psychoanalysis and the Cinema,* translated by Ben Brewster et al (Bloomington: Indiana University Press, 1982). In chapter 3, I address apparatus theories and temporality.

10. A recent collection of essays about contemporary museology makes the temporal function of the museum explicit. See *The Museum Time-Machine: Putting Cultures on Display,* edited by Robert Lumley (London: Routledge, 1988).

11. Stephen Kern, *The Culture of Time and Space (1880–1915)* (Cambridge, Mass.: Harvard University Press, 1983) and Wolfgang Schivelbusch, *The Railway Journey: The Industrialization of Time and Space in the Nineteenth Century* (Berkeley: University of California Press, 1986) provide important evidence of the transformations of time and space coincident with the emergence of the cinema. Kern claims that the cinema (along with the phonograph) "brought the past into the present more than ever before, changing the way people experience their personal past and the collective past of history" (38). See also Donald M. Lowe, *History of Bourgeois Perception* (Chicago: University of Chicago Press, 1982).

12. Miriam Hansen has provided an excellent critical history of the emergence of cinema spectatorship and its consequent transformation of the public sphere. Hansen's work draws on the German debates about the public sphere in the writings of Jürgen Habermas, Oskar Negt, and Alexander Kluge. Hansen relies on Kluge and Negt's conception of the "counter public sphere," an "oppositional" potential not present in much of the other post–Frankfurt school writings on the public sphere. Hansen argues that the category of spectator did not coincide with the invention of the cinema in the 1890s. Rather, she links the historical construction of the spectator to a shift (roughly between 1907 and 1917) in early cinematic style and modes of narration. See Miriam Hansen, *Babel and Babylon: Spectatorship in American Silent Film* (Cambridge, Mass.: Harvard University Press, 1991).

13. Although these technological changes are products of multinational capitalism in the First World, the global cultural imperialism of American culture is evident in the double-edged way that the Third World is both simultaneously a tourist haven and a consumer market for American culture. In the global schema, First World culture works in centripetal and centrifugal ways. Centripetal imperialism is introjective, incorporating the other—a Banana-Republic-anization (bringing the Third World to the First by mail order, the exotic made safe for tourism)—whereas centrifugal imperialism is projective, projecting onto the other—a Coca-colonization (bringing the taste of the First World into the Third).

In his book *Video Night in Katmandu and Other Reports from the Not-So-Far-East* (New York: Knopf, 1988), Pico Iyer has documented the impact of an implied *centrifugal imperialism:*

Yet in the Third World, a hunger for American culture is almost taken for
granted, and making it often means nothing more than making it in the Land
of the Free. Communist guerrillas in the Philippines fight capitalism while
wearing UCLA T-shirts. The Sandinista leaders in Nicaragua wage war against
"U.S. Imperialism" while watching prime-time American TV on private satellite
dishes. And many whites in South Africa cling to apartheid, yet cannot get
enough of Bill Cosby, Eddy Murphy and Mr. T. (12)

Recent statistics on VCR usage chart the unfortunate pervasiveness of this form of
cultural imperialism. Studies indicate that there is a higher VCR penetration in
"less diversified media environments." See Douglas A. Boyd, Joseph D. Straubhaar,
and John A. Lent, *Videocassette Recorders in the Third World* (New York: Longman,
1989); Gladys D. Ganley and Oswald H. Ganley, *Global Political Fallout: The VCR's
First Decade* (Cambridge, Mass.: Program on Information Resources Policy, Harvard University, 1987).

14. See Michel Foucault, *The Archeology of Knowledge* (New York: Harper and Row,
1972); Dominick LaCapra, *History and Criticism* (Ithaca, N.Y.: Cornell University
Press, 1985); Hayden White, *Metahistory* (Baltimore: Johns Hopkins University
Press, 1973) and *Tropics of Discourse* (Baltimore: Johns Hopkins University Press,
1978); Michel deCerteau, "History: Science and Fiction," in *Heterologies: Discourses
on the Other,* translated by Brian Massumi (Minneapolis: University of Minnesota
Press, 1986).

15. In film studies, historiography remains an area of polarized debate. See Robert C.
Allen and Douglas Gomery, *Film History: Theory and Practice* (New York: Alfred
A. Knopf, 1985); *Iris: A Journal of Theory on Image and Sound* 2, no. 2 (1984), which
is devoted to "Theory of Cinema History"; *Resisting Images: Essays on Cinema and
History,* edited by Robert Sklar and Charles Musser (Philadelphia: Temple Univer-
sity Press, 1990).

16. See *The New Historicism,* edited by H. Aram Veeser (New York: Routledge, 1989)
and Brook Thomas, *The New Historicism* (Princeton, N.J.: Princeton University
Press, 1991). Anton Kaes has drawn the comparison between the "spirit" of postmodernism and the New Historicism: both blur the boundaries between high art
and mass culture, past and present, decenter authority, propose a radical pluralism,
and so forth. See Anton Kaes, "New Historicism and the Study of German Literature," in *The German Quarterly* 62, no. 2 (Spring 1989): 210–220.

17. E. Ann Kaplan's study of music television, *Rocking Around the Clock: Music Television, Postmodernism and Consumer Culture* (New York: Methuen, 1987) was one
of the first book-length studies to apply the terminology of postmodernism to film
and television studies. Kaplan describes "postmodernist" aesthetic strategies in
MTV videos, and argues that the televisual apparatus is "itself postmodernist"(7).

As I will argue in chapter 3, Kaplan's claims for the specificity of the televisual apparatus also apply to other, earlier forms of "screen entertainment." Before television and before MTV there is a rich history of commodity-experiences that were not "historically situated" and that blurred—in a way that Kaplan maintains is unique to MTV—the "distinct separations and boundaries including that between past and present" (29).

In contrast to Kaplan's work on the textual forms of MTV as postmodernist, two recent books have addressed contemporary films as textual *responses to* postmodernism and postmodernity.

Jim Collins, *Uncommon Cultures: Popular Culture and Post-Modernism* (New York: Routledge, 1989) explores "forms of textuality . . . as responses to the complexities of contemporary cultural arenas, as responses to semiotic environments" (27) which are decentered and dispersed. Collins attempts "to develop an integrated theory of Post-Modernism as a situation and as a specific form of textuality that attempts to represent that situation" (42).

More recently in a study of post-Vietnam films and culture, Timothy Corrigan addresses "the contemporary or postmodern condition through which films are watched" and posits a "cinema without walls," transformed by the "new patterns of reception." See *Cinema without Walls: Movies and Culture After Vietnam* (New Brunswick, N.J.: Rutgers University Press, 1991).

18. See Mary Ann Doane, *The Desire to Desire* (Bloomington: Indiana University Press, 1988); Judith Mayne, *Private Novels, Public Films* (Athens: University of Georgia Press, 1988); Patrice Petro, *Joyless Streets: Women and Melodramatic Representation in Weimar Germany* (Princeton, N.J.: Princeton University Press, 1989); Jane Gaines and Charlotte Herzog, editors, *Fabrications: Costume and the Female Body* (New York: Routledge, 1990); Charles Musser, *The Emergence of Cinema: The American Screen to 1907* (New York: Charles Scribner and Sons, 1990); Hansen, *Babel and Babylon.*

19. See Kern, *Culture of Time and Space*; Schivelbusch, *Railway Journey* and *Disenchanted Night: The Industrialization of Light in the Nineteenth Century,* translated by Angela Davies (Berkeley: University of California Press, 1988); Rosalind Williams, *Dream Worlds: Mass Consumption in Late Nineteenth Century France* (Berkeley: University of California Press, 1982); Rachel Bowlby, *Just Looking: Consumer Culture in Dreiser, Gissing and Zola* (New York: Methuen, 1985); Elizabeth Wilson, *Adorned in Dreams: Fashion and Modernity* (London: Virago, 1985); Kathy Peiss, *Cheap Amusements: Working Women and Leisure in Turn-of-the-Century New York* (Philadelphia: Temple University Press, 1986).

20. To suggest that film history masks the loss of history that the film itself produces is an example of a "dyslexic" cultural analysis. Cultural dyslexia is a way of reading

culture in which every signifier cannily masks its reverse: antidrug rhetoric hides the contra war; the glamorization of motherhood disguises unwed pregnancy, poverty, and child abuse; discourse on the avant-garde disguises the diminished presence of the avant-garde; assertions of the death of narrative reappropriate narratology at another level; assertions that sexual difference is obsolete mask the reassertion of gender hierarchies, and so forth. Once one begins to read culture in this way, there are examples everywhere. In Paris today, for example, the "SITU" monitor—a videotext machine placed on boulevards to tell you WHERE you are and how to get where you are going—is a concomitant disguise for the very loss of SITU that the urban subject faces.

This form of dyslexia is indicated in the Baudrillardian formulation of the "deterrence operation" in which Disneyland is presented as imaginary to convince us that the rest is real. See Jean Baudrillard, *Simulations,* translated by Paul Foss, Paul Patton, and Philip Beitchman (New York: Foreign Agents Series, 1983), 25. Cultural dyslexia is not quite the same axis of simulation that Baudrillard describes when he talks about films (See *The Evil Demon of Images* [Sydney: Power Institute of Fine Arts, 1988]) but the confusion between representation and the real is similar. If, as Baudrillard describes, Three Mile Island was a reenactment of *The China Syndrome,* by the same logic, John Hinckley's fascination with Jodie Foster was a remake of *Taxi Driver,* the political career of Dan Quayle is a remake of *The Candidate.*

21. Michel Foucault, "Film and the Popular Memory," translated by Martin Jordan, in *Foucault Live,* edited by Sylvère Lotringer (New York: Semiotext(e), 1989), 92.

22. Anton Kaes, *From Hitler to Heimat: The Return of History as Film* (Cambridge, Mass.: Harvard University Press, 1990).

23. Ihab Hassan cites the "best history" of the term as Michael Kohler's "Postmodernismus: Ein begriffgeschichtler Überblick," *Amerikastudien* 22, no. 1 (1977). Hassan also attempts a brief history in "Toward a Concept of Postmodernism"(1982), reprinted in *The Postmodern Turn: Essays in Postmodern Theory and Culture* (Columbus: Ohio State University Press, 1987). Hassan's history begins in 1934 with the word *postmodernismo* in Federico de Onis's *Antologia de la poesia espanola y hispanoamericana,* followed by Arnold Toynbee's use of the word in *A Study of History* in 1947. Irving Howe ("Mass Society and Postmodern Fiction," *Partisan Review* 26, no. 3 [Summer 1959]) and Harry Levin ("What Was Modernism?" *Massachusetts Review* 1, no. 4 [August 1960]) both used the term lamentably for the passing of modernism. Charles Jencks also attempts to write a quick history of the term in *What Is Postmodernism?* (New York: St. Martin's Press, 1986), but he cribs directly from Hassan (who was, he asserts "by the mid 70's the self-proclaimed spokesman for the Postmodern").

Lyotard's *Postmodern Condition* played a key role in the dissemination of the term (and the subsequent debates) to English audiences. It should also be noted that the twist in translation from the French *le postmoderne* into the English *postmodernism* has produced some of the semantic confusion in terminology. Jencks's *What Is Postmodernism?* repeats the question of definition.

Lyotard's "Answering the Question: What Is Postmodernism?" originally appeared as "Reponse a la question: Qu'est-ce que le postmoderne?" in *Critique* no. 419 (April 1982) and is now included in *Postmodern Condition*. See also Lyotard's "Defining the Postmodern," in *ICA Documents 4* (London: ICA, 1985).

24. See my analysis of fashion advertisements that employ the adjective *postmodern*. "Mutual Indifference: Feminism and Postmodernism," in *The Other Perspective in Gender and Culture: Rewriting Women and the Symbolic,* edited by Juliet Flower MacCannell (New York: Columbia University Press, 1990), 39–58.

25. Christian Metz describes how film theoretical language, intending to be analytic *about* the object, gets caught up in the celebration *of* the object. See "Story/Discourse (A Note on Two Kinds of Voyeurism)," translated by Celia Britton and Annwyl Williams in *Imaginary Signifier*, 5.

26. Dick Hebdige, "Postmodernism and 'The Other Side,' " *Journal of Communication Inquiry* 10, no. 2 (Summer 1986):78. Hebdige's list of ever-expanding inclusivity may itself be a symptom of postmodernity. Todd Gitlin ("Hip Deep in Postmodernism," *New York Times Book Review*, November 6, 1988) described the list itself as a particularly postmodern trope.

27. When this project was first conceived the debates around postmodernism had not yet become the worn and trivialized discourse it is today. The most convincing case for banning the use of the term may have been made when the April 1988 issue of *Spy* magazine published their "Postmodern Guide to Everything." This article included a do-it-yourself PoMo kit, to turn your own household objects—pencil sharpeners, staplers, and so on—into "postmodern" objects.

Or, as Hassan quotes from William James's *Pragmatism* in *Postmodern Turn*:

First, you know, a new theory is attacked as absurd; then it is admitted to be true, but obvious and insignificant; finally it is seen to be so important that its adversaries claim that they themselves discovered it.

28. Walter Benjamin, *Das Passagen-Werk,* edited by Rolf Tiedemann (Frankfurt am Main: Suhrkamp, 1983), 54; and *Charles Baudelaire: A Lyric Poet in the Era of High Capitalism* (London: Verso, 1983), 170, 176.

29. See Jacques Lacan, *The Four Fundamental Concepts of Psycho-Analysis*, translated by Alan Sheridan (New York: W. W. Norton, 1978), 106:

In the scopic field, the gaze is outside, I am looked at, that is to say, I am a picture.

This is the function that is found at the heart of the institution of the subject in the visible. What determines me, at the most profound level, in the visible, is the gaze that is outside. It is through the gaze that I enter life and it is from the gaze that I receive its effects. Hence it comes about that the gaze is the instrument through which light is embodied and through which . . . I am *photographed.*

CHAPTER ONE

1. Jean-Louis Comolli, "Machines of the Visible," in *The Cinematic Apparatus,* edited by Teresa de Lauretis and Stephen Heath (New York: St. Martin's Press, 1980), 122–123.
2. Debord, *Society of the Spectacle,* aphorism number 1.
3. See Peter Galassi, *Before Photography: Painting and the Invention of Photography* (New York: Museum of Modern Art, 1981). The rhetoric of "crisis" pervades accounts of modernism in art history. Histories of rupture often neglect continuity.
4. *Emergence:* I've chosen this term as a preferred historiographic description that emphasizes the gradual formation of the cinema, emerging out of a wide and varied set of visual practices. See Foucault's discussion of "emergent capitalism" in *The Archeology of Knowledge,* 68–69. See also Musser, *Emergence of Cinema.*
5. Just as Debord depicted "the spectacle" as "not a collection of images, but a social relation among people mediated by images" (*Society of the Spectacle,* aphorism number 4), art historian Jonathan Crary has drawn the methodological distinction between accounts of the "visible tracks" (representations) and the history of the "observer":

   We've been trained to assume that an observer will always leave visible tracks, that is will be identifiable in terms of images. But here it's a question of an observer who takes shape in other, grayer practices and discourses. . . . *Rather than let a history of an observer be defined in terms of the changing forms of visual representations (which gives art works a kind of ontological priority), I think of an observer as an amalgam of many disparate events and forces.* (emphasis added)

   See Jonathan Crary, "Modernizing Vision," in *Vision and Visuality: Discussions in Contemporary Culture,* edited by Hal Foster (Seattle: Bay Press, 1988), 43, 48.
6. Michel Foucault, *Discipline and Punish,* translated by Alan Sheridan (New York: Pantheon Books, 1978) (*Surveiller et Punir* [Paris, 1975]).
7. See *Re-vision,* edited by Mary Ann Doane, Patricia Mellencamp, and Linda Williams (Los Angeles: AFI, 1984), 14.

   The dissociation of the see/being seen dyad [which the panoptic arrangement of the central tower and annular arrangement ensures] and the sense of permanent visibility *seem perfectly to describe the condition not only of the inmate in Bentham's prison but of the woman as well.* For defined in terms of her visibility, she carries her own Panopticon with her wherever she goes, her self-image a function of her being for another. (emphasis added)

John Berger's *Ways of Seeing* (London: Penguin Books, 1972) discusses an implicit panopticism: "A woman must continually watch herself. . . . from earliest childhood she has been taught and persuaded to survey herself continually" (46) and "the surveyor of woman in herself is male . . . thus she turns herself into an object—and most particularly an object of vision: a sight"(47). Berger's text initiated the common axiom of feminist criticism: "men act, women appear."

Whereas Laura Mulvey described the "sexual imbalance" of gendered visibility ("woman as image/man as bearer of the look") in her landmark essay "Visual Pleasure and Narrative Cinema" (*Screen* 16, no. 3 [Autumn 1975]), she did not equate this gendered looking with the panoptic model.

Joan Copjec cites the above passage from *Re-vision* as symptomatic of the misconceptions at the root of contemporary film theory, which has, for Copjec, entirely misread Lacan. (See "The Orthopsychic Subject," *October* 49 [Summer 1989]: 53–71.) Copjec's correction has the force of Lacanian fundamentalism; her refutation of the panoptic model is intended to recover Lacan from "Foucauldization" and to correct "film theory's" misrecognition of Lacan.

8. In her eloquent essay, "Technologies of Gender," de Lauretis persuasively argues against the theoretical constructions implied in the term "sexual difference" (woman as always and only defined in difference from, contrast to, relation with the man) and proposes, instead, a "subject constituted in gender." This gendered subject—which de Lauretis describes as "a subject not unified but rather multiple and not so much divided as contradicted"—is left out of Foucault and other Foucauldian-inspired accounts of the subject. See Teresa de Lauretis, *Technologies of Gender* (Bloomington: Indiana University Press, 1987), 2.

9. Michel Foucault, *The Order of Things: An Archaeology of the Human Sciences,* translated from *Les Mots et Les Choses* (New York: Random House, 1970), 319. Also see Martin Jay, "In the Empire of the Gaze: Foucault and the Denigration of Vision in 20th Century French Thought," in *Foucault: A Critical Reader,* edited by David Couzens Hoy (London: Basil Blackwell, 1986). Jay describes a deep French tradition of fascination with vision, from Cartesian philosophy to the poet art-critics like Baudelaire, Valery, Apollinaire. He situates Foucault in the antiocular discourse of twentieth-century French thought, in which "the denigration of vision supplanted its previous celebration." Whereas on the surface Foucault links *voir, pouvoir,* and *savoir,* as Jay indicates, the nature of his fascination is more complex.

10. Jeremy Bentham, *Panopticon, Works of Jeremy Bentham Published under the Super-intendence of His Executor, John Bowring*, 11 vols. (New York: Russell and Russell, 1962).

    For a discussion of Bentham see Foucault, *Discipline and Punish*, 195–228; Gilles Deleuze, *Foucault*, translated and edited by Sean Hand (Minneapolis: University of Minnesota Press, 1986); Mark Poster, *Foucault, Marxism and History* (Cambridge, Mass.: Polity Press, 1984); Jacques-Alain Miller, "Jeremy Bentham's Panoptic Device," translated by Richard Miller, *October* 41 (Summer 1987): 3–29.

11. See Richard D. E. Burton, "The Unseen Seer, or Proteus in the City: Aspects of a Nineteenth Century Parisian Myth," (*French Studies*, 42, no. 1 [January 1988]: 50–68) for a textual illustration of what Foucault confined to more institutionalized forms of the panoptic regime. Burton emphasizes the morphological similarities between nineteenth-century conceptions of the criminal, the detective, the capitalist, the flâneur, and the modern novelist. He aligns the "subjective, poetic or mythological transcriptions . . . in a wide range of literary works" in the period between 1815 and 1860 into the panoptic "leitmotiv."

12. Miller, "Jeremy Bentham's Panoptic Device." 4.

13. Foucault, *Discipline and Punish*, 204.

14. Ibid., 205.

15. Ibid., 201.

16. Ibid., 207.

17. Ibid., 202–203.

18. For a discussion of techniques of control in the contemporary workplace see the chapters "The Information Panopticon" and "Panoptic Power and the Social Text" in Shoshana Zuboff, *In the Age of the Smart Machine: The Future of Work and Power* (New York: Basic Books, 1984), 315–387. Zuboff discusses video surveillance and corporate systems management.

19. Whereas much of the reactive historical turn from 1970s cinematic "apparatus" theories had a Foucauldian base—in the need to historicize the "institution" of the cinema and return to the notion of the "social" subject—the panopticon model was not always explicitly invoked.

    The methodological turn to Foucault in feminist film studies may have seemed like a theoretical advance in 1983 and 1984. In a 1983 essay, de Lauretis noted the "growing interest in Foucault's work" and cited the "particular advantage of Foucault's historical methodology" which "appear[s] most relevant to cinema, to its elaboration of genres and techniques, to the development of audiences through tactical distribution and exhibition, to the ideological effects it produces (or seeks to produce) in spectatorship." (See *Alice Doesn't: Feminism, Semiotics, Cinema* [Bloomington: Indiana University Press, 1984], 84–85.) Also, in the introduction to her 1983 book, *Women and Film*, Ann Kaplan asserts "feminist theorists have been redefining history with Foucault in mind." (See *Women and Film: Both Sides of the Camera* [New York: Methuen, 1983], 3.)

But, paradoxically, as de Lauretis puts it in a later essay: "The understanding of cinema as a social technology, as a 'cinematic apparatus,' was developed in film theory contemporaneously with Foucault's work but independently of it." (The second part of her statement—"rather, as the word *apparatus* suggests, it was directly influenced by the work of Althusser and Lacan"—places the responsibility for the limitations of "apparatus theories" elsewhere.) To de Lauretis, the Foucauldian approach to an "institution"—whose "technologies" produce a subjectivity—did not adequately consider gender because, as de Lauretis argues, to Foucault "sexuality is not understood as gendered." (*Technologies of Gender,* 13.)

Foucault's work has also been invoked in film studies to suggest the potential for resistances to prescriptive or official discourses. See for example Pat Mellencamp, *Indiscretions* (Bloomington: Indiana University Press, 1990), 2; Dana Polan, *Power and Paranoia* (New York: Columbia University Press, 1986), 7–9.

20. And yet, as we will see in chapter 3, Baudry relied more on the subjective centering of Renaissance perspective and monocular vision than on the model of the imagined scrutiny of the panoptic subject.

21. Metz's description of the "all-perceiving subject" seems drawn on the panoptic guard (the seer) not on the panoptic subject (the seen). Yet, as Jacqueline Rose aptly points out, Metz's description of the "all-perceiving subject" was a subject deluded by perceptual verisimilitude; Metz did not question the erroneousness of the "all-perceiving" position. See Jacqueline Rose, "The Imaginary," in *Sexuality in the Field of Vision* (London: Verso, 1986).

22. Baudry, "The Apparatus: Metapsychological Approaches to the Impression of Reality in the Cinema," translated by Jean Andrews and Bertrand Augst in *Narrative, Apparatus, Ideology,* 316.

23. There were architectural projects that also relied on arrangements of visuality quite different from the panopticon model. Late eighteenth- and early nineteenth-century utopian projects, such as Robert Owen's (1771–1858) "parallelogram" and Charles Fourier's (1772–1837) *phalanstère,* conceived the arrangement of space and visuality along different lines. The panopticon used a central space to monitor (and hence control) its subjects who were confined and yet visible in the periphery. Both the phalanstery and the parallelogram included a central space as a courtyard for community education and recreation, which implied a collective and more fluid use of space. See Kenneth Frampton, *Modern Architecture: A Critical History* (London: Thames and Hudson, 1980); Anthony Vidler, "The Scenes of the Street: Transformations in Ideal and Reality 1750–1871" in *On Streets,* edited by Stanford Anderson (Cambridge, Mass.: MIT Press, 1986), 29–113.

24. Walter Benjamin, "The Work of Art in the Age of Mechanical Reproduction," in *Illuminations,* translated by Harry Zohn (New York: Schocken Books, 1969), 236.

25. The *panorama* (from Greek, *pan* = all; *hórama* = seeing) was a particular form of landscape painting with a 360-degree view. Richard Altick mentions one German (Johann Adam Breysig) and one American (William Dunlap) who conceived of a panorama independently of Barker. See Richard D. Altick, *The Shows of London* (Cambridge, Mass.: Harvard University Press, 1978), 128–140. For a discussion of Breysig, see also Stephan Oettermann, *Das Panorama: Die Geschichte eines Massenmediums* (Frankfurt am Main: Syndikat, 1980).

     In London, in 1794, a new building designed by the architect Robert Mitchell opened with two panoramas: the upper salon displayed the initial 1792 circular panorama of London from the Albion Sugar Mills in Southwark. The lower, larger salon in this new building displayed "The English Fleet anchored between Portsmouth and Isle of Wight."

26. Olive Cook, *Movement in Two Dimensions* (London: Hutchinson and Co., 1963), 32.

     In his excellent history of the panorama, Oettermann has also drawn the historical parallel between the panopticon and the panorama. Oettermann notes the coincident introduction of the two neologistic terms taken from the Greek—*pan-orama* and *pan-opticon.* Although the terms have an identical meaning (all-seeing) and the buildings have certain similarities, Oettermann notes that the two produce quite different looks (*Blicke*). See Stephan Oettermann, *Panorama,* 34–40.

27. Helmut Gernsheim and Alison Gernsheim, *L. J. M. Daguerre: The History of the Diorama and the Daguerrotype* (New York: Dover Publications, 1968), 6.

28. See Jac Remise, Pascale Remise, Regis Van de Walle, *Magie Lumineuse du Théâtre d'ombres à la lanterne magique* (Paris: Balland, 1979); *Magische Schatten,* edited by Hilmar Hoffmann and Walter Schobert (Frankfurt: Deutsches Film Museum Frankfurt, 1988); C. W. Ceram, *Archeology of the Cinema,* translated by Richard Winston (New York: Harcourt, Brace and World, 1965); Cook, *Movement in Two Dimensions;* Musser, *Emergence of Cinema.*

     The Ceram and Cook texts are marked by their explicit teleology. See, for example, Cook: "It is seldom remembered that there were almost as many houses showing entertainments of this kind in the London of a hundred and twenty years ago as there are cinemas today"(31) and

> Yet the film is no more the final manifestation of man's perennial interest in the living picture than were the Phantasmagoria, the Eidophusikon, or the Panorama. . . . Already the cinema is yielding to television as a mode of universal entertainment and the time may well come when the luxurious glittering picture palaces which are now an accepted feature of all our towns will be as rare as the Diorama in Regent's Park. (135)

29. See Musser, *Emergence of Cinema.*

30. A precursor of the panorama, the eidophusikon (from Greek, *eidolon* = image; *physike* = nature) was popular as pictorial entertainment dependent on movement and lighting effects. An invention of Strausbourg-born painter-turned-theatrical-scenery-designer Philip de Loutherbourg (1740–1812), whose stage devices had included moving ships, storm effects, and fires, the eidophusikon (or "Various Imitations of Natural Phenomena, represented by Moving Pictures") was marked by its miniature scale: a small stage (ten feet by six feet) displayed moving models accompanied by lighting and sound effects. Shipwrecks, storms, volcanoes, battles, and sunrises were its primary spectacles. See Gernsheim and Gernsheim, *L. J. M. Daguerre,* 43–44; Altick, *The Shows of London,* 116–127; and Oettermann, *Das Panorama,* 58–59.

31. For example, both the stereoscope and the phenakistoscope rely on a shared perceptual principle—based on the reconciliation of differences (à la Helmholtz's "differential hypothesis")—but the two apparatuses produce different effects. The stereoscopic spectator is concerned with overcoming binocular disparity, a spatial disjunction. The phenakistoscope viewer is perceptually overcoming a temporal disjunction.

32. "Paris—Capital of the Nineteenth Century," translated by Edmund Jephcott, in *Reflections* (New York: Harcourt Brace and Jovanovich, 1979), 150.

A short, but important remark on the translations of Benjamin seems appropriate here. This same passage was translated by Quinton Hoare in *Charles Baudelaire: A Lyric Poet in the Era of High Capitalism* (London: Verso, 1976), 162:

The town-dweller . . . made an attempt to bring the country into the town. In the *dioramas,* the town was transformed into landscape, just as it was later in a subtler way for the *flâneurs.* (emphasis added)

But in German, it is apparent that Benjamin was referring to *panoramas:*

Der Städter. . . . macht den Versuch, das Land in die Stadt einzubringen. Die Stadt weitet sich in *den Panoramen* zur Landschaft aus wie sie es auf subtilere Art später für den Flanierenden tut. (*Passagen-Werk,* 48, emphasis added)

Unfortunately, the English translation of the Benjamin text has perpetuated a confusion between the panorama and diorama. The panorama preceded the diorama and relied on significantly different techniques. But, to be fair, the English translations repeat a confusion that was also made by Benjamin. In the very next sentence

Benjamin writes: "1839 brennt das Daguerresche Panorama ab." Benjamin makes dramatic use of the coincidence of the 1839 fire and the invention of the daguerreotype, so it is worth making the correction: it was the destruction by fire of the diorama building on Rue Sanson that coincided with Daguerre's new invention.

Benjamin entitled the second section of this 1935 exposé "Daguerre oder die Panoramen." In *Reflections*, the section is translated as "Daguerre, or the Panoramas," but in *Charles Baudelaire*, the section is translated as "Daguerre or the Dioramas." The confusion is not so crucial with assertions like:

> While the dioramas [Panoramen] strove to produce life-like transformations in
> the Nature portrayed in them, they foreshadowed, via photography, the moving
> picture and the talking picture (*Charles Baudelaire*, 161.)

But when the translation reads that "Daguerre was a pupil of the *diorama*-painter Prevost, whose establishment was situated in the Arcade of the *Dioramas*" (emphasis added), the mistranslation is more misleading. In Paris, the *panorama* was located in a passage, called the Passage des *Panoramas*.

33. Altick, *Shows of London*, 180. The London Colosseum had a show called "A Trip Around the World" in 1785.

34. "Such deception is not meant to deceive . . . but to exist for its own sake, and it is content to amaze the viewer." Dolf Sternberger, *Panorama of the Nineteenth Century*, translated by Joachim Neugroschel (New York: Urizen Books, 1977), 13. Christian Metz will also maintain that the power of the cinematic signifier is that it is *imaginary*, not real.

35. See Altick, *Shows of London*, 141–162.

36. Fulton, later the inventor of the steam engine, assigned part of his interest in Barker's invention to another American businessman, James Thayer, who built the panorama on Boulevard Montmartre. See Heinz Buddemeier, *Panorama, Diorama, Photographie* (Munich: 1970).

37. Sternberger, *Panorama of the Nineteenth Century*, 13. The first panorama shown in London's Leicester Square was an unwitting example of a "captured historical moment": in the winter of 1791, Robert Barker's son, Henry, sketched a circular panorama of London from the rooftop of the Albion Sugar Mills in Southwark. In March 1791 the Albion Mills burned to the ground. By the time the painting was displayed in the spring of 1792, the image of the Albion Mills was only a memory. See Altick, *Shows of London*, 132.

38. Oettermann implies that the panoramic rotundas were literally replaced by the construction of the Passage des Panoramas. Both the panorama and the Passage were products of urban culture. Oettermann notes, offering the outdoors without renouncing the city. "It would seem to be no accident" (*doch scheint es kein Zufall*),

in Oettermann's account, that the panorama, which offered the viewer an unimpeded landscape view without the trouble of travel, was replaced by the Passage, which offered the flâneur indoor travel without weather.

Die Passagen waren der Tod der ersten französischen Panoramen, und doch scheint es kein Zufall, daß die erste Passage gerade durch die beiden Panoramarotunden hindurchging. . . . Das Panorama versprach einen freien landschaftlichen Ausblick, ohne dem Besucher die Mühen der Reise zuzumuten; die Passage versprach durch ihre Glas-Eisenkonstruktion einen Spaziergang im Freien, ohne den Elégant der Witterung auszusetzen. (*Panorama*, 123)

39. From Latin, *dio* = through; *horama*=view. The technique of the diorama is described in detail by Daguerre in his 1839 pamphlet, "Description des Procédés de Peinture et d'Eclairage Inventés par Daguerre et appliqués Par Lui Aux Tableaux du Diorama," in *Historique et Description des Procedes du Daguerreotype et du Diorama* (Paris: Alphonse Giroux, 1839).(This was reprinted in facsimile edition [Paris: Editions Rumeur des Ages, 1982.]) Daguerre provides a technical explanation of two canvases—a translucent canvas in front of an opaque canvas—and the manipulation of lights that shine through the transparent canvas from the front or onto the front canvas from the back. An expert in lighting and scenic effects, Daguerre collaborated with the painter Charles Marie Bouton.

In *Père Goriot* (1834), Honoré de Balzac includes the following sarcastic account of the fashion in naming these devices:

As a consequence of the recent invention of the optical illusion called the Diorama, which had quite surpassed the earlier Panoramas, artists and their friends had taken to ending every word they thought fit with "rama". . . . "And how's our little healthorama this evening?" . . . "It's perishing coldorama". . . . "There's just a healthy little nipporama in the air". . . . "it's as cold as hellorama". . . . "Aha! Here comes a mighty brothorama."

From Honoré de Balzac, *Père Goriot,* translated by Henry Reed (New York: New American Library, 1962), 53–54.

40. The *diaphanorama* (from Greek, *diaphane*= transparent) was an invention of Swiss landscape painter Franz Niklaus König (1765–1832). It consisted of watercolors on paper of varying degrees of transparency shown in a darkened room with light from both sides. Eight transparencies were first exhibited in Bern in the 1811 "Exposition du Diaphanorama de la Suisse" and traveled to Germany in 1812 and from 1819 to 1820, and to Paris from 1820 to 1821. See Gernsheim and Gernsheim, *L. J. M. Daguerre,* 14–15.

41. Ibid., 19–20. Cook provides a descriptive account written by an English spectator, Frederick Bakewell, of the opening exhibits, "Interior of Trinity Chapel, Canterbury Cathedral" and "The Valley of the Sarnen in Canton Unterwalden, Switzerland":

> The visitors, after passing through a gloomy anteroom, were ushered into a circular chamber, apparently quite dark. One or two small shrouded lamps placed on the floor served dimly to light the way to a few descending steps and the voice of an invisible guide gave directions to walk forward. *The eye soon became sufficiently accustomed to the darkness to distinguish the objects around and to perceive that there were several persons seated on benches opposite an open space resembling a large window. Through the window was seen the interior of Canterbury cathedral* undergoing partial repair with the figures of two or three workmen resting from their labours. The pillars, the arches, the stone floor and steps, stained with damp, and the planks of wood strewn on the ground, all seemed to stand out in bold relief, so solidly as not to admit a doubt of their substantiality. . . . The impression was strengthened by perceiving the light and shadows change, as if clouds were passing over the sun, the rays of which occasionally shone through the painted windows, casting coloured shadows on the floor. Then shortly the lightness would disappear and the former gloom again obscure the objects that had been momentarily illumined. The illusion was rendered more perfect by the sensitive condition of the eye in the darkness of the surrounding chamber.
>
> While gazing in wrapt admiration at the architectural beauties of the cathedral the spectator's attention was disturbed by sounds underground. *He became conscious that the scene before him was slowly moving away and he obtained a glimpse of another and very different prospect, which gradually advanced until it was completely developed and the cathedral had disappeared.* What he now saw was a valley surrounded by high mountains capped with snow. (*Movement in Two Dimensions*, 36–37, emphasis added)

The auditorium was set on rollers that rotated the platform by a single man who turned a crank. The admission was two francs for the amphitheatre and three francs for boxes. The London diorama was built in Regent's Park and opened in September 1823. A diorama was opened by Carl Wilhelm Gropius in Berlin in 1827.

42. The diorama was dependent on daylight. In Paris, it had continuous shows from 11 A.M. to 4 P.M. When the diorama opened in Regent's Park in London in 1823, it had continuous shows from 10 A.M. until 4 P.M. to 6 P.M., depending on the seasonal light. The London diorama was closed in the winter until the 1840s. The Paris diorama always had two scenes on exhibit. The first scene was enhanced by lighting changes for ten to fifteen minutes. When this was complete, the auditorium would rotate seventy-three degrees and the second scene would be shown.

43. The Gernsheims include a timetable of the paintings with their dates of exhibition (Gernsheim and Gernsheim, *L. J. M. Daguerre*, 182–184).

44. Ibid., 18.

45. Ibid.

46. Carl Wilhelm Gropius debuted the pleorama in Berlin in 1832. See Gernsheim and Gernsheim, *L. J. M. Daguerre*, 47. See also *Magische Schatten*, 88.

    Of course the concept of the pleorama is much like the later "Hale's Tours" introduced by George C. Hale of Kansas City in 1903, a mode of viewing in which the spectator sat in a simulation railway car and viewed a film taken from the front of a railway engine. See Raymond Fielding, "Hale's Tours: Ultrarealism in the Pre-1910 Motion Picture," in *Film Before Griffith*, edited by John L. Fell (Berkeley: University of California Press, 1983), 116–131.

47. In the "Daguerre or the Diorama" section of his 1935 exposé, "Paris—Capital of the Nineteenth Century," Benjamin writes:

    While the dioramas strove to produce life-like transformations in the Nature portrayed in them, they foreshadowed via photography, the moving picture and the talking picture. (*Charles Baudelaire*, 161)

48. As a historical addendum, Bentham's use of the term *panopticon* for his architectural structure should not be confused with the variety of other devices called panopticon. The *Oxford English Dictionary* mentions a use by Benjamin Franklin in 1768. In 1742, British clockmaker-showman brothers Edward and Christopher Pinchbeck produced a musical clock with six mechanically moving pictures. See Altick, *Shows of London*, 60.

    But as an architectural structure, there were buildings other than Bentham's prison that were called panopticons. Like other architectural forms new to the nineteenth century—the winter garden, the train station, the exhibition hall—the panopticon was a structure made possible by cast-iron construction. In 1852 a building deemed the "Royal Panopticon of Science and Art, An Institution for Scientific Exhibitions, and for Promoting Discoveries in Arts and Manufactures" opened in Leicester Square in London. With a Moorish exterior, the only similarity to the architectural plan of the panopticon prison was its theatrical atrium, designed for the spectators to see the center attractions. The key attraction in the Leicester Square panopticon was a luminous fountain that reached from floor to ceiling in the ninety-foot atrium rotunda and a pipe organ with four thousand pipes run by a steam bellows. But its main purpose was to exhibit Polytechnic pursuits, in short to turn science into entertainment. The panopticon initially drew crowds, but its charms were in its initial novelty and the entertainment did not draw in repeat business.

In 1857, the building was auctioned off, the organ was sold and a circus ring installed. (Altick, *Shows of London*, 490–496.)

49. In *Disenchanted Night,* Schivelbusch discusses the importance of the darkened auditorium and the highly illuminated image in "light-based" media from the magic lantern to the cinema screen: "The power of artificial light to create its own reality only reveals itself in darkness" (221).

50. Baudry emphasizes this immobility and enclosure for the cinematic spectator, as an extension of the prisoners in Plato's cave. Cinematic projection takes place in a closed space, separate from the external world: "Those who remain there, whether they know it or not (but they do not), find themselves chained, captured, or captivated." (Baudry, "Ideological Effects," 294.)

51. "If we had to nominate the first modernist, Baudelaire certainly would have been the man." (Marshall Berman, *All That's Solid Melts into Air* [New York: Simon and Schuster, 1982], 133.)

52. Charles Baudelaire, "The Painter of Modern Life," in *My Heart Laid Bare and Other Prose Writings* (London: Soho Book Company, 1986).

53. Ibid., 37.

54. Ibid., 34.

55. Charles Baudelaire, "Crowds," in *Paris Spleen* (1869), translated by Louise Varése (New York: New Directions, 1947), 20–21. "L'Homme des foules" (man of the masses) was also a figure from the writing of Edgar Allan Poe, whose story "The Man of the Crowd" (1840) Baudelaire mentions.

56. Ibid.

57. *Les Français, Peints Par Eux-Memes, Encyclopédie Morale du Dix-neuvième Siècle* (Paris: L. Curmer Editeut, 1841), 9.

58. Baudelaire, "Painter of Modern Life," 36.

59. I've chosen these two terms here to restate the paradox in Baudelaire's relation to spectation. *Scopophilia,* by now a well-known term, first taken from Freud's discussions of the perversions in "Three Essays on Sexuality," has come to be associated with the gendered pleasures in looking and feminist critiques of gendered voyeurism (as in "men look, women appear"). As a technical term, *scopophilia* refers to "pleasure in looking" and hence, as a neologistic twist on its technicality, *scopophobia* refers to the fear or dread of looking.

60. Baudelaire, "The Salon of 1859," in *Art in Paris 1845–1862.*

61. Ibid., 153.

Baudelaire's ambivalence toward photography is evident in the following passage:

> If photography is allowed to supplement art in some of its functions, it will
> soon have supplanted or corrupted it altogether, thanks to the stupidity of the
> multitude which is its natural ally. It is time, then, for it to return to its true
> duty, which is to be the servant of the sciences and arts—but the very humble

servant, like printing or shorthand, which have neither created nor supplemented literature. *Let it hasten to enrich the tourist's album and restore to his eye the precision which his memory may lack;* let it adorn the naturalist's library, and enlarge microscopic animals; let it even provide information to corroborate the astronomer's hypotheses; in short, let it be the secretary and clerk of whoever needs an absolute factual exactitude in his profession—up to that point nothing could be better. (159, emphasis added)

62. As fitting irony—given Baudelaire's fears of the relation between photography and history—the same year (1863) that "The Painter of Modern Life" was written, Baudelaire had his photograph taken by the portrait photographer Ettienne Carjat. This image of Baudelaire has become, next to the photograph of him taken by his friend Nadar in 1856, our image of him in historical memory.

63. Susan Sontag, *On Photography* (New York: Farrar, Straus and Giroux, 1977), 55.

64. Roland Barthes describes the photograph's virtual record as an "illogical conjunction" of spatial immediacy ("here-now") and temporal anteriority ("having-been-there"). The photograph's temporality of pastness ("for in every photograph there is always stupefying evidence of *this is how it was*") is, as Barthes claims, in "radical opposition" to the film's temporality. The film is not just composed of animated still images with the aura of "having-been-there" but is instead, Barthes implies, always received in the present tense, as a "being-there." See Roland Barthes, "Rhetoric of the Image," in *Image, Music, Text,* translated by Stephen Heath (New York: Hill and Wang, 1977), 44–45. We will return to discussion of the temporality of the filmic image in chapter 3.

65. Crary "embodies" the centuries (seventeenth, eighteenth, nineteenth, twentieth) as separate and motivated, a historiographic distinction that is, while important, often too tidily assumed. See Jonathan Crary, "Techniques of the Observer," *October* 45 (Summer 1988): 3–35; and Crary's book-length expansion of the October essay, *Techniques of the Observer* (Cambridge, Mass.: MIT Press, 1990).

66. Crary, "Techniques of the Observer," 4.
    This paradigm shift—away from the body into a more subjective source of vision—finds its origins, according to Crary, in Goethe's *Color Theory* (1810), a text that illustrates how the eye (a physiological organ) becomes the active producer of optical experience ("it arises from an image which now belongs to the eye"). Goethe describes the colors that are produced in the afterimage as "physiological colors" that belong to the *body* of the observer, not to the apparatus. Crary uses the following quote from Goethe as exemplary of this shift toward subjective vision:

Let a room be made as dark as possible; let there be a circular opening in the window shutter about three inches in diameter, which may be closed or not at pleasure. The sun being suffered to shine through this on a white surface, let the

spectator from some little distance fix his eyes on this bright circle thus
admitted. . . . The hole being then closed, let him look toward the darkest part
of the room; a circular image will now be seen to float before him.

The image of a spectator in a darkened room with (his) eyes fixed on a bright circle
seems, at first, to be a paradigm for the cinematic spectator; the familiar analogy of
the camera obscura as an informing instance for cinematic spectation. But Crary
refutes this teleology because it ignores the fundamental importance of the afterimage and subjective vision.

67. Ibid., 5.

68. When asked about the sexualized notion of psychic functioning found in the perceptual theories he cites, Crary responded that the "concept of sexuality" was not
present in the perceptual theories he was describing. The question here was asked
at a DIA Foundation Symposium by Jacqueline Rose, author of *Sexuality in the
Field of Vision.* See "Discussion" following "Modernizing Vision" in *Vision and
Visuality,* 45–49.

And yet, in an unelaborated footnote, Crary uses the following passage from
Goethe as an example of the subjectivity of vision:

Goethe provided a telling account of the subjectivity of the afterimage in which
the physiology of the attentive (male heterosexual) eye and its operation are
inseparable from memory and desire:

I had entered an inn towards evening, and, as a well-favored girl, with a
brilliantly fair complexion, black hair, and a scarlet bodice, came into the
room, I looked attentively at her as she stood before me at some distance in
half shadow. As she presently afterwards turned away, I saw on the white
wall which was now before me, a black face surrounded with a bright light,
while the dress of the perfectly distinct figure appeared of a beautiful sea
green.

From *Theory of Colors,* 22. See "Techniques of the Observer," 32. Goethe's account
is indeed telling, for it is clear that, to Goethe, attentive male heterosexual desire is
inseparable from subjective vision.

69. Crary, "Techniques of the Observer," 15.

70. Ibid.

71. Crary's work is not aimed at film history but he makes an implicit critique of the
film historical teleologies that neglect "nonveridical" forms of perception. Crary
attempts to distinguish between the frequently conflated optical devices that form
the list of "protocinematic" devices—from the thaumatrope to Plateau's phenakis-

toscope to Daguerre's diorama. But rather than explore the ranges of differences between these devices, he aligns them with either eighteenth- or nineteenth-century models of perception. Crary supplies a counterteleology that traces the history of devices fit into the nineteenth-century model. By supplanting the camera obscura with the stereoscope and phenakistoscope as more apt paradigms for the nineteenth-century observer, Crary slights two aspects that are fundamental features of cinematic spectatorship and are found in the panorama, the diorama and other forms of screen entertainment—the darkened room, which severs contact with the external world, and the projection of light.

72. From a 1978 interview with Luce Irigaray in *Les Femmes, la pornographie et l'erotisme,* edited by M. F. Hans and G. Lapougue. Quoted in Griselda Pollock's *Vision and Difference: Femininity, Feminism and the Histories of Art* (New York: Routledge, 1988), 50.

73. Baudry, "Ideological Effects," 292.

74. Michel deCerteau, *The Practice of Everyday Life,* translated by Steven Rendall (Berkeley and Los Angeles: University of California Press, 1984), xxi.

75. Baudelaire's *Les Fleurs du Mal* was published in 1857; it was first announced as *Les Lesbiennes.* The first edition was confiscated by the police following a judicial order. Baudelaire was charged with obscenity, fined 300 francs and required to delete six poems from all future editions. The three lesbian poems of *Les Fleurs du Mal*— "Lesbos," "Delphine et Hippolyte," and "Femmes damnées"—were deemed indecent by the French court. In these poems, Baudelaire cast the lesbian as a heroic yet pitiable force:

Wandering far from mankind, condemned
to forage in the wilderness like wolves,
pursue your fate, chaotic souls, and flee
the infinite you bear within yourselves!
(Baudelaire, *Les Fleurs du Mal,* 128)

or

Sisters! I love you as I pity you
for your bleak sorrows, for your unslaked thirsts,
and for the love that gorges your great hearts!
(Baudelaire, *Les Fleurs du Mal,* 130)

Benjamin offers an explanation of Baudelaire's fascination with the lesbian, suggesting that he gives a "purely sexual accent" to "masculine traits" that appear in women as a result of their incorporation in the processes of commodity production:

The figure of the lesbian woman belongs in the most precise sense among the heroic models of Baudelaire. . . . The 19th century began to incorporate women wholesale into the process of commodity production. All theoreticians agreed that their specific femininity was thus threatened; masculine traits would in the course of time appear also in women. Baudelaire affirmed these traits; but at the same time wished to deny their economic necessity. Thus it is that he comes to give a purely sexual accent to this evolving tendency in women. (39)

See Benjamin, "Central Park," translated by Lloyd Spencer, *New German Critique* 34 (Winter 1985): 32–58. Wolff argues that the lesbian was a hero(ine) of modernity solely because she was "mannish." See Janet Wolff, "The Invisible Flâneuse: Women and the Literature of Modernity," *Theory, Culture and Society* 2, no. 7 (1985).

76. *"A une passante"* is the poem that Benjamin discusses in the *Flâneur* section of "The Paris of the Second Empire in Baudelaire," 44–45.

See also William Chapman Sharpe, "Poet as *Passant:* Baudelaire's 'Holy Prostitution,' " in *Unreal Cities: Urban Figuration in Wordsworth, Baudelaire, Whitman, Eliot, and Williams* (Baltimore: Johns Hopkins University Press, 1990).

77. Charles Baudelaire, *Les Fleurs du Mal,* poem 26, translated by Richard Howard (Boston: David R. Godine, 1983).

78. "Der Blick des Flaneurs" in Benjamin, "Paris—Capital of the Nineteenth Century," 170; *Passagen-Werk,* 54.

79. Walter Benjamin, "The Paris of the Second Empire in Baudelaire," in *Charles Baudelaire,* 36.

80. As a key description of the effect of mass culture, Siegfried Kracauer uses the term *Zerstreuung* (distraction). See "Kult der Zerstreuung," translated by Tom Levin, *New German Critique* 40 (Winter 1987): 91–96. See also Heide Schlupmann, "Kracauer's Phenomenology of Film," in the same issue.

Also Hans Robert Jauss, in his essay "Reflections on the Chapter 'Modernity' in Benjamin's Baudelaire Fragments" (in *On Walter Benjamin,* edited by Gary Smith [Cambridge, Mass.: MIT Press, 1988], 176–185) points to Benjamin's omission of Baudelaire's "Painter of Modern Life" essay.

81. In 1927, in Paris, Benjamin read to Gershom Scholem the first drafts of his projected study of the Paris arcades. See Gershom Scholem, *The Story of a Friendship,* translated from the German by Harry Zohn (London: Faber and Faber, 1982), 135.

82. Benjamin, "Paris—Capital of the Nineteenth Century," 170.

83. Susan Buck-Morss, "The Flâneur, the Sandwichman and the Whore: The Politics of Loitering," *New German Critique* 39 (Fall 1986): 99–140.

84. In "The Paris of the Second Empire in Baudelaire," Benjamin has a rather strange passage in which he projects the soul of the flâneur into the soul of the commodity.

If, as Marx would have had it, a commodity could speak, it would say, to quote Benjamin, quoting Baudelaire:

"The poet enjoys the incomparable privilege of being himself and someone else
as he sees fit. Like a roving soul in search of a body, he enters another person
whenever he wishes. For him alone, all is open; if certain places are closed to
him, it is because in his view they are not worth inspecting." The commodity
itself is the speaker here. Yes, the last words give a rather accurate idea of what
the commodity whispers to a poor wretch who passes a shop-window containing
beautiful and expensive things.

Rather than identifying with the prostitute, a commodity that *could* speak, Benjamin has placed himself on the shelf as a silent commodity that envies the (male) poet who "like a roving soul in search of a body" can enter "another person whenever he wishes." These were not only the privileges of the poet, but of the flâneur who possessed an urban mobility denied to women.

In her study of women and Weimar Germany, Patrice Petro sees Benjamin's reading of "A une passante" as an indication of his ambivalence to woman and mass culture. As she aptly indicates:

We may suspect that *women's relationship to modernity was entirely different from*
what was commonly projected onto the figure of woman during Weimar period.
Indeed, it would seem that women's relationship to modernity and mass culture
has all too frequently been confused with male desire, and with male
perceptions of gender difference. (*Joyless Streets,* 68, emphasis added)

85. Pollock, *Vision and Difference,* 53.
86. See T. J. Clark, *The Painting of Modern Life: Paris and the Art of Manet and his Followers* (New York: Knopf, 1985).
87. Kathy Peiss discusses the dance hall and the amusement park as sites of "heterosocial" interaction. Elizabeth Wilson, Rachel Bowlby, Susan Porter Benson, and others have described the department store as a public urban space for women. See Peiss, *Cheap Amusements;* Wilson, *Adorned in Dreams;* Susan Porter Benson, *Counter Cultures: Saleswomen, Managers, and Customers in American Department Stores, 1890–1940* (Urbana: University of Illinois Press, 1986); William R. Leach, "Transformations in a Culture of Consumption: Women and Department Stores 1980–1925," *The Journal of American History* 71, no. 2 (September 1984); Bowlby, *Just Looking;* Michael B. Miller, *The Bon Marché: Bourgeois Culture and the Department Store 1869–1920* (Princeton: Princeton University Press, 1981).

88. In an unelaborated note in *Passagen-Werk* (544), Benjamin mentions that in Paris, in 1857, women were forbidden to ride on the roof of public buses.

89. Bowlby, *Just Looking,* 6.

90. See Miller, *Bon Marché;* Benson, *Counter Cultures.*

91. Macy's ladies tearoom opened in 1878 and by 1902 was a restaurant catering to twenty-five hundred customers. Marshall Field's in Chicago opened a tearoom in 1890 and by 1902 the restaurant took up the entire floor. See Wilson, *Adorned in Dreams.* For elaboration of these transformations see Leach, "Transformations"; Bowlby, *Just Looking.*

92. Guiliano Bruno has elaborated on the flâneuse as spectator in early Italian cinemas in the train stations and arcades of Milan. See "Streetwalking in Plato's Cave," *October* 59 (1992).

93. Wolff, "Invisible Flâneuse." Wolff has included this as a chapter in *Feminine Sentences: Essays on Women and Culture* (Berkeley and Los Angeles: University of California Press, 1990).

94. In her Ph.D. thesis, Anke Gleber traces the German origins of female flânerie in the work of Christa Wolf and others. See "Flanerie oder die Lektüre der Moderne: Franz Hessel und Paul Gurk. Mit einem Exkurs zur neueren deutschen Literatur," Ph.D. diss., University of California at Irvine, 1988.

95. Certainly the work of female literary modernists such as Gertrude Stein (*Everybody's Autobiography, The Autobiography of Alice B. Toklas*), H. D. (*Palimpsest, The Usual Star*), and Dorothy Richardson (*Pilgrimage*) provides accounts of women in public urban settings of modernity. For a recent compilation of female modernists, see *The Gender of Modernism: A Critical Anthology,* edited by Bonnie Kime Scott (Bloomington: Indiana University Press, 1990).

    Carroll Smith-Rosenberg argues the need for a reconceptualization of nineteenth-century women's history which relies less on traditional historical sources and more on private letters and journals. See "Hearing Women's Words: A Feminist Reconstruction of History," in *Disorderly Conduct: Visions of Gender in Victorian America* (New York: Oxford University Press, 1985).

96. Pollock, "Modernity and Spaces of Femininity," in *Vision and Difference,* 50–90.

97. Benjamin, "Paris—Capital of the Nineteenth Century," 170.

98. See Bowlby, *Just Looking.* Bowlby describes shopping as a "new feminine leisure activity" (19). See also T. J. Jackson Lears, "From Salvation to Self-Regulation: Advertising and the Therapeutic Roots of the Consumer Culture, 1880–1930," in *The Culture of Consumption: Critical Essays in American History 1880–1980,* edited by Richard Wightman Fox and T. J. Jackson Lears (New York: Pantheon Books, 1983), 1–39.

99. deCerteau, *Practice of Everyday Life.*

PASSAGE I

1. Émile Zola, *The Ladies Paradise (Au Bonheur des Dames)* (Berkeley and Los Angeles: University of California Press, 1991), 8.
2. Ibid., 16–17.
3. Ibid., 378.
4. Ibid., 208.
5. Ibid., 236.
6. Ibid., 72.
7. Ibid., 208. See Miller, *Bon Marché;* Williams, *Dream Worlds.*
8. See Ian Watt, *The Rise of the Novel* (Berkeley: University of California Press, 1957); Mayne, *Private Novels, Public Films.*
9. Kristin Ross, "Shopping," introduction to *The Ladies Paradise,* Émile Zola (Berkeley and Los Angeles: University of California Press, 1991), xiii.
10. Ibid., xiv.
11. Zola, *Ladies Paradise,* 87, 223, 366.
12. Ibid., 87.
13. Williams, *Dream Worlds;* see also Nancy F. Cott, *The Grounding of Modern Feminism* (New Haven: Yale University Press, 1987).
14. For a further discussion of *A Question of Silence,* see Lucy Fischer, *Shot/Counter-Shot: Film Tradition and Women's Cinema* (Princeton: Princeton University Press, 1989), 282–300; Linda Williams, "A Jury of Their Peers: Marlene Gorris's *A Question of Silence,*" in *Postmodernism and Its Discontents,* edited by E. Ann Kaplan (London: Verso, 1988), 107–115.

CHAPTER TWO

1. Benjamin, "Work of Art," 236.
2. Ibid.
3. Jean Epstein, "Grossisement," translated by Stuart Liebman as "Magnification," *October* 3 (Spring 1977): 15.
4. Jean Epstein, "A Conversation with Jean Epstein," *L'ami du Peuple,* May 11, 1928, translated by Bob Lamberton, Anthology Film Archives; quoted in Annette Michelson, "Reading Eisenstein, Reading Capital," *October* 2 (Summer 1976): 33.
5. See Béla Balázs, "The Face of Man," in *Theory of Film: Character and Growth of a New Art* (New York: Dover Publications, 1970); Gertrud Koch, "Béla Balázs: The Physiognomy of Things," *New German Critique* 40 (Winter 1987): 167–177.
6. Benjamin, "Work of Art," 220.
7. Benjamin also discusses photography and mechanical reproduction in his earlier essays, "Short History of Photography," translated by Stanley Mitchell, *Screen* 13, no. 1 (Spring 1972) and "On Mimetic Faculty," in *Reflections.*

8. "Technical reproduction," Benjamin wrote, "can put the copy of the original into situations which would be out of reach for the original itself" ("Work of Art," 220). Hence, mechanical reproduction answered

> the desire of contemporary masses to bring things "closer" spatially and humanly, which is just as ardent as their bent toward overcoming the uniqueness of every reality by accepting its reproduction." (223)

"The film," he describes in a long footnote, "virtually causes mass distribution . . . because the production of a film is so expensive" (244).

9. Miriam Hansen's excellent essay, "Benjamin, Cinema and Experience: 'The Blue Flower in the Land of Technology,' " *New German Critique* 40 (Winter 1987): 179–224, provides the most detailed exegesis yet of the "Work of Art" essay, especially her discussion of the distinction between *Bild* (image) and *Abbild* (copy), and her contextualization of Benjamin's notion of *Erfahrung* (experience). Hansen maintains that Benjamin's concept of aura contains a "complex temporality" (189):

> Not only are distance and proximity entwined in a single metaphor of psychic ambivalence, but their political significance is bound up with the question of temporality. (217)

In Hansen's reading of Benjamin's work, "time has a conceptual priority over space" (189).

10. The fragments of Benjamin's *Passagen-Werk,* edited by Rolf Tiedemann, were published in two volumes in 1983 (Frankfurt am Main: Suhrkamp, 1983); the German edition was translated into French and published in 1989 as *Paris, Capitale du XIX Siecle: le livre des passages,* traduit par Jean Lacoste (Paris: Les Editions du Cerf, 1989). Further references to *Passagen-Werk* will be noted as *PW.*

   The two-volume Suhrkamp edition contains a lengthy "Zeugnisse zur Entstehungsgeschichte" (Summary of the Project's Origins and Progress) which carefully reconstructs Benjamin's progress on the project. The project has its earliest origins in April and May 1927 in Paris. Benjamin worked on it from the winter of 1928 to the end of 1929 and then again beginning 1934. The exposé "Paris—Capital of the Nineteenth Century" was written in German at Horkheimer's urging; the essay "Paris of the Second Empire in Baudelaire" was written in French in 1938. "Some Motifs on Baudelaire" was the only piece of the intended Arcades Project that was published in Benjamin's lifetime (in *Zeitschrift für Sozialforschung,* 1939). The thirty-six "convoluts" of "Notes and Materials" for the *Passagen-Werk* were hidden in the

Bibliotheque Nationale during the war, rescued by George Bataille and Pierre Missac after the war. The Tiedemann survey—summarized by David Frisby in his chapter on Benjamin, "The Prehistory of Modernity," *Fragments of Modernity: Theories of Modernity in the Work of Simmel, Kracauer and Benjamin* (Cambridge, Mass.: MIT Press, 1986)—has been translated as "Dialectics at a Standstill: Approaches to the *Passagen-Werk*," in *On Walter Benjamin*.

Although the broad strokes of Benjamin's intentions for the work are apparent in the reduced exposés, "Paris—Capital of the Nineteenth Century" (1935) and "Paris of the Second Empire in Baudelaire" (1938), the scope of the *Passagen-Werk* is only hinted at in these drafts. As in any stock made from reducing its original ingredients, the recipe list of Konvoluts gives us only an indirect indication of the disparate materials that Benjamin tried to blend: Arcades, Fashion, Catacombs, Haussmannization, Iron Construction, Advertisements, Grandville, the Ragpicker, Baudelaire, the Museum, the Flâneur, Prostitution, Theory of Knowledge, The Streets of Paris, Fourier, Marx, Photography, Dolls, the Automat, and Daumier.

Susan Buck-Morss's *Dialectics of Seeing* (Cambridge, Mass.: MIT Press, 1989) provides an excellent concordance to the massive Arcades Project. For a discussion of the "Work of Art" essay in relation to the *Passagen-Werk*, see Susan Buck-Morss, "Benjamin's *Passagen-Werk*: Redeeming Mass Culture for Revolution," *New German Critique* 29 (Spring/Summer 1983): 211–241.

11. *PW*, 1030. "Aber die Lumpen, den Abfall: die will ich nicht beschreiben sondern vorzeigen."

12. Theodor W. Adorno, "A Portrait of Walter Benjamin," translated from the German by Samuel and Sherry Weber, in *Prisms* (Cambridge, Mass.: MIT Press, 1986), 240.

This assessment of Benjamin's method should be compared to Benjamin's discussion, in the "Work of Art" essay, of the importance of Freud's *Psychopathology of Everyday Life:* "This book isolated and made analyzable things which had heretofore floated along unnoticed in the broad stream of perception" ("Work of Art," 235).

13. Ibid., 233.

14. Was in den Passagen verkauft wird sind Andenken. Das Andenken ist die Form der Ware in den Passagen. Man kauft immer nur Andenken an die und die Passage." (*PW*, 1034)

15. "Both sides of these passageways, which are lighted from above, are lined with the most elegant shops, so that such an arcade is a city, even *a world, in miniature*" (Benjamin, "Paris of the Second Empire in Baudelaire," 36–37).

16. The *Passagen-Werk* was left in fragments, ruins. Benjamin's posthumous editor, Rolf Tiedemann, describes the project as a building not built, but whose floor plans and construction materials have been left:

The fragments of the *Passagen-Werk* can be compared to the materials used in building a house, the outline of which has just been marked in the ground or whose foundations are just being dug. . . . The five or six sections of each exposé should have corresponded to the same number of chapters in the book or, to continue the analogy, to the five or six floors of the projected house. Next to the foundation we find the neatly piled excerpts, which would have been used to construct the wall; Benjamin's own thoughts would have provided the mortar to hold the building together. ("Dialectics at a Standstill," 264)

Benjamin described his method in telegraphic form in Konvolut N of *Passagen-Werk*:

The work must raise to the very highest level the art of quoting without quotations marks. Its theory is intimately linked to montage.

And:

Method of this work: *literary montage.* I need say nothing. Only show. I won't steal anything valuable or appropriate any witty turns of phrase. But the trivia, the trash: this, I don't want to take stock of, but let it come into its own the only way possible: use it. (emphasis added)

See Walter Benjamin, "N [Theoretics of Knowledge; Theory of Progress]," *Philosophical Forum* 15, nos. 1–2 (Fall-Winter 1983–1984): 5–6.

17. Buck-Morss, *Dialectics of Seeing*, x.

When Benjamin took his own life in September 1940, the only part of the Arcades Project that had been published was the small essay, "Uber einige Motive bei Baudelaire," *Zeitschrift für Sozialforschung* 8 (1939): 50–89. (Translated as "On Some Motifs in Baudelaire.")

Buck-Morss calls her long-awaited book-length study of Walter Benjamin's *Passagen-Werk* a "picture book of philosophy" which "proceeded mimetically, extrapolating from the *Passagen-Werk*." If, as Buck-Morss claims, Benjamin's writing was "only a series of captions to the world outside the text," then she has provided an excellent concordance to those irretrievable images. In a brave and brilliant maneuver, Buck-Morss has surpassed the generation of Benjamin exegetes to extrapolate on Benjamin's significance in relation to contemporary culture.

Peter Jukes's *A Shout in the Streets: An Excursion into the Modern City* (New York: Farrar Straus, 1990) is a Benjaminian assemblage of photographs and quotes from a wide range of sources. Part montage, part essay, the book attempts to represent the modern urban experience in a variety of chance encounters, juxtapositions, and planned intersections.

18. The architecture of Benjamin's unfinished *Passagen-Werk* was intended to, in its very structure, present dialectical images. Even though they are not dialectical pairings, the section headings of his 1935 exposé— I. Fourier or the Arcades, II. Daguerre or the Panoramas, III. Grandville or the World Exhibition, IV. Louis-Philippe or the Interior, V. Baudelaire or the Streets of Paris, VI. Haussmann or the Barricades—form analogical-dialectical relations to each other. Benjamin wanted to superimpose these widely disparate aspects of nineteenth-century culture onto each other—to suggest that the impetus behind the arcades was related to the impetus behind the panorama; and that this was related to the concept of an interior for the new private citizen; which was, in turn, related to Baudelaire's sense of flânerie and to Haussmann's designs for Paris.

19. Pierre Missac discusses the repeated trope of *Bruch* (rupture) and *Bruchstück* (fragment) in Benjamin's work, in "From Rupture to Shipwreck," in *On Walter Benjamin*, 210–224.

   In *Fragments of Modernity*, Frisby discusses Kracauer, Simmel, and Benjamin as exemplary diagnosticians of the fragmentary experience of time, space, and causality in modernity.

20. *PW*, 1035.

21. Benjamin, "N [Theoretics of Knowledge; Theory of Progress]," 6.

22. In "Work of Art" Benjamin's knowledge of Russian cinema is made known in cryptic asides. In discussions of the actor, Benjamin mentions Vertov's *Three Songs for Lenin* ("Work of Art," 231) and quotes Pudovkin's *Filmregie und Film manuskript* in a footnote (247).

   Otherwise, we can read the essay for clues to his awareness of Soviet montage theory:

> The directives which the captions give to those looking at pictures in illustrated magazines soon become even more explicit and more imperative in *the film where the meaning of each single picture appears to be prescribed by the sequence of all preceding one.* (226, emphasis added)

> *We do not deny that in some cases today's films can also promote revolutionary criticism of social conditions,* even distribution of property. However, our present study is no more specifically concerned with this than is the film production of Western Europe. (231, emphasis added)

In 1927, Benjamin wrote a piece on Eisenstein's *Potemkin*, "Zur Lage des Russichen Filmkunst," *Gesammelte Schriften*, vol. 3. (Frankfurt: Suhrkamp, 1982), 747–751.

23. See Sergei Eisenstein, "Notes for a Film of *Capital*," and Annette Michelson's excellent exegesis, "Reading Eisenstein, Reading *Capital*," *October* 2 (Summer 1976): 21, 38.

24. Eisenstein's theorization of intellectual montage, although evidenced in his film *October* (edited at the beginning of 1928), was not written up until 1929. "Dialectic Approach to Film Form" was written in April 1929.

25. Eisenstein wrote this in a letter to Moussinac dated December 16, 1928. The letter, quoted in Moussinac's biography of Eisenstein, is requoted in Jay Leyda and Zina Voyow's *Eisenstein at Work* (New York: Pantheon, 1982), 35.

26. Susan Sontag refers cryptically to the *Passagen-Werk* as a "sublimated version of photographer's activity," in *On Photography*, 76. Elsewhere, Buck-Morss has described the *Passagen-Werk* as "like a script of a film documentary.") See Buck-Morss, "Walter Benjamin—Revolutionary Writer II," *New Left Review* 129 [1981]: 94); Anson Rabinbach described it as a "pictorial history without photographs," in "Critique and Commentary/Alchemy and Chemistry: Some Remarks on Walter Benjamin and This Special Issue," *New German Critique* 17 (Spring 1979): 3–14.

27. Walter Benjamin, *Briefe*, edited by Gershom Scholem and Theodor W. Adorno (Frankfurt: Suhrkamp, 1966), 783. For an detailed account of Adorno's reactions to Benjamin see Susan Buck-Morss, *The Origin of the Negative Dialectics* (New York: 1977). Adorno's essay, "Fetish Character of Music," was a direct reaction to Benjamin's "Work of Art" essay. Pierre Missac describes the Benjamin-Adorno correspondence as "acrimonious exchanges" (Missac, "From Rupture to Shipwreck," 213).

28. Theodor W. Adorno, "Introduction to Benjamin's *Schriften*," translated by R. Hullot-Kentor, in *On Walter Benjamin*, 10.

29. May 20, 1935. *Correspondence of Walter Benjamin and Gershom Scholem, 1932–1940* (New York: Schocken Books, 1989), 159.

30. Lautréamont's famous dictum, "as beautiful as the chance encounter of a sewing machine and an umbrella on a dissection table," suggested the expressive potential of unexpected juxtaposition. Benjamin found, in the surrealists, a model for taking the hodge-podge juxtaposition and clutter of urban life. See Walter Benjamin, "Surrealism: The Last Snapshot of the European Intellegentsia," in *Reflections*.

31. *PW*, 1057.

32. Benjamin, "Paris—Capital of the Nineteenth Century," 176.

33. Tiedemann, "Dialectics at a Standstill," 268.

34. Tiedemann maintains that when Benjamin submitted his "Early Drafts" to Horkheimer and Adorno in 1929, Benjamin "at that time had read hardly anything by Marx." Tiedemann suggests that "it is entirely possible [that Benjamin] was influenced" by their suggestions that "it was impossible to speak sensibly about the nineteenth century without considering Marx's analysis of capital" (Tiedemann,

"Dialectics at a Standstill," 275) and that Benjamin "apparently only began to look around in the first volume of *Capital* after completing the exposé" (276).

Marshall Berman compares Benjamin to Greta Garbo in *Ninotchka*, torn between the lure of Parisian fashion and his Marxist conscience. See Marshall Berman, *All That's Solid Melts into Air* (New York: Simon and Schuster, 1982).

35. Karl Marx, *Capital: A Critique of Political Economy*, vol. 1, translated by Ben Fowkes (New York: Vintage Books, 1977), 125.

36. To cite the famous passage from *Das Kapital:*

> The commodity form, and the value-relation of the products of labor within which it appears have absolutely no connection with the physical nature of the commodity and the material relations arising out of this. It is nothing but the definite social relation between men themselves which assumes here, for them, the fantastic form of a relation between things. . . . I call this the fetishism which attaches itself to the products of labor as soon as they are produced as commodities. (165)

37. Karl Marx, *Theories of Surplus Value*, translated by G. A. Bonner and Emile Barns (New York: International Publishers, 1952), 190.

38. Benjamin, "Work of Art," 231. *Das Kunstwerk im Zeitalter seiner technischen Reproduzierbarkeit* (Frankfurt: Suhrkamp Verlag, 1963), 27–28.

39. I am indebted here to Thomas Y. Levin's translations of Adorno's writing on the gramophone and the record. See his excellent essay, "For the Record: Adorno on Music in the Age of Its Technological Reproducibility," and the three Adorno essays: "Curves of the Needle" (1928), "The Form of the Phonograph Record" (1934), "Opera and the Long-Playing Record" (1969), in *October* 55 (Winter 1990): 23–66.

Adorno's writings on these technological means of reproduction demonstrate, as Levin points out, his commitment to "the mechanics of indexicality" and led him to compare the phonograph with the photograph. The second essay, "The Form of the Phonograph Record," was influenced by Benjamin's *Trauerspiel* work, but prefigured the discussion of "aura" in Benjamin's "Work of Art" essay.

In a description that suggestively predicts "karaoke" and "lip-synching" technology, Adorno remarks on the "mirror function" of the gramophone:

> What the gramophone listener actually wants to hear is himself and the artist merely offers him a substitute for the sounding image of his own person. . . . Most of the time records are virtual photographs of their owners—flattering photographs—ideologies. (54)

Accordingly, Adorno notes a "problematic" consequence of the separation of body from voice. Adorno speculates that the male voice reproduces better than the female voice because "the female voice requires the physical appearance of the body that carries it." Without this bodily presence, the female voice sounds "needy and incomplete." (This, Adorno offers, also explains Caruso's "uncontested dominance" as a recording artist.)

Adorno's 1934 essay "The Form of the Phonograph Record" was written under the pseudonym Hektor Rottweiler. Remarking on the his master's voice in "Curves of the Needle," Adorno argues: "The dog on records listening to his master's voice off of records through the gramophone horn is the right emblem for the primordial effect which the gramophone stimulated" (54).

40. Adorno, "Form of the Phonograph Record," *October* 55 (Winter 1990): 58–59.

41. Similarly, contemporary expenditures on the movie ticket, the videocassette, and the theme park ticket do not buy a tangible product. As the multibillion dollar profits of theme parks (in excess of the movie-division earnings of Disney and Universal) illustrate, the imaginary transit offered in experience is a prized commodity.

42. Karl Marx, *Grundrisse der Kritik der politischen Oekonomie* (Berlin: Dietz Verlag, 1953), 599–600. Translated and edited by David McLellan in *The Grundrisse* (New York: Harper and Row, 1970), 148.

43. As a vivid illustration of this paradox of the "leisure-worker" see Philip K. Dick's prophetic *The Three Stigmata of Palmer Eldritch* (Garden City, N.J.: Doubleday, 1965).

44. But capitalism can also turn "aura" into a commodified aspect. In the contemporary marketplace, for example, foods are marketed to sell the cachet of regional aura— the "Maui" onion, the "New Zealand" tomato, and so forth.

45. Schivelbusch, *Railway Journey*.

46. See Daniel Bell, *The Coming of Post-Industrial Society* (New York: Basic Books, 1973).

Bell describes the "emergent features" of a "post-industrial society." In Bell's distinctions, preindustrial societies, based on agriculture, mining, fishing, and timber, were predominately *extractive*. Industrial societies used machine technology and were predominately concerned with *fabricating*. Postindustrial societies are shaped by intellectual technology and are primarily concerned with *processing* information and knowledge. These social formations are overlapping and not exclusive. The growth of personal services—hotels, restaurants, travel, entertainment—is a feature of "post-industrial society."

For a critique of Bell, see Daniel Lyon, *The Information Society: Issues and Illusions* (New York: Harper and Row, 1988).

47. Williams, *Dream Worlds,* 106.
48. Thorstein Veblen, *The Theory of the Leisure Class,* in *The Portable Veblen,* edited by Max Lerner (New York: Penguin Books, 1976), 125.
49. By the end of the nineteenth century, women had become the primary domestic consumers. See Jean Gordon and Jan McArthur, "American Women and Domestic Consumption, 1800–1920: Four Interpretive Themes," *Journal of American Culture* (n.d., after 1983); Remy G. Saisselin, *The Bourgeois and the Bibelot* (New Brunswick, N.J.: Rutgers University Press, 1984); Williams, *Dream Worlds;* Judith Williamson, *Consuming Passions: The Dynamics of Popular Culture* (London: Marion Boyers, 1987); Wilson, *Adorned in Dreams;* Stuart Ewen and Elizabeth Ewen, *Channels of Desire: Mass Images and the Shaping of American Consciousness* (New York: McGraw-Hill, 1982); Bowlby, *Just Looking.* In this context, Bowlby discusses Marx's description of the consumer-consumed relation in sexual terms.
50. Agora: from Greek, *ageirein* = to assemble, gathering place, especially the market. *Agoraphobia* literally means fear of the market, but has become a term in contemporary symptomatology which refers to fear of open spaces of the public sphere.
51. The first paragraph of Benjamin's "Paris—Capital of the Nineteenth Century" announces: "Sie sind die Vorläufer der Warenhäuser."
52. Dorothy Davis, *A History of Shopping* (London: Routledge and Kegan Paul, 1966), 291.
53. In her biography, *Eighty Years and More (1815–1897)* (London: T. Fisher Unwin, 1898), Elizabeth Cady Stanton tells the story of the Congressman's Wife who needed a new stove but waited for her husband to buy it for her. As quoted in Lloyd Wendt and Herman Kagan, *Give the Lady What She Wants* (Chicago: Rand McNally and Co., 1952), Stanton always ended her story of the Congressman's Wife with the rally cry: "GO OUT AND BUY." Although the story as related in her biography seems to match Wendt's account, a search through Stanton's speeches did not turn up this exact slogan.

    See also Williams's discussion of the alliance between feminism and the consumer movement at a later date: the first international conference of Shoppers Leagues in 1904. See Williams, *Dream Worlds,* 276–321.
54. One of Thomas Cook's early female tourists wrote:

> Many of our friends thought us too independent and adventurous to leave the shores of England and thus plunge into foreign countries not beneath Victoria's sway, with no protecting relatives, but we can only say that we hope this will not be our last excursion of this kind. We could venture anywhere with such a guide and guardian as Mr. Cook for there was not one of his party but felt perfectly safe when under his care.

Quoted in Maxine Feiffer, *Tourism in History: From Imperial Rome to the Present* (New York: Stein and Day, 1985), 170. See also Geoffrey Trease, *The Grand Tour* (New York: Holt, Rinehart and Winston, 1967); John A. Jakle, *The Tourist: Travel in Twentieth Century North America* (Lincoln: University of Nebraska Press, 1985).

55. Cook's first tour was organized for the Leicester Temperance Society in July 1841. For a reduced group fare of a shilling apiece, nearly six hundred men and women traveled on the Midland Railway to Loughborough for an all-day Temperance Rally. See Edmund Swinglehurst, *Cook's Tours: The Story of Popular Travel* (Poole, Dorset: Blanford Press, 1982); John Pudney, *The Thomas Cook Story* (London: Michael Joseph, 1953).

The relation between alcohol consumption and tourism and cinema is a subject for further analysis. In 1910, the Massachusetts Commission on Cost of Living reported, "It is worthy to note that wherever the 'motion picture' houses are opened, the patronage of liquor saloons in the neighborhood shows a falling off." (Quoted in Carolyn Shaw Bell, *Consumer Choice in the American Economy* [New York: Random House, 1967], 36.)

In one of D. W. Griffith's many attempts to defend the still-fledgling *pictograph* as socially redeemable entertainment, Griffith described the cinema as a saloon surrogate, displacing one site for consumption with another. "I believe in the motion picture not only as a means of amusement," said Griffith in an interview in 1915,

> but as a moral and educational force. Do you know that there has been less drinking in the past five years and that it is because of the motion pictures? It is absolutely true. . . . No man drinks for the sake of drinking. He drinks because he has no place to go. Man is a moving animal. The bigger the man the more he has need of activity. It isn't so with women. Their natures are different. The motion pictures give a man a place to go beside a saloon. He drops in to see a picture. *He has been somewhere. He has seen something.* He comes out and goes home in a different state than if he had gone to a saloon. The domestic unities are preserved.

In this defense, a transformation is as much incurred by the activity of getting out of the house as by what is *seen* in the theater. Griffith's tone is not surprising. (Nor are his assumptions about women—leaving the female spectator, and the female alcoholic, simply unaddressed. The "moral and educational force" is aimed, here, at a male subject.) Griffith's quasi-theoretic speculations about the relation of cinema to alcoholism (the concomitant similarities of incorporation, habituation, desire for loss of self, replacement with other) are twisted into a suggestion of the cinema as *cure*, an effective substitute for drinking and vice, a potential superintendent of domestic unity. As an argument for the cinema as an instrument of social reform, Griffith does not defend it in terms of narrative content, but describes instead the sense of *destination* offered, a place, a *somewhere* outside of the home. But Griffith also used the family and its unity as a regulatory narrative force—all threats to its sanctity were central devices for catalyzing his one-reel dramas; the restoration of its hold central to his ideas of narrative closure.

56. To pursue the subjective effects of tourism, it is helpful to briefly distinguish between exploration, travel, and tourism. *Exploration* implies an excursion into the entirely unknown, uncharted, and never repeatable. *Travel* has a more predictable itinerary but still has possibilities for misadventures and a latitude for unplanned experiences. *Tourism*, on the other hand, prepared by mass publicity and cliché, is designed to encode the foreign in the familiar, to introduce the new and exotic from a vantage mitigated by comfort and expectations. The correlations between tourism and structured fantasy seem quite suggestive—a cruise has its own narrative codes involving departure, engagement, and conclusion.

57. Roland Barthes, "Dining Car," in *The Eiffel Tower and Other Mythologies,* translated by Richard Howard (New York: Hill and Wang, 1984), 144.

Thomas Pynchon, in his novel *V.,* (New York: Lippincott, 1963) makes frequent reference to what he terms "Baedeker land." One of the characters, in fact, comes to live "entirely within the Baedeker world—as much a feature of the topography as the other automata: waiters, porters, cabmen, clerks" (58–59). Another exhibits "the honest concern and frustration of any English tourist confronted with a happening outside the ken of his Baedeker or the power of Cook's to deal with it" (174). Of those (packaged) tourists, Pynchon wonders, "What was it that drove them to Thomas Cook & Son in ever-increasing flocks every year to let themselves in for the Campagna's fevers, the Levant's squalor, the septic foods of Greece?" Pynchon's reply (to his own question) is, tellingly, gendered: "To return to Ludgate Circus at the desolate end of every season having caressed the skin of each alien place, a peregrine or Don Juan of cities but no more able to talk of any mistress's heart than to cease keeping that interminable Catalogue, that non picciol' liboro" (168–169).

58. Dean MacCannell, *The Tourist: A New Theory of the Leisure Class* (New York: Schocken, 1989), 11. In his introduction to the 1989 edition of the book, MacCannell expertly draws the parallels between postmodernism and tourism:

The need to be postmodern can thus be read as the same as the desire to be a
tourist: both seek to empower *modern* culture and its conscience by neutralizing
everything that might destroy it from within. (xiii)

59. Altick, *Shows of London,* 478.

"Appetite-whetters for the real thing": Hansen has shown how the discourse about cinema in the trade press from 1910 to 1916 often argued for the cinema as a substitute for the privileges of mass tourism. See Miriam Hansen, "Universal Language and Democratic Culture: Myths of Origin in Early American Cinema," in *Mythos und Aufklärung in Der Amerikanischen Literatur (Myth and Enlightenment in American Literature),* edited by Dieter Meindl and Friedrich W. Horlacher (Erlangen, 1985), 321–351.

Hansen also traces this line of argument about the cinema's compensatory function for those unable to travel in chapter 3 of *Babel and Babylon.* Quoting a 1908 article on exhibition:

> He would bring to the heart of the Ghetto the heart of Nature itself, and even though devoid of color and freshness and odor, he would at least suggest something of that flowering world which is farthest away from asphalt and brick.

From "Where They Perform Shakespeare for Five Cents," *Theatre Magazine* 8.92 (October 1908): 265; quoted in Hansen, *Babel and Babylon,* 110.

60. See also Robert Harbison, *Eccentric Spaces* (New York: Alfred Knopf, 1977). Harbison's eccentric and brilliant book draws connections between nineteenth-century topographical fictions and architectural spaces, gardens, sanctums, and iron and glass structures.

61. *PW,* 1060–1067. Benjamin wrote this short piece in 1929, and although it was never published, it seems to be one of the few (in addition to the 1935 and 1939 exposés) finished passages from *Passagen-Werk.* In his reflection on the Grandville lithograph, "The Flâneur of the Universe," Benjamin draws the connection between the Saint-Simonian ideas of interplanetary travel and communication and the familiar flânerie of the passages.

62. Also, Kracauer's dissertation in 1915 was on iron construction (*Eisenbau*).

63. Walter Benjamin, "Der Saturnring oder Etwas von Eisenbau," in *PW,* 1060–1067. Translation mine.

In Konvolut G of *Passagen-Werk,* "Exhibitions, Advertisements, Grandville," Benjamin notes: "If the commodity is a fetish, Grandville is its magician priest" (*PW,* 249). Buck-Morss documents that Benjamin's interest in Grandville was spurred by Disney films in the 1930s.

64. "Der Saturnring oder Etwas von Eisenbau." Translation mine.

65. Baltard's *Les Halles* was torn down in the late 1970s to build what is now the extensive underground shopping mall, still deemed Les Halles.

66. See Schivelbusch, *Railway Journey;* Lynne Kirby, "The Railroad and the Cinema, 1895–1929: Technologies, Institutions and Aesthetics," Ph.D. diss., University of California at Los Angeles, 1989.

67. Georg Kohlmaier and Barna von Sartory, *Houses of Glass: A Nineteenth Century Building Type* (London and Cambridge, Mass.: MIT Press, 1986), 2.

68. Ibid., 1.

69. Vidler, "Scenes of the Street," 81.

70. "Dialektik der Flanerie: das Interieur als Straße (Luxus); die Straße als Interieur (Elend)." *PW,* 1215.

71. See Schivelbusch, *Disenchanted Night.*

72. Vidler, "Scenes of the Street," 94–95.

73. Le Corbusier, *The City of Tomorrow and Its Planning,* translated from *Urbanisme* by Frederick Etchells (New York: Dover Publications, 1987), 131.

74. Davis, *History of Shopping,* 191–192.

75. Charles Knight (1851) quoted in Alison Adburgham, *Shops and Shopping 1800–1914* (London: George Allen and Unwin, 1964), 96, and in Schivelbusch, *Disenchanted Night.* For a discussion of the history of mirrors, see Benjamin Goldberg, *The Mirror and Man* (Charlottesville: University of Virginia, 1985). Goldberg's chapter, "Seventeenth and Eighteenth Centuries," details the mid-seventeenth-century changes in methods for casting glass which helped to produce larger mirrors, free of bubbles, and flat planar surfaces that gave increasingly precise reflections.

76. Baudrillard describes this "calculus of objects" on display in *La Société de consommation* (Paris: Gallimard, 1970).

77. From 1897 to 1902, Baum edited a trade journal, *The Show Window: A Monthly Journal of Practical Window Trimming.* For an excellent analysis of the relation of Baum's work on window display to the representation of advertising and consumerism in *The Wonderful Wizard of Oz,* see Stuart Culver, "What Manikins Want: The Wonderful World of Oz and the Art of Decorating Dry Goods Windows," in *Representations* 21 (Winter 1988): 97–116.

   L. Frank Baum, Frederick Kiesler, Vincente Minelli, and Andy Warhol each began their careers as window dressers.

78. L. Frank Baum, *The Art of Decorating Dry Goods Windows and Interiors* (Chicago: Show Window, 1890), 146.

79. Ibid., 82.

80. Davis, *History of Shopping,* 292. Also see William Leach, "Strategies of Display and the Production of Desire," in *Consuming Visions: Accumulation and Display of Goods in America, 1880–1920,* edited by Simon J. Bronner (New York: Norton, 1989), 23–36.

81. See Charles Eckert, "The Carole Lombard in Macy's Window," *Quarterly Review of Film Studies,* 3, no. 1 (Winter 1978); Doane, *Desire to Desire;* Jane Gaines, "The

Queen Christina Tie-Ups: Convergence of Show Window and Screen," in the special issue "Female Representation and Consumer Culture," edited by Michael Renov and Jane Gaines, *Quarterly Review of Film and Video* 11, no. 1 (Winter 1989): 35–60. *Window-Shopping* is also the American title of Chantal Akerman's 1986 musical set in a shopping mall.

82. Mark Girouard, *Cities and People* (New Haven: Yale University Press, 1985).

83. N. M. Karamzin, *Letters of a Russian Traveller* (New York: 1957), quoted in Johann Friedrich Geist, *Arcades: History of a Building Type*, translated by Jane O. Newman and John Smith (Cambridge, Mass.: MIT Press, 1985), 215.

84. Quoted in Vidler, "Scenes of the Street," 50.

85. Honoré de Balzac, *Lost Illusions*, translated by Herbert J. Hunt (Middlesex, England: Penguin Books, 1971), 260–266.

86. This description is from Vidler, "Scenes of the Street," 53, 77.

87. In an excellent etymology of the sixteenth- and seventeenth-century uses of the term "market" to refer to both *process* and *place,* Jean-Christophe Agnew has discussed the theatrical nature of the "act" of consumption:

> A certain theatricality, quite divorced from civic ceremony, attaches itself to a placeless market in which impersonality and impersonation have suddenly thrust themselves forward as vexing issues. . . . With its indefinite extension in space and in time, the liminal threatens to become coextensive with all that a deritualized market touches. Life thereby becomes a multiplicity of thresholds, a profusion of potential "passages" or opportunity costs which run alongside experience itself, infusing public life with the intimation of private calculation and private life with the specter of public exchangeability." (112)

See "The Threshold of Exchange: Speculations on the Market," *Radical History Review* 21 (Fall 1979): 99–118. For a related discussion of consumption as spectacle see Richard Sennett, *The Fall of Public Man* (New York: Vintage, 1974).

88. Geist, *Arcades.* Geist provides an excellent and thorough international architectural history of the arcades. See also Bertrand Lemoine, *Les Passages Couvert en France* (Paris: Délégation à l'Action Artistique de la Ville de Paris, 1989); Patrice de Moncan and Christian Mahout, *Les Passages de Paris* (Paris: Seesam Editions, 1990).

89. Geist, *Arcades,* 12, 54.

90. Louis Aragon, *Paris Peasant,* translated by Simon Watson Taylor (London: Picador, 1980), 28–30.

91. Ibid., 48.

92. Ibid., 49.

93. Ibid., 36.

94. Gershom Scholem, *Walter Benjamin: The Story of a Friendship* (London: Faber and Faber, 1982), 135. Benjamin's reaction to the Aragon novel was so unsettling that, as he wrote to Adorno in 1935, his heartbeat was so strong when he read it in bed in the evenings that he had to put the book out of his hand:

> Da steht an ihrem Beginn Aragon—der Paysan de Paris, von dem ich des abends im Bett niemehr als zwei bis drei Seiten lesen konnte, weil mein Herzklopfen dann so stark wurde, daß ich das Buch aus der Hand legen mußte. (*PW,* 1117)

95. Franz Hessel, *Spazieren in Berlin* (Vienna and Leipzig: Dr. Hans Epstein Verlag, 1929). This volume has been reprinted as *Ein Flaneur in Berlin* (Berlin: Arsenal, 1984).

96. Franz Hessel, "Von der schwierigen Kunst spazieren zu gehen," in *Ermunterung zum Genuß,* edited by Karin Grund and Bernd Witte (West Berlin: Brinkmann & Bose, 1981), 54. See also *Ein Flaneur in Berlin;* Eckhardt Köhn, *Strassenrausch: Flanerie und kleine Form Versuch zur Literaturgeschichte des Flaneurs von 1830–1933* (Berlin: Das Arsenal, 1989).

97. Walter Benjamin, *Berliner Chronik* (Frankfurt am Main: Suhrkamp Verlag, 1970):

> In jenen frühen Jahren lernte ich "die Stadt" nur als den Schauplatz der "Besorgungen" kennen. . . . Eine Reihe unerforschlicher Massive nein Höhlen von Waren—das was "die Stadt." (60)

Translated as, "A Berlin Chronicle," in *Reflections:*

> In those early years I got to know the "town" only as the theater of purchases. . . . An impenetrable chain of mountains, no, caverns of commodities—that was "the town." (40)

98. Hannah Arendt, "Introduction" to Walter Benjamin's *Illuminations,* 19.

99. "Telescopage der Vergangenheit durch die Gegenwart," *PW,* 588. The Konvolut that contains this descriptive phrase, "Erkenntinistheoretisches, Theorie des Fortschritts," was translated in *The Philosophical Forum* 15, nos. 1–2 (Fall 1983–1984): 1–40.

100. Benjamin reviewed Hessel's book *Spazieren in Berlin* in his essay, "Die Wiederkehr des Flaneurs": "The city as a mnemotechnical expedient to solitary walking, calls up one's childhood and youth, more as a story." (Benjamin, *Angelus Novus* [Frankfurt am Main: Surkampf Verlag, 1966], 416).

101. Ibid., 416–422. "Brandmauern ihr Schreibpult, Zeitungskioske ihre Bibliotheken, Briefkästen ihre Bronzen, Bänke ihr Boudoir und die Caféterrasse der Erker" (418).

102. Benjamin, "Paris of the Second Empire," 36–37.

103. Benjamin quotes Balzac, "Paris—Capital of the Nineteenth Century," 157.

104. Geist, *Arcades,* 156.

105. Ibid.

106. Ibid., 157.

107. Siegfried Kracauer, "Abschied von der Lindenpassage," quoted in Geist, *Arcades,* 160. (The translation was changed to retain the word "passage.")

> Jetzt, unterm neuen Glasdach und im Marmorschmuck, gemahnt die ehemalige Passage an das Vestibül eines Kaufhauses. Die Läden dauren zwar fort, aber ihre Ansichtkarten sind Stapelware, ihr Welt-panorama ist durch de Film überholt und ihr anatomisches Museum längst keine Sensation mehr.

See Siegfried Kracauer, "Abschied von der Lindenpassage," in *Straßen in Berlin und anderswo* (Berlin: Arsenal, 1987), 29.

108. Geist, *Arcades,* 158.

109. Kracauer, "Abschied," 25; translated in Geist, *Arcades,* 158. (Again, the Geist translation was changed to keep the word "passage.")

110. Kracauer, "Abschied," 26; Geist, *Arcades,* 159.

111. Ibid.

112. Ibid.

113. In France, Bon Marché opens in 1852 (the Eiffel and Boileau store was built between 1869 and 1887); Printemps and Samaritaine were founded in 1870, Galleries Lafayette was founded in 1895. In the United States, Alexander Tunney Stewart opened his store "The Marble Palace" in New York in 1846; Marshall Field's opened in Chicago in 1879 and moved into its current store in 1902; Wanamaker's opened in Philadelphia in 1911; Lord & Taylor opened in New York in 1914.

    H. Pasdermadjian, *The Department Store: Its Origins, Evolution and Economics* (London: Newman Books, 1954) was one of the earliest definitive histories of the department store. See also Miller, *Bon Marché;* Wendt and Kogan, *Give the Lady;* Susan Porter Benson, *Counter-Cultures: Saleswomen, Managers, and Customers in American Department Stores 1890–1940* (Urbana: University of Illinois Press, 1986); Susan Porter Benson, "Palace of Consumption and Machine for Selling: The American Department Store 1880–1940," *Radical History Review* 21 (Fall 1979): 199–225; Leach, "Transformations," 319–342; Klaus Strohmeyer, *Wärenhauser: Geschichte, Blüte und Untergang im Warenmeer* (Berlin: Verlag Klaus Wagenbach, 1980).

114. Siegfried Giedion, *Time, Space, and Architecture: The Growth of a New Tradition* (Cambridge, Mass.: Harvard University Press, 1941), 234.

115. *PW,* 571. "Denn der gemalte Sommerhimmel, der aus Arkaden in den Arbeitssaal der pariser Nationalbibliothek hinuntersieht, hat seine träumerische, lichtlose Decke über ihr ausgebreitet."

Translated in *The Philosophical Forum* 15, no. 1–2 (Fall 1983–1984): 1–40.

116. See Saisselin, *The Bourgeois and the Bibelot* (New Brunswick, N.J.: Rutgers University Press, 1984).

The 1894 Baedeker to Paris described:

> The GRAND MAGASINS DE NOUVEAUTES . . . form a very important feature of modern Paris, and owing to the abundant choice of goods they offer are gradually superseding the smaller shops. Perhaps the most important of these establishment is the *Bon Marché*. . . . the *Grand Magasins du Louvre,* in the Place du Palais Royal, with reading and writing rooms, and a buffet where refreshments are dispensed gratis.

See Karl Baedeker, *Paris and Environs* (Leipsic: Karl Baedeker, 1894), 35.

117. In Paris in 1825, Le Grand Bazar opened on Rue St. Honore, in 1827, Bazar de l'Industrie, in 1829, Bazar de Boufflers, and in 1830, Galerie de Fer. Dry goods stores known as *magasins de nouveautés* dealt with textile goods—silks, woolens, shawls, and lingerie changed the retailing market in the 1830s and 1840s.

118. Giedion, *Time, Space, and Architecture,* 234.

119. Ewen and Ewen, *Channels of Desire,* 69.

120. In 1857, the first passenger elevator in a commercial department store was used in the cast-iron building at the corner of Broadway and Broome in New York. Macy's and Wanamaker's installed electric lights in the late 1870s, Marshall Field's in 1882; the three stores added ventilating systems in the 1880s.

121. Porter Benson, *Counter-Cultures,* 18–20.

122. Altick supplies the statistic that the first passenger elevator was used in the London Coliseum in 1832. Pasdermadjian records that the first elevator was installed at Strawbridge and Clothier in Philadelphia in 1865; and in Macy's and Wanamaker's in the 1880s (Pasdermadjian, *Department Store,* 25); Porter Benson also supplies statistics on escalators: in 1911, seventeen stores had them; in 1936, six hundred stores had them (*Counter-Cultures,* 39). Pneumatic tubes were introduced to Macy's in 1893.

123. Porter Benson, *Counter-Cultures,* 3.

Pasdermadjian describes this:

> The free entrance principle also revealed itself as a powerful asset. It gave the woman purchaser the opportunity to "shop" that is to say to go about through the various departments of a department store, or the corresponding

departments of different department stores, comparing qualities, prices, styles and values to her heart's content. In itself the principle of "shopping" was not new. It was already present in the public food markets. The originality of the department store consisted in the introduction of it into fields from which it had been banished: the textile and home furnishing trades. (*Department Store*, 12)

Or as Robert A. M. Stern dramatically put it:

Merchants like Field and Wanamaker, who orchestrated the transformation of the utilitarian dry goods store into a palace of consumption, were canny enough to realize that labor-saving devices combined with cheap domestic help were enabling affluent women, long relegated to the domestic hearth, to assume a major role in the urban drama. Politicians and lawyers could act out their public roles in the templelike settings of statehouse and courthouse, merchants and bankers could pursue their tasks in equally impressive surroundings, and now, with the department store, women could play their part in a setting that was the equivalent and more.

From Robert A. M. Stern, *Pride of Place: Building the American Dream* (Boston: Houghton Mifflin), 1986, 230–231.

124. Siegfried Kracauer, "Die kleinen Ladenmädchen gehen ins Kino," in *Das Ornament der Masse* (Frankfurt am Main: Suhrkamp, 1963). As Patrice Petro has demonstrated, "The cinema, in particular, became one of the few places in German cultural life that afforded women a prominent position and a privileged access." Petro argues that the "growing visibility" of Weimar women (at work and at the movies) explains both the defensive reaction toward women in various discourses during the Weimar years and also helps to account for the suspicions toward the mass cultural forms that attracted women as spectators. See Patrice Petro, "Modernity and Mass Culture in Weimar: Contours of a Discourse on Sexuality in Early Theories of Perception and Representation," *New German Critique* 40 (Winter 1987): 141; *Joyless Streets: Women and Melodramatic Representation in Weimar Germany* (Princeton: Princeton University Press, 1989). For a further analysis of Kracauer's discussion of female spectatorship see Heide Schlüpmann, "Phenomenology of Film: On Siegfried Kracauer's Writings of the 1920s," and Sabine Hake, "Girls and Crisis: The Other Side of Diversion." in *New German Critique* 40 (Winter 1987): 97–114; 147–164.

125. For a discussion of the historical interactions between film viewing and shopping see: Jeanne Allen, "The Film Viewer as Consumer," *Quarterly Review of Film Studies* 5, no. 4 (Fall 1980): 481–499; Eckert, "Carole Lombard," 1–21; Gaines, "Queen Christina Tie-Ups," 35–61.

126. Benjamin, "Paris—Capital of the Nineteenth Century," 165; *PW*, 50.
127. *PW*, 588.
128. *The Crystal Palace Exhibition Illustrated Catalog,* reprint of unabridged special issue of *The Art-Journal* 1851 (New York: Dover Publications, 1970), xi.
129. "une tache d'encre l'ombre odieuse de l'odieuse colonne de tôle boulonée." The public protest signed by outraged artists (including Guy de Maupassant and Alexandre Dumas) is quoted in Richard D. Mandell, *Paris 1900* (Toronto: University of Toronto Press, 1967), 19–20.
130. Roland Barthes writes evocatively of the panoramic vista from the Eiffel Tower as a "new sensibility of vision," which is almost responsible for the structuralist method:

Every visitor to the Tower makes structuralism without knowing it. . . . he separates and groups: Paris offers itself to him as an object virtually prepared, exposed to the intelligence, but which he must himself construct by a final activity of the mind. . . . This activity of the mind, conveyed by the tourist's modest glance, has a name: decipherment. (10–11)

See Roland Barthes, "The Eiffel Tower," in *The Eiffel Tower and Other Mythologies,* translated by Richard Howard (New York: Hill and Wang, 1979), 3–19.

Stephan Oettermann writes on the freeing of the gaze ("die Befreiung des Blickes") as a result of the panoramic aerial perspective of the balloonist. See Oettermann, *Das Panorama,* 7–19.

131. This included Italy, Turkey, Great Britain, Norway, Spain, Monaco, Sweden, Serbia, Russia, Germany, Belgium, Switzerland, Austria-Hungary, Japan, and the United States. The United States was insulted at first because it was not at first offered a place in the front row.
132. [La sensation était extraordinaire, et beaucoup de spectateurs éprouvaient le même vertige que celui que donne une ascension vrai. La vue animée de Paris, entre autres avec le flot de ses voitures et ses passants arrêtes qui regardaient le ciel, constituait une nouveauté sensationnelle.] For Grimoin-Sanson's description of the cinéorama see "Le cinéma des origines," *Cinema D'Aujourd'hui* 9 (Automne, 1976): 94–99. Translation mine.
133. For a detailed history of this form of exhibition, see Raymond Fielding, "Hale's Tours: Ultrarealism in the Pre-1910 Motion Picture," in *Film Before Griffith,* edited by John L. Fell (Berkeley: University of California Press, 1983), 116–131.
134. The Galérie des Machines was the largest of the iron and glass halls. The Grand Palais had glass and steel domes that, like Paxton's Crystal Palace built for the 1851 London Exhibition, vaulted a spectacular interior space full of painting and sculp-

ture. In "Le Palais de l'Optique" one could see either a magnified drop of water from the Seine or look through a telescope to the moon; under the Trocadero was a diorama-filled cavern of automobiles and bicycles.

135. See Mandell, *Paris 1900*.

136. Musser, *Emergence of the Cinema*, 278.

137. Although in all likelihood this story is apocryphal, many historians cite it with authority. For a moderately cynical account, see Paul Hammond, *Marvelous Méliès* (New York: St. Martin's Press, 1975).

138. Musser implies a continuity match between the day and night panoramas, linked by the continous panning movement of the camera. In Musser's description (Musser uses a different title than the Library of Congress), *Pan-American Exposition by Night* was:

a technical tour de force that began with a smooth, sweeping panorama of the electric tower during the day and continued at night in the same direction and at the same pace, with the lights of the tower providing a decorative image. . . . The time-change was modeled on a popular stereopticon convention–day-to-night dissolving views. (*Emergence of the Cinema*, 317)

From my viewing of the two films, *Circular Panorama of Electric Tower* and *The Panorama of Esplanade at Night,* a rough continuity based on direction and movement would have been possible if the films were exhibited together without titles separating them, but the day panorama and the night panorama are taken from different camera distances and positions.

Although Musser's description seems to differ only slightly from mine, his suggestion that the two films were "edited" together, into one smoothly executed pan, would mean that the panoramic film may have aimed for spatial verisimilitude but equally challenged a verisimilitude of the temporal.

139. Tom Gunning, "The Cinema of Attraction(s): Early Film, Its Spectator and the Avant-Garde," *Wide Angle* 8, nos. 3-4 (1986): 63–70; also republished in *Early Cinema: Space, Frame, Narrative,* edited by Thomas Elsaesser (Bloomington: Indiana University Press, 1991), 56–62.

140. Ibid., 58.

141. Ibid., 57, 61. See also Tom Gunning, "An Unseen Energy Swallows Space: The Space in Early Film and Its Relation to American Avant Garde Film," in *Film Before Griffith,* 355–366.

142. See Gary Kyriazi, *Great American Amusement Parks: A Pictorial History* (Seacaucus, N.J.: Castle Books, 1976); John F. Kasson, *Amusing the Millions: Coney Island at the Turn of the Century* (New York: Hill and Wang, 1978); Peiss, *Cheap Amusements.*

143. See Peiss, *Cheap Amusements.*

144. The Giralda tower was also copied in the Los Angeles Waterworks Building, which now houses the Margaret Herrick Library of the Academy of Motion Pictures. It seems fitting that a library dedicated to the history of motion pictures should be housed in a building that is an architectural simulation of a foreign monument.

145. The Elephant Hotel built in 1882 was a 122-foot-high structure in the shape of an elephant; one front leg contained a cigar store, the other front leg contained a diorama. The entrance was up one hind leg, the exit down the other. A building in the shape of an elephant would fit into what Robert Venturi and Denise Scott Brown call a "duck." See Robert Venturi, Denise Scott Brown, and Steven Izenour, *Learning from Las Vegas* (Cambridge, Mass.: MIT Press, 1972).

146. Kasson, *Amusing the Millions,* 50.

147. In a 1991 PBS documentary, "Coney Island: Sodom by the Sea," Ric Burns compiled films of many of Coney Island's attractions. As they exited the "Blow-Hole Theater," both men and women were blown by a strong air current that lifted women's skirts and whisked off men's hats in a spectacle of display for passersby and for the crowds waiting to enter.

    Writer and filmmaker Lynne Tillman has drawn the historical relation between Freud's collection of antiquities and his fascination with Coney Island:

    > Monuments to voyeurism and exhibitionism, Coney's houses of mirth, mayhem and curiosity may have been homes away from home for Freud, who could have produced magnificent associations from rides and spectacles, to obsessions and sessions, to neurotic displays and case histories. Or he may have viewed Coney Island as the place where his theories were enacted in theaters of pleasure and danger, instincts and their vicissitudes.

    See "Madame Realism in Freud's Dreamland," *Art in America* 79, no. 1 (January 1991): 88–95.

148. See Charles Musser, "The Travel Genre in 1903–1904: Moving toward Fictional Narrative," *Iris* 2, no. 1 (1984): 47–59; reprinted in *Early Cinema*, 123–132.

149. Dr. Martin Arthur Couney, in Pilat and Ranson, *Sodom by the Sea: An Affectionate History of Coney Island* (1941), quoted in Kasson, *Amusing the Millions,* 112.

150. Scott Bukatman has suggested a relation between Disneyland and the shopping mall, and has further correlated the "mutually reinforcing symbiosis of the Disney-land/world/mall" with the "implosive reality of television." See Scott Bukatman, "There's Always a Tomorrowland: Disney and the Hypercinematic Experience," *October* 57 (Summer 1991): 55–78.

151. Geist, *Arcades,* 490.

152. While the Musée Grevin is still in the Passage Jouffroy today, it has another branch in the underground shopping mall of Les Halles, proving, as does the placement of multiplex cinemas and Videotheque in Les Halles, that these spectacles are extensions of a mobilized gaze past shop windows.

A comparison of the 1894 and the 1910 Baedeker guides illustrate some of these changes. In Section 9—Theatres, Circuses, Music Halls—the 1894 Baedeker (Baedeker, *Paris and Environs*) claims, "Panoramas, which a few years ago were fairly numerous, seem to be losing their vogue once more" (32). In the section on Boulevard Montmartre, the 1894 guide describes the right side of the Seine:

> The cafés become more numerous, and the shops more attractive. On the left stand the *Théâtre des Variétés*. On the same side is the *Passage des Panoramas*, and opposite to it the *Passage Jouffroy*. These two arcades, with their handsome shops, are generally thronged with foot-passengers, especially towards evening. In the Passage Jouffroy are the *Musée Grévin* and the *Petit Casino*. (76)

In the 1910 edition (Karl Baedeker, *Paris and Environs* [Leipzig: Karl Baedeker, 1910]), Section 9—Theatres, Music Halls, Balls, Circuses—lists:

> The MUSEE GREVIN, Boul Monmartre 10, adjoining the Passage Jouffroy, founded by the celebrated draughtsman Grevin, is a collection of wax figures, resembling Madame Tussaud's in London. . . .
> At the THEATRE ROBERT HOUDIN, Boul des Italiens, 8, acrobatic performances and exhibitions of conjuring are given in the afternoon and cinematograph shows in the evening.
> CINEMATOGRAPHS [eight listed]. (44)

153. Quoted in Terry Ramsaye, *Million and One Nights* (New York: Simon and Schuster, 1926), 152–161.

154. *The Time Machine* has a complex bibliographic history, a total of seven versions, only five of which survive. An early draft, the 1888 "Chronic Argonauts," contained only a vague idea of time travel. Between March and June loosely connected articles appeared in the *National Observer*. The novel was serialized in five installments in *The New Review* from January to May 1895 and then published as a book at the end of May. See Bernard Bergonzi, "The Publication of *The Time Machine* 1894–1895" (reprinted from *Review of English Studies* 11 [1960]: 42–51) in *Science Fiction: The Other Side of Realism,* edited by Thomas D. Carlson (Bowling Green, Ohio: Bowling Green University Press, 1971), 204–215.

155. H. G. Wells, *The Time Machine* (New York: Bantam Books, 1982) 8–12.

156. Ibid., 21.

157. Ibid.

158. Ibid., 38.

159. Ibid., 107.

160. Quoted in Ramsaye, *Million and One Nights*, 152–161. This was reprinted in *Focus on the Science Fiction Film*, edited by William Johnson (Englewood Cliffs, N.J.: Prentice-Hall, 1972), 18–26. The following references will be to the Johnson edition.

161. Ramsaye, *Million and One Nights*, 23. The Paul patent application included features of forward and backward movement through time. Ramsaye writes, "The photoplay of today moves backward and forward through Time with facile miracle from the Present into the Past and Future by the cutback, flashback, and vision scenes" (22).

162. Quoted in Ramsaye, *Million and One Nights*, 152–161.

163. The material base of the two famed "fathers" of cinema—Lumière and Méliès—demonstrates that their cinematic experiments were, in each case, made possible by family fortunes that capitalized on two distinct aspects of nineteenth-century life: the Lumière family fortune was made at a photographic plate manufacturer in Lyon; the Méliès family fortune was made from a shoe factory in Montreuil. The photographic plate fortune was made on the obsession to make static visual records (the "virtual" gaze) and the shoe factory fortune was made on the pedestrian flâneur who wore out his shoe leather in an era of city pavements (the "mobilized" gaze). Both family "fortunes" subsidized the sons' experiments.

Of course, there were other inventors, a list that includes Georges Demeny, William Friese-Green, W. K. L. Dickson, and others, but if we consider Lumière and Méliès as paradigms of the two aesthetic lineages that Bazin, Kracauer, and others trace through the history of cinema, the material base of their aesthetics suggest a logic.

PASSAGE II

1. See Musser, "Travel Genre." Musser cites the number of travel films in 1902 and 1903; in the Vitagraph 1903 catalog, half of the features listed were travel subjects, in the 1903 Edison catalog, after *Life of an American Fireman*, sixty-one of the next sixty-two films copyrighted were travel films.

2. The paper print in the Museum of Modern Art collection has these shots in slightly different sequence: HOLD UP IN ITALY, CLIMBING THE PYRAMIDS OF EGYPT, KISSING THE BLARNEY STONE, DOING PARIS, CLIMBING THE ALPS, MUDBATHS OF GERMANY. The MOMA print also has the seasick stateroom scene between Egypt and the Blarney stone.

3. As a contemporary illustration of the virtual replacement for tourism, videotaped "tours" are marketed as both substitute and souvenir:

Select, plan, enjoy and *even remember* your vacation dreams when you return. . . . The next best thing to being there, a Travelview International video captures a "sense of place" impossible to achieve with still photography or brochures. $29.95

YES! *I want to travel the world from the comfort of my own home.* Please send me the following videos (VHS only). (*Tours and Resorts* magazine, July 1989, emphasis added)

Philip K. Dick recurrently uses the concept of memory and virtual tourism. See especially his 1965 story, "We Can Remember It For You Wholesale," in which a "miserable little salaried employee" named Douglas Quail lives in a smog-infested Chicago suburb and fantasizes about visiting Mars. He goes to "Rekal Incorporated" for an "extrafactual memory implant." These preplanned memory packets of "ersatz interplanetary travel" come with "proof artifacts"—ticket stub, color postcards, and movie film. Yet Quail, it turns out, has actually been to Mars and he cannot tell whether his memory of the planet is a false memory or a real one. Because his real memory (of being an Interplan assassin on Mars) is dangerous, the only solution for Quail is to have an Interplan psychiatrist implant a more extreme extrafactual memory. See "We Can Remember It for You Wholesale," in *The Collected Stories of Philip K. Dick,* vol. 2 (New York: Citadel Twilight Books, 1990), 35–52. The 1989 film *Total Recall* was based on this story.

4. Benjamin, "Work of Art," 226. See Annette Michelson's discussion of *Paris Qui Dort* in the context of Dziga Vertov's montage strategies in "*The Man with the Movie Camera:* From Magician to Epistemologist," *Artforum* 10, no. 7 (1972): 62–72.

    Michelson relates that Dziga Vertov saw *Paris Qui Dort* in Paris in 1926 and planned to make a similar film of Moscow asleep. Vertov's *Man with a Movie Camera* (1929) begins with static shop windows, still mannequins, and motionless factory machines that "come alive" as the city awakens. Vertov's film makes a more direct reference to the cinema camera's capacity to manipulate—stop, reverse, speed up—motion and hence, time.

5. Michelson, "*Man with the Movie Camera.*"

6. *La Jetée* has been written about eloquently by many: Bruce Kawin, "Time and Stasis in *La Jetée,*" *Film Quarterly* 36, no. 1 (Fall 1982): 15–20; Terrence Rafferty, "Marker Changes Trains," *Sight and Sound* 53, no. 4 (Autumn 1984): 284–288; Constance Penley, "Time Travel, Primal Scene, and Critical Dystopia," *Camera Obscura* 15 (Fall 1986): 66–84; reprinted in *Close Encounters: Film, Feminism and Science Fiction,* edited by Constance Penley, Elisabeth Lyon, Lynn Spigel, and Janet Bergstrom (New York: Routledge, 1990), 63–80.

7. Pal won five Academy awards for special effects (*Puppetoons*, 1943; *Destination Moon*, 1950; *When Worlds Collide*, 1951; *The War of the Worlds*, 1953; *The Time Machine*, 1960).

8. Jean Painlevé, *Hyas et Stenorinques, Crustaces Marins* (1925), *Les Oursins* (1925).

9. *Bill and Ted's Excellent Adventure* begins in a typical southern California hyper-suburb, San Dimas, where wanna-be rockers and air-guitarists Bill and Ted are given a class assignment for a "history report." The two travel in a telephone booth–time machine through fiber optic wormholes. "History" is a scavenger hunt and they bring back souvenirs (Napoleon, Beethoven, Socrates) to Southern California. The film ends with a "world tour" through the centuries played as a rock concert in the school gymnasium to a standing ovation. Bill and Ted don't have to crack a book to learn history.

10. In addition to the examples discussed, there have been relatively few attempts to make films with explicit time-travel narratives: *The Times Are Out of Joint* (Gaumont, 1909), *Time Flies* (1944), *Time Slip* (1955).

Penley discusses the time-travel narrative and its reliance on unconscious primal fantasies. Penley's eloquent description of how, in *The Terminator,* every element of domestic technology "turns noir" reads the film "in relation to a set of cultural and psychical conflicts, anxieties and fantasies." Penley argues that dystopic science fiction is a symptom of what Jameson diagnoses as an incapacity to imagine the future. See Penley, "Time Travel."

CHAPTER THREE

1. Christian Slater in *Pump Up the Volume* (written and directed by Allan Moyle, 1990); compare this pronouncement to Arendt's despairing diagnosis:

> The wasteland of the American suburb, or the residential districts of many towns, where all of street life takes place on the roadway and where one can walk on the sidewalks, now reduced to footpaths, for miles on end without encountering a human being, is the very opposite of Paris. What all other cities seem to permit only reluctantly to the dregs of society—strolling, idling, flânerie—Paris streets actually invite every one to do.

Hannah Arendt in her Introduction to Benjamin's *Illuminations,* 21.

2. As Faith Popcorn predicts:

> In Orwell's classic *1984,* the state controlled the screen. In the year 2000, the consumer will control the screen. The computerized shopping screen.
>
> The home cocoon will be the site of the future shopping center. . . . Once home distribution takes hold, stores will gradually become obsolete.

Popcorn foresees that the "going-out-to-shop experience" will only prevail in empo- riums that merge "the atmosphere of department stores/malls with a three-ring circus . . . shopping will seem like visiting Las Vegas or Disney World." See Faith Popcorn, "The End of Shopping," in *The Popcorn Report* (New York: Doubleday, 1991), 164–168. For a history and analysis of the Home Shopping Network, see Mimi White, "The Television Viewer and the Culture of Shop-at-Home Con- sumption," chapter of the forthcoming book *Tele-Advising: Therapeutic Discourse and American Television* (Chapel Hill: University of North Carolina Press, 1992).

3. In a chilling document of market calculation entitled "The Miniaturization of Com- munications," Don Pepper, an executive vice president of a Madison Avenue "busi- ness development" research group, has assessed the change from production econ- omies to "consumer information economies." Pepper predicts the future of communications in the format change from *package* to *conduit*:

    Conduits are on-line, on-stream, continuously broadcast or continuously transmitted. Packages are discreet, tangible things you can take with you . . . a video cassette is a package. . . . In fifty years or so, you'll have almost no packages at all. . . . *You'll no longer be able to go down to the store and buy a video cassette or rent one, because there won't be any such store. Instead you'll pick up your phone and dial a toll free number. You'll hook up your modem on your laser compact disc recorder, and the film you want will be encoded on the disc.* (emphasis added)

    From Don Pepper, "The Miniaturization of Communications," paper delivered to the American Advertising Federation, June 13, 1989. Text courtesy of Lintas: New York.

    The cable television "Viewer's Choice" channel already delivers a "pay per view" movie to any cable subscriber who calls a toll-free number to request it.

4. For recent debates on "virtual reality" technology see *Mondo 2000,* nos. 1, 2, 3; *Virtual Reality: Theory, Practice, and Promise,* edited by Sandra K. Helsel and Judith Paris Roth (Westport, Conn.: Meckler Publishing, 1991); Howard Rheingold, *Vir- tual Reality* (New York: Simon and Schuster, 1991); Myron W. Krueger, *Artificial Reality I* (Reading, Mass.: Addison-Wesley Publishing, 1990) and *Artificial Reality II* (Reading, Mass.: Addison-Wesley Publishing, 1990); Gareth Branwyn, "Salon Virtual," *Utne Reader,* March-April 1991.

5. For an excellent parallel to my discussion, see Peter Gibian, "The Art of Being Off- Center: Shopping Center Spaces and Spectacles," an essay in two parts in *Tabloid: A Review of Mass Culture and Everyday Life,* nos. 4, 5 (1981). Gibian begins with an analysis of Toronto's Eaton Centre and also discusses the historical roots of public spaces of spectacle and consumption. See also: Meaghan Morris, "Things to Do

with Shopping Centres," *Center for Twentieth Century Studies,* working paper no. 1 (Fall 1988).

6. Edgar Lion, *Shopping Centers: Planning, Development and Administration* (New York: John Wiley and Sons, 1976), 1–2.

   The patterns of development in the United States followed regional economic growth; in the 1950s shopping center growth was in California and the Northeast, in the 1960s numbers grew in California and in the South, in the 1970s in Texas, Florida, and Georgia. In 1981, half of the shopping centers in the United States were located in ten states. See John A. Dawson, *Shopping Center Development* (New York: Longman Publications, 1983).

7. When the Bullock's Wilshire Boulevard store opened in Los Angeles in 1928, it revolutionized department store entrances by favoring the driver, instead of the street pedestrian. The grand entrance to the store, complete with an elaborate mural mosaic as a paean to transportation, faced the back parking lot behind the store. The driver was, for the first time, directly equated with the shopper.

8. For a further discussion of "sales breed sales" logic see Pasermadjian, *Department Store,* 12: "It seems that *sales breed sales* and that the most dissimilar objects lend each other mutual support when they are placed next to one another" (emphasis added).

9. See Barry Maitland, *Shopping Malls: Planning and Design* (New York: Construction Press, 1985); Michael J. Bednar, *Interior Pedestrian Spaces* (New York: Whitney Library of Design, 1989); Robert A. M. Stern, "Great Places Within" in *Pride of Place.*

10. Quoted in Leon Whiteson, " 'This is Our Time': And Architect Jon Jerde Is Trying to Write a 'Different Urban Script' for L.A.," *Los Angeles Times,* January 20, 1988.

11. New York City has remained an outpost of resistance to mall culture. As a symptom of the 1980s financial boom, Donald Trump's gilt-encrusted Trump Tower had limited success as a commercially mixed atrium mall. The Marcos-developed Herald Center was less successful. Even before it was repossessed from Imelda Marcos's New York holding company in 1988, the mall had not approached full occupancy. Herald Center conducted a strange relation between the exterior geography of the city and its interior restructuring; each floor was named and designed along the thematics of a New York shopping neighborhood: Soho, Columbus Avenue, Central Park, Madison Avenue, Broadway, Fifth Avenue, Herald Square, The Village. The mall planners for Herald Center intended the space to be a safe haven from the urban reality of New York street life, but New Yorkers and tourists alike preferred the real neighborhoods over their vertically-stacked theme-park equivalents.

12. See Raphael Ghermezian and Hironao Ryoji, *The Proposals for the Largest-Scale Commercial Zone Development: The World's Largest Shopping Center West Edmonton*

Mall and IMI (Tokyo: IMI, 1990). Souvenir booklets of the West Edmonton Mall describe its immensity: 110 acres with 828 stores and services, including 210 "ladies fashion" stores, 35 menswear stores, 55 shoe stores, 35 jewelry stores, 11 major department stores, 23 movie theatres, 110 restaurants, and 2 car dealerships. *West Edmonton Mall: Official Souvenir Book* (Edmonton: Chris Cam Publication, 1989).

Two recent essays have discussed the theme park nature of the West Edmonton Mall. See Margaret Crawford, "The World in a Shopping Mall," in *Variations on a Theme Park: The New American City and the End of Public Space,* edited by Michael Sorkin (New York: Hill and Wang, 1992); Tracy C. Davis, "The Theatrical Antecedents of the Mall that Ate Downtown," *Journal of Popular Culture* 24, no. 4 (Spring 1991). Davis provides an informed discussion of the mall's replacement of regional specificity with the "paratheatrical" idioms of entertainment—zoos, eateries, winter-gardens—found in traveling fairgrounds and stationary theme parks. After quoting a critic who describes Disneyland in terms of cinematic montage, Davis almost argues for the metaphor of mall as cinema, but instead opts for the metaphor of video game:

> Progress through the Mall is like a succession of scenes, as one passes a kinetic perpetual motion sculpture, animal cages, the ice palace, the waterpark, the galleon, the medieval waxwork dungeons, shops, shops and more shops. An obscure corner of the Mall features a walk-through video game which arms patrons with ray guns and automatically computes their score as they progress through a three-dimensional maze of monsters and extra-terrestials. *This produces a similar sensation to the Mall as a whole—the game just makes the conventions more overt than they are elsewhere.* (13, emphasis added)

In constructing a "world in miniature," the West Edmonton Mall only indirectly addresses its Canadian location. Most of the "attractions" (Bourbon Street, Europa Boulevard) are non-Canadian. Only a small controversial exhibit of Canadian moose acknowledged its regional specificity. Denying the geographic or climatic externals is a frequent strategy in mall planning. Malls in the desert or temperate south—the Houston Galleria and Palm Desert Town Center in California, for example—contain ice skating rinks as if to defy the desert climate.

To compete with West Edmonton's claim to "world's largest," the same Canadian developers, the Ghermezians, have an even more massive "Mall of America" under construction in Bloomington, Minnesota.

13. Whether or not a mall is a truly "public" space has been the subject of a number of First Amendment (freedom of speech) lawsuits. If the mall is a public space, then religious and political organizations have the "right to free speech," to leaflet, and so forth; if the mall is a privately owned commercial space, these rights do not apply.

14. See deCerteau, *Practice of Everyday Life*. In his analysis of "pedestrian speech acts" (97), deCerteau describes the spatial nowhere produced by "walking as a space of enunciation" (98). For deCerteau: "To walk is to lack a *place*" (103).

15. See Barthes, "Dining Car" in *The Eiffel Tower*.

16. Foucault identifies "heterotopias" as heterogenous social spaces in which "all the other real sites that can be found within the culture are simultaneously represented, contested, and inverted." See Michel Foucault, "Other Spaces: The Principles of Heterotopia," *Lotus* 48/49 (1986): 9–17; "Of Other Spaces," *Diacritics* 16, no. 1 (Spring 1986): 22–27.

    In a 1990 pamphlet, the Los Angeles Forum for Architecture and Urban Design published a set of imaginative design alternatives for the Los Angeles shopping mall, the Beverly Center. Organized by Aaron Betsky, the design project addresses the absence of monumental spaces in Los Angeles: "Today there is little place for permanent symbols in a city based on exile, automobile movement and evanescent images." See Aaron Betsky, *Proposals: 33-D6-E6: Rethinking the Beverly Center* (Los Angeles: Los Angeles Forum for Architecture and Urban Design, 1990).

17. Mike Davis, *City of Quartz* (London and New York: Verso, 1990): 240–244. Foucault, *Discipline and Punish*, 195–228.

18. Dody Tsiantar, "Big Brother at the Mall," *Newsweek* (July 3, 1989): 44.

19. Quoted in "All Shopped Out?," *Utne Reader* (September-October 1989).

20. Jean Baudrillard, "Consumer Society" (1970) in *Jean Baudrillard: Selected Writings*, edited by Mark Poster (Stanford, Calif.: Stanford University Press, 1988), 30.

21. Benjamin, "Paris of the Second Empire," 36–37; Baudrillard, "Consumer Society," 32. Baudrillard describes Parly 2, the planned community between Paris and Orly airport, which has a giant shopping center, tennis courts, pools, and library.

22. Baudrillard, "Consumer Society," 31.

23. William Kowinski, *The Malling of America* (New York: Morrow, 1985), 18, 22, 23.

24. Benjamin, "Paris—Capital of the Nineteenth Century," 176.

25. Ira G. Zepp, Jr., *The New Religious Image of Urban America: The Shopping Mall as Ceremonial Center* (Westminster, Md.: Christian Classics, 1986), 73.

26. Morris, "Things To Do," 5.

27. Ernest Hahn, "The Shopping Center Industry," in *Shopping Centers and Malls*, edited by Robert Davis Rathbun (New York: Retail Reporting, 1986), 6–7.

28. In Veblen's era, "conspicuous consumption" served the purpose of demarcating wealth. Purchases through mail order or toll-free telephone numbers and the Home Shopping Network privatize the act of consumption into a form of "inconspicuous" consumption where the purpose of shopping does not have an immediate public consequence, but is reduced to the pleasures involved in the act of purchase— choice, acquisition, a sense of a "bargain."

29. The illusion of choice and the construction of consumer desire has been argued forcefully and historically illustrated in Stuart Ewen, *Captains of Consciousness: Advertising and the Social Roots of the Consumer Culture* (New York: McGraw-Hill, 1976); Ewen and Ewen, *Channels of Desire;* Williamson, *Consuming Passions.*

30. Recent university studies at USC, UCLA, and the University of Minnesota treat compulsive shopping as an addiction, not unlike gambling or alcoholism. These studies demonstrate that this addiction largely occurs in, but is not confined to, women. Compulsive spending has been made easier in a credit economy: personal bankruptcy increased 462 percent between 1950 and 1975. See "Mall Mania" in *University of California, Berkeley, Wellness Letter* (Berkeley: University of California, February 1988):1–2.

    Compulsive shopping is one of many disturbances based on the consumption model—binge shopping and impulse buying are others and one can easily imagine other diagnostic terms. Shopping *bulimia,* for example, would refer to a form of binge-and-purge purchasing—buying and then returning merchandise—made easier in credit economies where money is only abstractly exchanged. Agoraphobia (literally, excessive fear of the market) has as its equally common converse, *agoraphilia* (literally, excessive love of the market).

31. See Elaine Showalter, "The Female Malady" in *Women, Madness and English Culture 1830–1980* (New York: Pantheon Books, 1985), 145–164.

32. Carolyn Wesson, *Women Who Shop Too Much: Overcoming the Urge to Splurge* (New York: St. Martin's, 1990).

33. Jane Gallop, "Nurse Freud: Class Struggle in the Family," unpublished paper quoted in Showalter, "Female Malady," 160.

34. A recently marketed electronic board game, Mall Madness (Milton Bradley, 1990), has each player choose a color (yellow, red, blue, green) and a shopper piece (boy or girl). The game is recommended for ages nine and older. The object of Mall Madness is to be the first to buy six different items and get back to the parking lot. The game involves moving through the mall spaces according to directions from the electronic microchip "Voice of the Mall." Each shopper is given an ATM card and a credit card. The Voice announces sales ("There is a sale in the camera shop") and gives each player a number of spaces to move ("Red, move five"). The Voice also provides setbacks, as in "Go to the Restroom," or "You left your lights on, go to the parking lot," or when making a purchase, "Long line, try again later" or "I'm sorry we're out of stock, try again later." The player's mall flânerie is limited by the number of spaces that the Voice commands and is motivated by the strictly consumer objectives of buying the most and the fastest.

35. "I Shop Therefore I Am" is the text on an untitled work by Barbara Kruger, 1987.

36. Kowinski, *Malling of America,* 20. Kowinski catches some of these apparatical sim-

ilarities, but does not develop them. "Watching TV, we can be everywhere without being anywhere in particular . . . the mall is like three dimensional television." (74)

37. Kowinski, *Malling of America*, 62.

38. Ibid., 376.

39. Several writers have recently correlated mall subjectivity with televisual, but not cinematic, spectatorship. In an unpublished paper, "An Ontology of Everyday Distraction—the Freeway, the Mall and Television," Margaret Morse has argued that the mall and the freeway are analogous to television as modes of distraction. See also Bukatman, "There's Always a Tomorrowland," 55–78.

40. Following the historical precedents of department store "tie-ins" in display windows and merchandising (see Miriam Hansen, "Adventures of Goldilocks: Spectatorship, Consumerism and Public Life," *Camera Obscura* 22 [1990]: 51–71; Janes Gaines, "The Queen Christina Tie-Ups," *Quarterly Review of Film and Video* 11, no. 1 [1989]: 35–60), Warner Bros. has recently opened Studio Stores in malls in Beverly Hills, Chicago, Fairfax, Virginia, and Danbury, Connecticut, which sell videotapes. stuffed animals, and clothing all licensed from Warners cartoon characters. Disney has more than 120 stores in malls worldwide. At this writing, Disney promises to have another hundred or so stores in Japan alone to follow the opening of Tokyo Disneyland.

41. Douglas Gomery, "Thinking about Motion Picture Exhibition," *Velvet Light Trap* no. 25 (Spring 1990): 6.

42. Mary Ann Doane appeals to Joan Riviere's concept of a gender-mobile "masquerade" to describe the imaginary activity of the female spectator. See Mary Ann Doane, "Film and the Masquerade: Theorising the Female Spectator," *Screen* 23, nos. 3–4 (1982): 74–87.

43. Charles Moore, Peter Becker, and Regula Campbell, *The City Observed: Los Angeles* (New York: Vintage Books, 1984), 232.

44. Dziga Vertov described the Kino-Eye as "the microscope and telescope of time, as the negative of time." See Dziga Vertov, "The Birth of Kino-Eye" (1924) in *Kino-Eye: The Writings of Dziga Vertov*, edited by Annette Michelson (Berkeley: University of California Press, 1984), 41. André Breton wrote about film's "power to disorient." See André Breton, "As in a Wood," in *The Shadow and Its Shadow: Surrealist Writings on Cinema*, edited by Paul Hammond (London: British Film Institute, 1978), 43.

45. Hugo Munsterberg, *The Film: A Psychological Study*, 1916, reprint (New York: Dover Publications, 1970), 95.

46. Ibid., 74.

47. Ibid., 77.

48. Ibid., 78.

49. Erwin Panofsky, "Style and Medium in the Motion Pictures," *Bulletin of the Department of Art and Archeology* (Princeton, N.J.: Princeton University, 1934); reprinted in *Film Theory and Criticism,* edited by Gerald Mast and Marshall Cohen, third edition (New York: Oxford University Press, 1985), 218.

50. Henri Bergson, *Matter and Memory,* translated by N. M. Paul and W. S. Palmer (New York: Zone Books, 1991), 135.

51. See Gilles Deleuze, *Le Bergsonisme* (Paris: Presses Universitaires de France, 1966); *Bergsonism,* translated by Hugh Tomlinson and Barbara Habberjam (New York: Zone Books, 1988).

52. Deleuze, *Bergsonism,* 74.

53. Henri Bergson, *Creative Evolution,* translated by Arthur Mitchell (New York: Modern Library, 1944), 332–334. For a recent discussion of Bergson's encounter with the chronophotographs of Etienne-Jules Marey see Anson Rabinbach's excellent book on time, motion, and labor in the nineteenth century, *The Human Motor: Energy, Fatigue and the Origins of Modernity* (Berkeley: University of California Press, 1990).

54. William Boddy discusses the "new experience of time" produced by early radio broadcasts of time signals and by the time-clock structure of radio programming. See "The Rhetoric and Economic Roots of the American Broadcasting Industry," *Cinetracts* 2, no. 2 (Spring 1979):37–55. For additional accounts of these changes in the standardization of time, see Susan J. Douglas, *Inventing American Broadcasting, 1899–1922* (Baltimore: Johns Hopkins University Press, 1987). Andrew Ross has brilliantly detailed the subjective impact of the twenty-four-hour Weather Channel as the contemporary global epitome of these changes in the conception of time. See Andrew Ross, *Strange Weather: Culture, Science, and Technology in the Age of Limits* (London: Verso, 1991), 238–244.

55. See Kern, *Culture of Time and Space.*

56. Gilles Deleuze, *Cinema 1: The Movement-Image,* and *Cinema 2: The Time-Image,* translated by Hugh Tomlinson and Barbara Habberjam (Minneapolis: University of Minnesota Press, 1986).

    For an excellent critique of Deleuze's first volume, see Edward Dimendberg, "The Grand Deleuzian Fog: A Review of *Cinema I: The Movement-Image* by Gilles Deleuze," *Canadian-American Slavic Studies* 22 (1988): 199–209.

57. Deleuze, *Cinema 2,* xi.

58. Ibid., 105.

59. Ibid., 125.

60. Ibid., 81.

61. Like many of his novels, Philip K. Dick's *Time Out of Joint* (1959) has a narrative in which the temporality of the fictional world is deceptively ordered. The protagonist, Ragel Gumm, supports himself by anticipating patterns in a supposedly random newspaper contest until he discovers that it is neither random nor does he live

in the time frame that makes it appear random. *Time Out of Joint* was translated to French, *Le Temps Désarticule* (Paris: Calman-Levy), in 1975.

62. André Bazin, "The Ontology of the Photographic Image," in *What Is Cinema?*, vol. 1, translated by Hugh Gray (Berkeley: University of California Press, 1971), 9–10, 14.

63. See Bazin, "Ontology of the Photographic Image," 15.

Bazin exalted directors who put their "faith in reality" and not in the image, filmmakers who followed the holy grail of "total cinema," who enjoined cinema's ability to render the artist absent. ("All arts are based on the presence of man, only photography derives an advantage from his absence," ibid., 13.)

64. See André Bazin, "Myth of Total Cinema" and "Ontology of the Photographic Image," in *What Is Cinema?*, vol. 1, 21.

65. Bazin's work has been frequently challenged for its teleology, historiographic oversights, and idealist assumptions.

One of the most profound indictments of Bazin's "integral realism" is found in the work of Noël Burch, who decries Bazin's theories as the "quintessence of a bourgeois ideology of representation." Burch scours historical documents about protocinematic devices and "primitive" films to find alternatives to such realist aspirations. Covering much of the territory that film historians such as Deslandes and Sadoul have mapped, Burch returns to many of the contemporary recorded reactions to photography and the cinema, noting the nineteenth-century *disinterest* in spatial verisimilitude or mimesis. Yet Burch does not remark on the number of contemporaneous responses that were about the transformations of temporality— the ways in which photographs of a dead loved one haunted the world of the living, changing, in effect, the boundaries of death and life. See Noël Burch, "Charles Baudelaire v. Dr. Frankenstein," *Afterimage*, 8/9 (Spring 1981): 5. See also "Porter, or Ambivalence," *Screen* 19, no. 4 (Winter 1978–1979) and "A Parenthesis on Film History" in *To a Distant Observer* (Berkeley: University of California Press, 1979).

Burch's assessment would agree with Baudry's discussion of the psychical source (the "desire inherent to a participatory effect deliberately produced, sought for, and expressed by cinema") for the invention of the cinema. See "Apparatus," 307. Baudry also describes the "state of artificial regression" or a "return to a primitive narcissism" which the cinema produces as a possible determining desire and that we have been lead to produce mechanisms that simulate the unconscious or secondary processes (313).

66. The English translation *apparatus* was used to refer to French work on the cinema which considered the "cinematic apparatus" as *dispositif,* a more general sense of device and arrangement which includes the metapsychological effects on the spectator and was not simply the "apparatus" as *appareil,* the machine. See *The Cinematic Apparatus,* edited by Teresa de Lauretis and Stephen Heath (New York: St.

Martin's Press, 1980) and *Apparatus,* edited by Theresa Hak Kyung Cha (New York: Tanam Press, 1980). Joan Copjec argues that film theorists borrowed this term from Gaston Bachelard's attempts to add to phenomenology, a phenomeno-technology. See "The Orthopsychic Subject: Film Theory and the Reception of Lacan," *October* 49 (Summer 1989).

67. Baudry, "Ideological Effects," 290.

Baudry's "Ideological Effects" was first printed in *Cinéthique,* nos. 7–8 (1970); "Apparatus" was first printed in *Communications,* no. 23 (1975). Both essays have been reprinted in translation in *Apparatus,* edited by Theresa Hak Kyung Cha and in *Narrative, Apparatus, Ideology,* edited by Phil Rosen.

68. Baudry, "Apparatus," 315.

69. Baudry's further argument is that an "ideological effect" is produced by organizing an image from the centered view of Renaissance perspective, a view that is produced by the camera obscura and then reproduced by the photographic camera itself. In these images, monocular vision and centered perspective organize the spectator-subject's relation to the space of representation.

70. Ibid., 314.

71. Copjec challenges the misconceptions of (a generalized) "film theory" that mistakenly, in her reading, appropriates Lacan. Although Copjec may have correctly diagnosed the elision that many film theorists have made between Foucauldian and Lacanian theories, she rather ungenerously misreads some specific film theorists— Metz, Baudry, and Comolli—to charge them with the "ignorance of" the "true" Lacan. Copjec argues that "film theory" mistakenly conceives of the screen as a mirror, and has missed "Lacan's more radical insight" that "the mirror is conceived as screen." See "Orthopsychic Subject."

72. Metz, *Le signifiant imaginaire: Psychoanalyse et Cinéma* (Paris: Union générale d'Editions, 1977); translated by Ben Brewster in *The Imaginary Signifier.*

73. See Metz's "little piece of science fiction" used to illustrate the nonmandatory aspects of cinema spectatorship:

One goes to the cinema because one wants to and not because one has to force oneself. . . . imagine what would happen in the absence of such a state of affairs: we should have to suppose the existence of some special police force (no less) or some statutory system of *a posteriori* inspection (= a stamp in one's identity card on admission to a cinema) to force people to go to the cinema. (*Imaginary Signifier,* 7–9)

74. The dramatic demographic changes in consumer lifestyles are evident in the history of "home use" videotaping. In 1956, Ampex introduced a two-inch videotape for television signals to be recorded on magnetic tape. The two-inch tape helped to facilitate program schedules in separate time zones (programs from the East coast

could be recorded and transmitted via coaxial cable and later rebroadcast). In 1976, Sony introduced their one-half-inch home system, the Betamax. Akio Morita, CEO of Sony, coined the term "timeshift" to describe the radical potentials of videotaping. In 1977, 1 percent of TV homes had VCRs; in 1984, 10 percent of households had VCRs; Nielson Media Research reports in 1989, 65.5 percent of American households had VCRs, up from the 1984 figure of 14 percent ("VCR Penetration Rises to 65.5%," *Daily Variety,* July 25, 1989). Current statistics show that household "penetration" of VCRs is moving toward 80 percent. Recent (1991) statistics show that while the number of VCRs soars, recording use declines. Average monthly recordings were down from 10.3 in 1987 to 7.3 in 1991. See Lauren Lipton, "VCR (Very Cool Revolt)," *Los Angeles Times,* August 4, 1991.

In 1976, Universal/MCA and Disney brought a legal challenge to the technology of home taping, suing the Sony Corporation for copyright infringement. The Supreme Court decided in January 1984 in favor of Sony, allowing home users to the right to tape movies. In 1978, Fox sold videocassette rights to fifty movies from its archives; other major studios quickly released their archives to videotape for home rental. In 1988, two billion videocassettes were rented. In 1990, a national video rental store, Blockbuster, modeled its display and marketing after the supermarket.

See *Social and Cultural Aspects of VCR Use,* edited by Julia R. Dobrow (Hillsdale, N.J.: Lawrence Erlbaum Associates, 1990); Ganley and Ganley, *Global Political Fallout;* James Lardner, *Fast Forward: Hollywood and Japan VCR Wars* (New York: Norton, 1989); Douglas A. Boyd, Joseph D. Straubhaar, and John A. Lent, *Videocassette Recorders in the Third World* (New York: Longman, 1989).

See also Sean Cubitt, *Timeshift: On Video Culture* (New York: Methuen, 1990) and Ien Ang, "The Streamlined Audience Disrupted; Impact of New Technologies," in *Desperately Seeking the Audience* (London and New York: Routledge, 1991), 68–77. Ang discusses the changes in ratings demography caused by the VCR. The "multichannel environment" has meant that the three networks have lost their hold on prime time. "Zapping" between channels has made audience measurement more difficult. "Zipping" (fast-forwarding through taped programming) has made advertisers wary. Ang argues that the heterogenous informal daily practices of "actual audiences" for television are too polymorphic and diverse to be reduced to a single discursive construct, the "television audience."

75. David Bordwell, Janet Staiger, and Kristin Thompson, *The Classical Hollywood Cinema* (New York: Columbia University Press, 1985), xiv.

76. It is no accident that Baudry is not mentioned in the Bordwell, Staiger, and Thompson text. "Apparatus" theories did not contain historically specific or textually specific support for their generalized model of spectatorship. Metz and Thierry Kuntzel are mentioned, but only in the context of Metz's discussion of "sequence" and crosscutting and Kuntzel's discussion of "segment" and "classical scene."

77. Gerald M. Mayer, "American Motion Pictures in World Trade," *The Annals of the American Academy of Political and Social Science* 254 (November 1947): 34; as quoted in Doane, *Desire to Desire,* 37.

78. Baudrillard, *Simulations,* 55.

79. See Tania Modelski's account of the rhythms of domestic spectatorship for viewers of soap operas in *Loving with a Vengeance* (New York: Methuen, 1984).

80. Remote "wands" used for pauses, "zips" (fast forward) and "zaps" (changing channels) have accelerated the spectator's flânerie.

    If Benjamin compared flânerie to the distracted style of newspaper journalism in the feuilleton, it does not take much to consider the televisual spectator who zaps with the remote button as the contemporary equivalent of the radio listener whose channel-switching *aural flânerie* Adorno had already described. (See Buck-Morss, "Flâneur," 105).

81. Kaplan, *Rocking Around the Clock,* 145.

82. As I mentioned in the Introduction, Kaplan's claims for the specificity of the televisual apparatus also apply to earlier forms of "screen entertainment." In two unelaborated historical passages in *Rocking Around The Clock,* Kaplan supplies an account of television and the "changing relation between subject and image":

    Television in this way seems to be at the end of a whole series of changes begun at the turn of the century with the development of modern forms of advertising and of the department-store window. (44)

    And:

    The change involved began at the turn of the century with the development of advertising and of the department-store window; it was then further affected by the invention of the cinematic apparatus, and television has, we've seen, produced more changes. (151)

    Kaplan also claims MTV's postmodern specificity in its "reflection" of adolescent subjectivity. MTV, Kaplan argues, "reflects young people's condition" (5), and "mimics the cultural formation of contemporary teenagers appearing to live in a timeless but implicitly 'futurized' present" (29).

83. "I will be arguing that MTV produces a kind of decenteredness, often called 'postmodernist' " (5); "television may itself be seen as a postmodernist phenomenon in its very construction of a decentered historical spectator" (32).

84. Kaplan, *Rocking Around the Clock,* 28.

85. Cubitt, *Timeshift,* 31.

86. Kaplan, *Rocking Around the Clock,* 149.

87. See Beverle Houston, "Viewing Television: The Metapsychology of Endless Consumption," *Quarterly Review of Film Studies* 9, no. 3 (Summer 1984): 183–195.

88. See Raymond Williams, *Television: Technology and Cultural Form* (New York: Schocken Books, 1975); Stephen Heath and Gillian Skirrow, "Television: A World in Action," *Screen* 18, no. 2 (Summer 1977).

89. Williams, *Television,* 26.

90. See Lynn Spigel, "Installing the Television Set: Popular Discourses on Television and Domestic Space 1948–1955," *Camera Obscura* no. 16 (January 1988): 11–48; William Boddy, *Fifties Television: The Industry and Its Critics* (Champaign: University of Illinois Press, 1990).

91. See also Avital Ronnell, *The Telephone Book: Technology, Schizophrenia, Electric Speech* (Lincoln: University of Nebraska Press, 1990).

92. The technology of coaxial cable emphasizes this two-way individual-to-individual form of telecommunication. Not only do cable television franchises frequently share wires with the telephone company, but the coaxial cable itself allows signals to travel in two directions, so that home users can communicate their responses *back* to the cable company.

93. See Jane Feuer, "The Concept of Live TV: Ontology as Ideology," in *Regarding Television,* edited by E. Ann Kaplan (Los Angeles: American Film Institute, 1983), 12–23.

94. In *Practice of Everyday Life,* Michel deCerteau uses the metaphor of apartment rental—space borrowed by a transient—to illustrate the elsewhere produced by reading:

> the procedures of contemporary consumption appear to constitute a subtle art of "renters" who know how to insinuate their countless differences into the dominant text (xxii).

Although deCerteau details the spatial displacement of reading, he says little about temporal displacement. We not only "rent" fictional spaces, but we "rent" other times. These displacements become less figurative when viewing movies and videotapes. One can literally rent another space and time when one borrows a videotape to watch on a VCR.

95. "Third Window," 185–197.

96. Promotional video monitors arrayed in the theater lobbies or on the sidewalk outside of theaters serve as video window displays to upcoming films.

97. In Rene Clair's 1924 film, *Paris Qui Dort,* a Parisian scientist, Docteur Crase, has a ray machine that could stop, accelerate, or reverse time. See Annette Michelson's discussion of "temporality apprehended as movement in space" in this film by Rene Clair and in Vertov's *Man with a Movie Camera,* in "Docteur Crase and Mr. Clair."

98. "Life in the Data-Cloud," interview with Jaron Lanier, *Mondo 2000*, no. 2 (Summer 1990): 46.

99. Quoted in John Perry Barlow, "Being in Nothingness: Virtual Reality and the Pioneers of Cyberspace," *Mondo 2000*, no. 2 (Summer 1990): 34–44.

100. Ibid., 36.

101. Trish Hall, " 'Virtual Reality' Takes Its Place in the Real World," *New York Times*, July 8, 1990.

102. One chilling example of this technological prescience is an interactive video program, "Combat Trauma," designed by the Interactive Media Laboratory at Dartmouth Medical School. The program, designed to train military medical personnel in combat medicine and triage, was used at Bethesda Naval Hospital from 1989 to 1990.

    A sophisticated interactive video game using laser discs and a keyboard, the narrative "story told using traditional cinematic vocabulary" simulates a emergency medical (MASH) unit in desert camouflage, in the middle of a desert war. Causalities are coming in at a fast rate and decisions must be made quickly in the conditions of a hot, windy desert combat zone. When I saw "Combat Trauma" in December 1990, 90 percent of the Bethesda staff had been deployed to the Persian Gulf. They had all trained on the virtual game.

103. *Dataglove* is a trademarked term for a Lycra glove with fiber optic wiring from wrist to fingertip, which reads the motion of the hand and the individual fingers. VPL licensed their $8800 Dataglove to Mattel to be marketed as a Nintendo interactive device for $85.

104. The race to patent requisite neologisms led the Sausalito based company, Autodesk (a division of Auto/CAD), to register the word *cyberspace* as a patented trademark. This prompted William Gibson, author of the "cyberpunk" novel *Neuromancer* whose fictional use of the term has become almost nonfictional, to retaliate and apply for a trademark of the name "Erich Gullichsen," one of Autodesk's founders.

105. "A Lexicon of Cyberspeak," Leep Systems advertisement, *Mondo 2000*, no. 2 (Summer 1990): 1.

106. Williams, *Television,* 25.

107. Lanier, "Life in the Data-Clond," 51.

108. Jean Baudrillard, *America*, translated by Chris Turner (London: Verso, 1988), 56.

109. In, for example, Michael Jackson's "Makes no difference if you're black or white" video, the fast dissolves that alternate between faces of various races, genders, ages, ethnicities, and sexualities carry the blurring of multicultural identity to a visual extreme.

110. See Daniel Boorstin, *The Image: A Guide to Pseudo-Events in America* (New York: Harper Colophon Books, 1961); Joshua Meyrowitz, *No Sense of Place: The Impact of Electronic Media on Social Behavior* (New York: Oxford University Press, 1987).

111. The Sharper Image catalog features Artagraph reproductions of modernist "masterpieces." The two-page catalog copy reads:

> THE GREAT MASTERS ARE PAINTING AGAIN. TECHNOLOGY
> RECREATES ART ORIGINALS—DOWN TO THE FINEST BRUSH
> STROKE. Developed over eight years by Artagraph Reproductions Technology
> of Canada, the patented Artagraph process creates a precise, three-dimensional,
> oil-on-canvas duplicate of the original painting. . . . The finished, three-
> dimensional Artagraph reproduction now perfectly replicates the texture of the
> original. . . . Each comes with a certificate of authenticity and a lifetime
> warranty.

The paintings available are *Starry Night*, by Vincent Van Gogh ($799), *Bouquet of Flowers*, by Paul Gauguin ($599), and *The Artist's Garden at Giverny*, by Claude Monet ($699).

112. News stories frequently illustrate this confusion. On August 7, 1989, during an earthquake preparedness simulation drill in Santa Clara County, California, the area was rocked by a 5.2 quake. Vice President Dan Quayle's wife, Marilyn, who was in Sacramento with the disaster relief teams, did not feel the earthquake but when she turned on the television she thought, "Gee, this is interesting, they've got the simulation on the news." (See *New York Times*, "Drill for Earthquake Jolted by Real Thing," August 9, 1989; *Los Angeles Times*, August 9, 1989.)

On August 2, 1989, the news of the possible hanging of an American marine, Colonel Higgins, was covered by accounts that questioned the authenticity of the videotape (itself a video illustration of what Foucault described as "the spectacle of the scaffold" in *Discipline and Punish*). In the *Los Angeles Times*, this story was paired with a story about the debut of the ABC "electronic time machine" news program, *Yesterday, Today, Tomorrow* (*Los Angeles Times*, August 2, 1989).

PASSAGE III

1. Edward Bellamy, *Looking Backward* (Boston and New York: Houghton Mifflin, 1926), 102.
2. The Bradbury Building was the architect's only famous building. Charles Moore relates that Wyman was convinced by the spirit of his dead brother—through a Ouija board—that this commission would make him famous. It did. See Moore et. al., *The City Observed*, 24–25.
3. Moore, *The City Observed*, 24.
4. Marvin Trachtenberg, "The Ghostly Trains of Gae Aulenti," *Art in America* 76, no. 1 (January 1988): 104–106.
5. Ibid., 105.

CHAPTER FOUR

1. "Where Is Your Rupture?" is the title of a piece by Andy Warhol from 1960. Michelson has also used this as the title to a lecture on Warhol's work (given May 10, 1990 at the Getty Institute, Santa Monica, California). See Annette Michelson, "Where Is Your Rupture: Mass Culture and *Gesamtkunstwerk*," *October* 56 (Summer 1991): 43–63.

2. Malcolm Bradbury and James McFarlane suggest that the historian of modernism must engage in "cultural seismology," recording and measuring each aesthetic tremor and seeking out its epicenters. It is not surprising that the same geological language appears in the periodizing rhetoric of the "rupture" between modernism and postmodernism. See "The Name and Nature of Modernism," in *Modernism*, edited by Malcolm Bradbury and James McFarlane (New York: Penguin Books, 1976).

3. Jochen Schulte-Sasse, "Modernity and Modernism, Postmodernity and Postmodernism: Framing the Issue, "*Cultural Critique* no. 5 (Winter 1986–1987): 5–22, makes a forceful assertion of this terminological clarification. Of course, some of the difficulties with terminology have come from translations: the German term (*die Postmoderne*) or the French term (*le Postmoderne*) has been transformed into postmodern*ism*. Cf. Jean Francois Lyotard's "Réponse à la question: qu'est-ce que le postmoderne?" (*Critique* no. 419 [April 1982]), which became, "Answering the Question: What is Postmodernism?" translated by Regis Durand, in *Postmodern Condition*.

   Clearly, although theorists and critics agree that postmodernism marks a crisis in cultural authority, they seem split along the divide of the ideological effects of such a crisis. Following Jameson, the critic Hal Foster has underlined the schisms that break between "neo-conservative" and "post-structuralist" postmodernism. See Hal Foster, "Postmodernism: A Preface," in *Anti-Aesthetic* and "(Post)Modern Polemics," *New German Critique* 33 (Fall 1984). "Neo-conservative" postmodernism operates as a retrenchment *in* or reassertion *of* traditional premodern values, a nostalgic yearning for a past that was disturbed by the rupture of modernism, while "poststructuralist" postmodernism operates as a subversion of past values (both premodern and modern) through reappropriation or pastiche and somehow shifts the authority of those values. In psychological terms, Foster's division amounts to an object relations split: good object postmodernism versus bad object postmodernism. Habermas, in Foster's example, has denounced the antimodernist roots of postmodernism which he feels have subverted the completion he wishes of the modernist project, while Lyotard seems to find, if not emancipatory potential in the postmodern, a more philosophically positive valence, turning postmodernism into a good object. See Jürgen Habermas, "Modernity versus Postmodernity, *New German Critique* 22 (Winter 1981); "Modernity—An Incomplete Project," in *Anti-*

Aesthetic; "The French Path to Postmodernity," *New German Critique* 33 (Fall 1984); Lyotard, *Postmodern Condition;* Fredric Jameson, "The Politics of Theory," *New German Critique* 33 (Fall 1984).

4. See Irving Howe, "Mass Society and Postmodern Fiction," *Partisan Review,* 26, no. 3 (Summer 1959); Levin, "What Was Modernism?" *Massachusetts Review* 1–4 (August 1960); Ihab Hassan, "POSTmodernISM: A Paracritical Bibliography," *New Literary History* 3, no. 1 (Fall 1971).

5. See Charles Jencks, "The Rise of Postmodern Architecture," *Architecture Association Quarterly,* no. 4 (1975); "Footnote on the Term Postmodern Architecture," in *Language of Postmodern Architecture* (New York: Rizzoli, 1984), 8.

6. See Sally Banes, *Terpsichore in Sneakers: Postmodern Dance* (New York: Houghton Mifflin, 1980). Banes discusses the trajectory from "modern" dance of Loie Fuller and Martha Graham to the "performance" work of Trisha Brown, Yvonne Rainer, and David Gordon. Emphasizing "ordinary movements," these "dancers" eliminated narrative, decoration, and allusion from their works.

7. See Kaplan, *Rocking Around the Clock;* Collins, *Uncommon Cultures;* Corrigan, *Cinema without Walls;* Guiliana Bruno, "Ramble City: Postmodernism and *Blade Runner*," *October* 41 (1987): 61–74; Dana Polan, " 'Above All Else to Make You See': Cinema and the Ideology of Spectacle," in *Postmodernism and Politics,* edited by Jonathan Arac (Minneapolis: University of Minnesota Press, 1986), 55–69; Meaghan Morris, "Tooth and Claw; Tales of Survival and Crocodile Dundee," in *Universal Abandon?,* edited by Andrew Ross (Minneapolis: University of Minnesota Press, 1988): 105–127.

8. See "Footnote on the Term Postmodern Architecture," 8–9. Jencks takes credit for the first use of the term *postmodern architecture* in an article he wrote in 1975. Given its current overusage, one has the sense that Jencks is sorry that he could not have patented the word.

9. Jencks, *Language of Postmodern Architecture,* 6. This is oddly similar to Baudelaire's definition of modernity as half "ephemeral" and half "eternal and unchanging." See Baudelaire, *Painter of Modern Life,* section on "Modernity," in *My Heart Laid Bare,* 37.

10. Jameson cites the Bonaventure Hotel (although he spells it Bonaventura) as a key model of postmodern urban space. See "Postmodernism: The Cultural Logic of Late Capitalism," 80–85. In a less utopian, but eloquent passage about the Bonaventure Hotel, urban geographer Edward Soja describes:

the Bonaventure Hotel, an amazingly storeyed architectural symbol of the
splintered labyrinth that stretches miles around it. Like many other Portman-
teaus which dot the eyes of urban citadels in New York and San Francisco,
Atlanta and Detroit, the Bonaventure has become a concentrated representation

of the restructured spatiality of the Late Capitalist city: fragmented and fragmenting, homogenous and homogenizing, divertingly packaged yet curiously incomprehensible, seemingly open in presenting itself to view but constantly pressing to enclose, to compartmentalize, to circumscribe. *Everything imaginable appears to be available in this micro-urb, but real places are difficult to find, its spaces confuse an effective cognitive mapping, its pastiche of superficial reflection bewilder coordination and encourage submission instead.* Entry by land is forbidding to those who walk but do not drive, but entrance is nevertheless encouraged at many different levels, from the truly pedestrian skyways above to the bunker-like inlets below. Once in, however, it becomes daunting to get out again without assistance. In so many ways, architecture recapitulates and reflects the sprawling manufactured environments of Los Angeles. (emphasis added)

See Edward Soja, *Postmodern Geographies: The Reassertion of Space in Critical Social Theory* (London: Verso, 1989), 234–235.

11. The architecture critic for the *Los Angeles Times,* Sam Hall Kaplan, described the invasion of this architectural paradigm as an "attack of the mini-malls!" that "slice up sidewalks with curb cuts, destroy the scale and massing of street scapes, hide store fronts behind rows of automobiles and generally discourage pedestrian life." See "Mini-malls: Scenario for a Horror Film," September 30, 1984, republished in *L.A. Follies* (Los Angeles: Cityscape Press, 1989).

12. Jencks divides postmodern styles into six separate categories: historicism, straight revivialism, neo-vernacular, ad-hoc urbanist, metaphor/metaphysical, and postmodern space. Jencks, *What Is Postmodernism?,* 35.

13. Jameson, "Politics of Theory," 54.

14. In the final chapter of their massive and detailed account of Hollywood's "historical hegemony," Bordwell, Staiger, and Thompson's *Classical Hollywood Cinema,* Bordwell and Staiger address "alternative modes of film practice." Although Bordwell and Staiger suggest a typology of formal oppositions which extends beyond the easy binarism (pleasure and unpleasure; depth and flatness; invisibility of technique and foregrounded materiality) which so frequently describes alternative practices, "national cinemas" are placed in the position also occupied by oppositional and avant-garde practices.

15. Standish Lawder, in his study *The Cubist Cinema* (New York: New York University Press, 1975), draws parallels between cubist painting and film and focuses on the relation of painters such as Picasso, Survage, and Kandinsky to the cinematic experimentations of Richter, Eggeling, and Ruttman.

P. Adams Sitney is drawn toward literary, not visual, paradigms for "avant-garde" filmmaking. In his book, *Visionary Film* (New York: Oxford University Press, 1974), Sitney situates the American avant-garde in terms of the "potent tradition of Romantic poetics" (ix).

16. Lawder in *Cubist Cinema* equates modernism in painting with the avant-garde film movement:

> The avant-garde film movement [was] . . . created for the most part, by painters and poets whose principal medium was not film. . . . In its broadest outlines, the *avant-garde film movement follows a course similar to modern painting.* (35, emphasis added)

Noncommercial and non-narrative are determinant features for Lawder's "avant-garde."

Sitney's use of the term *avant-garde* is slightly different, although the salient features of noncommercial and non-narrative remain. Sitney defines the "avant-garde" as "independent" from traditional forms of cinema:

> Insofar as it calls itself independent or avant-garde, admirably introducing a negative element into its epithet, it reflects back upon another cinema, itself unnamed an undefined, against the darkness of which it shines.

From *The Avant-Garde Film: A Reader of Theory and Criticism* (New York: New York University Press, 1978), vii.

17. Critical and theoretical writing about film in the twenties employed the term *avant-garde* to refer to "alternative" filmmaking efforts; the term *modernism* is, however, a more retrospective critical term. (Here the historiography of literary movements provides an fitting example: Ezra Pound did not call himself a modernist, he was an "imagist"; T. S. Eliot, a "classicist.") Cubist, expressionist, and surrealist movements have been retrospectively deemed modern*isms*—often obscuring the nuances of their differences from each other and from the project of the "avant-garde." And with each of the *isms*—cubism, impressionism, expressionism, surrealism—there was a different relation between an artistic or literary "avant-garde" and its cinematic applications. Hence to assume a retrospective homogeneity between this range of modernism(s) is a problematic and inaccurate gesture.

For histories that conflate the avant-garde with modernism, see Lawder, *Cubist Cinema;* Malcolm LeGrice, *Abstract Film and Beyond* (Cambridge, Mass.: MIT Press, 1977); *The Essential Cinema: Essays on the Films in the Collection of Anthology Film Archives,* edited by P. Adams Sitney (New York: New York University Press, 1975); David Curtis, *Experimental Cinema* (New York: Dell Publishers, 1971); *The New American Cinema: A Critical Anthology,* edited by Gregory Battcock (New York: E. P. Dutton, 1967); Sheldon Renan, *An Introduction to the American Under-*

ground Film (New York: E. P. Dutton, 1967); Parker Tyler, *Underground Film: A Critical History* (New York: Grove Press, 1969).

18. See Peter Bürger, *Theory of the Avant-Garde,* translated by Michael Shaw (Minneapolis: University of Minnesota Press, 1984); Andreas Huyssen, *After The Great Divide* (Bloomington: Indiana University Press, 1988).

19. Debates about the continued existence of an "avant-garde" became quite heated in 1987 when the Los Angeles County Museum mounted a show called "The Avant-Garde in the '80's." See exhibition catalog by Howard N. Fox, *Avant-Garde in the Eighties* (Los Angeles: Los Angeles County Museum of Art, 1987). See also Diana Crane, *The Transformation of the Avant-Garde: The New York Art World 1940–1985* (Chicago: University of Chicago Press, 1987).

20. David Bordwell argues that the growth of film magazines and ciné-clubs were integrally related to the growth of impressionism as a movement and to the building of a "film culture" in France. (David Bordwell, "French Impressionist Cinema: Film Culture, Film Theory, Film Style," Ph.D. diss., University of Iowa, 1974); see also Richard Abel's discussion of the importance of writing about cinema in the formation of the French avant-garde in Richard Abel, *French Cinema: The First Wave 1915–1929* (Princeton: Princeton University Press, 1984), 241–272. For a discussion of the internationalist importance of writing about the cinema in *Close Up,* see Anne Friedberg, "Writing about Cinema: *Close Up* (1927–1933)," Ph.D. diss., New York University, 1983.

   While the journals *Le Film* and *Cinéa* were marked pioneers in the campaign for the cinema as an art and *Cinéa-Ciné-pour Tous* and *Gazette des Septieme Arts* contained articles that were directly theoretical, *Close Up,* unlike all of its French predecessors, began with a strong distaste for Hollywood film. The French journals—although containing articles by Delluc, Epstein, and Dulac which explored the essential qualities of the cinematic—were also journals that revered Chaplin, DeMille, Sennett, and others. *Close Up* writers seemed suitably uninterested in Hollywood and turned toward the work of German and Soviet filmmakers for their arguments about cinema's aesthetic potentials. The French taste for American culture and the popular film (the vogue for Chaplin and the Pearl White serials) meant that types of cinema valorized as "art" were often products of popular culture. The French sought to discover what was uniquely cinematic about these films, but they often sacrificed concern with cinema experiment to the fascination with the narrative and performance values of American cinema.

21. *Gazette des Septieme Arts,* begun by Riciotto Canudo in 1923, is a direct illustration of the discursive campaign for cinema-as-an-art. *Close Up,* which began in 1927, marked its commencement with advertisements in the periodical *transition* for "a monthly magazine to begin battle for film art," in *Ciné* as "L'Art Cinematographique," and in *Film und Volk* as "CLOSE UP, die erste internationale Revue für

Filmkunst." In 1928, when it changed its cover format, the subheading "The Only Magazine Devoted to the Film as an Art" was added.

22. See Bordwell, *French Impressionist Cinema.*

23. Abel, *French Cinema,* 280–281.

24. Huyssen, *After the Great Divide,* vii. Eight of the ten essays included in this collection were originally published in *New German Critique* between 1975 and 1984.

25. See also Tania Modleski's "Femininity as mas(s)querade: a feminist approach to mass culture," in *High Theory/Low Culture,* edited by Colin MacCabe (New York: St. Martin's Press, 1986) for an earlier discussion of this rhetorical treatment.

26. "The Great Divide": The language of topography, of mapping boundaries, schisms, borderlines, certainly seems adequate to the semantic quagmire of the postmodern. Huyssen's work performs a ground-breaking and comprehensive account of the relation of modernism(s) to postmodernism(s). He uses this concept of the "Great Divide" as an aesthetic North Star to set his compass through the *terra incognita* of discourse in the postmodern debate. See my review, "The Mercator of the Post-modern: Mapping the Great Divide," *Camera Obscura* 18 (1987).

27. J. Hoberman, "After Avant-Garde Film," in *Art After Modernism: Rethinking Representation,* edited by Brian Wallis (New York: The New Museum of Contemporary Art, 1984), 59–73.

28. Peter Wollen, "The Two Avant-Gardes," *Studio International* 190, no. 978 (November–December 1975): 77–85.

29. Hoberman, "After Avant-Garde Film," 72.

30. J. Hoberman, "Avant to Live: Fear and Trembling at the Whitney Biennial," *Village Voice,* June 16, 1987.

31. Letter to editor, *Village Voice,* July 14, 1987.

32. Caryn James, "For Avant-Garde Films, A Struggle to Stay Avant," *New York Times,* June 29, 1989.

33. Fredric Jameson, "Postmodernism," and "Postmodernism and Consumer Society." At the time of writing, two collections of Jameson's writings have just come out. *Signatures of the Visible* (New York: Routledge, 1990) and *Postmodernism, or the Cultural Logic of Late Capitalism* (Durham: Duke University Press, 1991) reprint many of Jameson's previously published essays. *Signatures of the Visible* reprints essays on *The Shining* (from *Social Text* 4 [1981]), *Dog Day Afternoon* (from *College English* 38 [1977]), and *Diva* (from *Social Text* 6 [1982]). It remains to be seen how Jameson will revise or elaborate his discussion of film and postmodernity. Another book, *The Geopolitical Aesthetic: Cinema and Space in the World System* is forthcoming in 1992 (Bloomington: Indiana University Press, 1992).

34. For an excellent critique of Jameson's writing on film, see Kathleen Rowe, "Class and Allegory in Jameson's Film Criticism," *Quarterly Review of Film and Video* 12, no. 4 (Fall 1991).

35. Jameson, "Postmodernism," 68.

36. Peter Dews, in his introduction to *Habermas: Autonomy and Solidarity* (London: Verso, 1986), 1–34, compares the similarities between the "end of ideology" debate of English-speaking political scientists (Daniel Bell and others) in the late 1950s and early 1960s with the theories of Lyotard and the French neo-Nietzscheans.

37. This is Daniel Bell's term from *Coming of Post-Industrial Society.*

38. Charles Newman, in *The Postmodern Aura: The Act of Fiction in an Age of Inflation* (Evanston: Northwestern University Press, 1985), argues the relationship of cultural production to economic base. Newman wants to describe the *inflationary discourse* of postmodernism as one of the symptoms:

> Theory becomes an infinitely expandable currency, the ultimate inflation hedge. *Theory more than any work of art is most easily translated into Hype,* which is the conceptual engine of our overstimulated culture. (14, emphasis added)

Bell lists theoretical languages as a feature of "post-industrial society." Jameson also finds that "theoretical discourse" is a symptom of the postmodern.

39. Jameson, "Postmodernism," 57.

40. Jameson, "Postmodernism and Consumer Society," 123.

41. Jameson, "Postmodernism," 55.

42. Ibid., 56.

43. Ibid., 57.

44. Ihab Hassan points out how the teleologies and antecedents are only assumed once a typology of postmodern culture is described. See "Toward a Concept of Postmodernism" and "Prospects in Retrospect," in *Postmodern Turn.* Lyotard, while bemoaning the periodizing implications of the term *post*modern, defines it as a changed relation to meaning and places the "transformations which, since the end of the nineteenth century, have altered the game rules for science, literature, and the arts" in the "context of a crisis of narratives." (See *Postmodern Condition,* xxiii.)

45. Jameson, "Postmodernism," 60.

46. An excellent exhibit of the commercial roots of Warhol's later work was curated by Donna M. DeSalvo for the Grey Art Gallery, New York University, March 14–April 29, 1989. See Donna M. DeSalvo, "Mexican flowers": catalogue 111–113 in *Success Is a Job in New York: The Early Art and Business of Andy Warhol"* (New York: Grey Art Gallery and Study Center and The Carnegie Museum of Art, 1989)

> Warhol made frequent use of rubber stamps and other reproductive devices, specifically to hasten production. This technique enabled him to produce not one, but three versions of a basket of Mexican flowers slated for a 1961 cover of

Vogue's Interior Living. As his first art director Tina Fredericks noted, "One of the wonderful things about Andy is that he was very quick, he would literally come back with something overnight, while other peopled would spend lots of time fooling with the drawing." (9)

47. Jameson describes two accounts for the death of the subject ("Postmodernism," 64): a historicist explanation based on the dissolution of classical capitalism and the nuclear family, and a poststructuralist explanation that claims the subject never really existed but was produced as an ideological illusion. There might also be a third explanation for the postmodern fragmentation of the subject: that we are subjects in a culture of fragmentary images, and no images of a unified subject exist.

48. See Annette Michelson's discussion of the "part object" nature of Warhol's work in "Where Is Your Rupture," *October* 56.

49. See Stephen Koch, *Stargazer: Andy Warhol's World and His Films* (New York: Praeger Publishers, 1973). In *Andy Warhol* (New York: Studio Vista, 1971), Peter Gidal argues that Warhol does not use conventional filmic continuity and narrative progression in his serial painting. *Jackie* (1965) and *Seven Decades of Sidney Janis* (1967) have what Gidal claims is an antinarrative seriality that anticipates Warhol's film work. Also see *Andy Warhol: The Film Factory,* edited by Michael O'Pray (London: BFI Publishing, 1989).

50. Jameson, "Postmodernism," 55.

51. Fredric Jameson, "Postmodernism and Utopia," in *Utopia Post Utopia: Configurations of Nature and Culture in Recent Sculpture and Photography* (Boston: Institute of Contemporary Arts, 1988). See especially, 12, 31.

   Jameson describes the "sense of loss" as:

   memory of deep memory . . . nostalgia for nostalgia, for the grand older extinct questions of origin and telos, of deep time and Freudian Unconscious (dispatched by Foucault at one blow in the *History of Sexuality*) and for the dialectic also. (12)

52. Ibid.

53. Ibid., 11.

54. Ibid., 12.

55. Ibid., 14.

56. Caryn James, "Post-Modernism Edges into the Film Mainstream," *New York Times,* July 23, 1990.

57. In his recent book, *Looking Awry: An Introduction to Jacques Lacan through Popular Culture* (Cambridge, Mass.: MIT Press, 1991), Slavoj Zizek enters the debate on the

break between modernist and postmodernist film style. Challenging the concept of a historical rupture, Zizek asserts "we are even tempted to say that postmodernism in a way precedes modernism" (145). In Zizek's terms, postmodernist style "consists . . . in displaying the object directly, allowing it to make visible its own indifferent and arbitrary character" (143). Applying this definition to film stylistics, Zizek argues that Hitchcock is postmodernist because his approach is to show terror in ordinary objects rather than withholding them. Antonioni's *Blow Up* is modernist, for example, ("perhaps the last great modernist film") because "the play is set in motion by a central absence." See "The Obscene Object of Postmodernity," in *Looking Awry*, 141–153.

58. Linda Hutcheon, "An Epilogue: Postmodern Parody: History, Subjectivity and Ideology," *Quarterly Review of Film and Video*, 12, nos. 1–2 (1990): 125. This is also a section of her book, *The Politics of Postmodernism* (New York: Routledge, 1989), 107–117.

59. Frank McConnell, *Storytelling and Mythmaking* (New York: Oxford University Press, 1979), details the continuities and differences between literary and filmic modes of storytelling.

60. The televisual apparatus, of course, also has this capacity. Yet the technology of the cinema serves as a historical prelude to the televisual.

61. There are countless examples in early cinema: Michael Chanan discusses a British film, *Let Me Dream Again* (1900), which was remade by Zecca as *Reve et Realité* in 1901. See Chanan, *The Dream That Kicks: The Prehistory and Early Years of Cinema in Britain* (London: Routledge and Kegan Paul, 1980), 324–325.

62. For a discussion of these practices, see Benjamin B. Hampton, *History of the American Film Industry* (New York: Dover Publications, 1970); Ralph Cassady, Jr., "Monopoly in Production and Distribution" and Jeanne Thomas Allen, "Afterword," both in *The American Movie Industry: The Business of Motion Pictures*, edited by Gorham Kindem (Carbondale: Southern Illinois University Press, 1982).

63. For an account of the production circumstances of *Perils of Pauline*, see Fred J. Balshofer and Arthur C. Miller, *One Reel a Week* (Berkeley: University of California Press, 1967).

64. Abel, *French Cinema*, 76, 83.

65. See, for example, Bruno, "Ramble City." Bruno discusses the *Blade Runner* as a diegetic illustration of the logic of postmodernism: "*Blade Runner* presents a manifestation of the schizophrenic condition. . . . Replicants are condemned to a life composed only of a present tense; they have neither past nor memory" (70).

In Bruno's reading, the character J. F. Sebastion is a "literalization" of postindustrial condition; the replicants are a "literalization of Baudrillard's theory of postmodernism."

66. See the collective text by the editors of *Cahiers du Cinéma*, "John Ford's *Young Mr. Lincoln*," translated by Hélène Lackner and Diana Matias, *Screen* 13, no. 3 (Autumn 1972). (This text was originally published in *Cahiers du Cinéma*, no. 223 [1970].) In this "reading" of the film, the Cahiers collective examines the "structuring absences" between the film as text and specific historical events:

> Insofar as we can distinguish the historicity of their inscription: the relation of these films to the codes (social, cultural . . .) for which they are a site of intersection, and to other films, themselves held in an inter-textual space. (5–6)

67. For an excellent and thorough bibliography, see "The Literature of Film Exhibition" in the issue "Exhibition/Conditions of Reception" of *Velvet Light Trap*, no. 25 (Spring 1990): 81–119.
68. Jameson, "Postmodernism and Utopia," 11.
69. Boorstin, *Image*.
70. Debord, *Society of the Spectacle*, 158.
71. Baudrillard, "Ecstasy of Communication," 129.
72. Meyrowitz, *No Sense of Place*, vii.
73. A phrase coined by urban studies theorist Edward Relph in *The Modern Urban Landscape* (Baltimore: Johns Hopkins University Press, 1987).
74. For a related critique of Benjamin's theory of art, see Bürger, *Theory of the Avant-Garde*, 27–34. Bürger challenges Benjamin's technodeterminist notions of mode of reception.

CONCLUSION

1. D. W. Griffith, "Five Dollar 'Movies' Prophesied," *The Editor*, April 24, 1915, excerpted as "Some Prophecies: Film and Theatre, Screenwriting, Education," in *Focus on D. W. Griffith*, edited by Harry M. Geduld (Englewood Cliffs, N.J.: Prentice-Hall, 1971), 35. (My emphasis added.) I use this quote to frame an examination of the narrative conventions for representing madness in Griffith's Biograph films. See Anne Friedberg, " 'A Properly Adjusted Window': Vision and Sanity in D. W. Griffith's 1908–1909 Biograph Films," in *Space, Frame, Narrative: Early Cinema*, edited by Thomas Elsaesser (Bloomington: Indiana University Press, 1990), 326–335.
2. Jameson, "Postmodernism and Consumer Society," 125.
3. Adorno, "Introduction to Benjamin's *Schriften*," 10.
4. Benjamin, "Work of Art," 236.

5. Roland Barthes, "Rhetoric of the Image," 44–45:

> The type of consciousness the photograph involves is indeed truly unprecedented, since it establishes not a consciousness of the *being-there* of the thing (which any copy would provoke) but an awareness of its *having-been-there*. What we have is a new space-time category: Spatial immediacy and temporal anteriority, the photograph being an illogical conjunction between the *here-now* and the *there-then*. . . . Film can no longer be seen as animated photographs: the *having-been-there* gives way to a *being-there* of the thing.

6. Clearly, my argument diverges from theories of bodily-determined subjectivity, and instead emphasizes the more fluid social, historical, and discursive determinants to subjectivity. David Rodowick has recently asserted this point quite bluntly:

> Subjectivity does not devolve from the body; it cannot be defined ontogenetically nor can it be simply divided into masculine and feminine identities assured from birth by chromosome count, hormonal balances, or types of genitalia. Subjectivity is defined by social and historical processes that are irreducible to singular categories, and its forms and potentialities are always in flux.

See D. N. Rodowick, *The Difficulty of Difference: Psychoanalysis, Sexual Difference and Film Theory* (New York: Routledge, 1991), 139–140. Rhona Berenstein has elaborated on the fluidity of gender and sexual orientation in cinema spectatorship in her discussion of "spectatorship as drag," in "I Spy with My Little Eye: Spectatorship and Classic Horror Cinema," in "Attack of the Leading Ladies," Ph.D. diss., University of California at Los Angeles 1992.

7. See "Translator's Preface" in Jacques Derrida, *Of Grammatology,* translated by Gayatri Chakravorty Spivak (Baltimore: Johns Hopkins University Press, 1974), xvii. See also Jacques Derrida, "Freud and the Scene of Writing," in *Writing and Difference,* translated by Alan Bass (Chicago: University of Chicago Press, 1978), 196–231.

8. Peter Brunette and David Wills have taken Derrida's notion of "writing" and applied it to film. See *Screen/Play: Derrida and Film Theory* (Princeton: Princeton University Press, 1989).

9. Bergson, *Matter and Memory,* 74.

10. For two exemplary attempts to realign cinematic texts with their historical contexts see Doane, *Desire to Desire,* and Sandy Flitterman-Lewis, *To Desire Differently: Feminism and the French Cinema* (Urbana: University of Illinois Press, 1990).

11. Annette Michelson, "Film and the Radical Aspiration," in *The Film Culture Reader*, edited by P. Adams Sitney (New York: Praeger, 1970), 406.

12. Otto Friedrich, *City of Nets: A Portrait of Hollywood in the 1940s* (New York: Harper and Row, 1986), 2.

13. Philip K. Dick has recurrently used the concept of "memory implant." See especially his treatment of the "extrafactual memory implant" in his 1965 story, "We Can Remember It for You Wholesale," in *The Collected Stories of Philip K. Dick*, vol. 2 (New York: Citadel Twilight Books, 1990), 35–52.

14. See Claudia Springer, "The Pleasure of the Interface," *Screen* 32, no. 3 (Autumn 1991): 303–323.

15. Frederic Jameson, "Nostalgia for the Present," *South Atlantic Quarterly* 88, no. 2 (Spring 1989): 526.

16. Doane and Hedges, *Nostalgia and Sexual Difference*. More recently, Susan Faludi has assessed the antifeminist trends in the media and in popular culture. See Susan Faludi, *Backlash: The Undeclared War Against American Women* (New York: Crown Publishers, 1991).

17. For a discussion of the signification of vintage clothing see Kaja Silverman, "Fragments of a Fashionable Discourse," in *Studies in Entertainment,* edited by Tania Modleski (Bloomington: Indiana University Press, 1986), 139–152. Silverman assesses the "sartorial reticence" of American feminists and argues in defense of the critical potential of a "different sartorial system": "thrift shop dressing" in vintage or retro clothing:

> By recontextualizing objects from earlier periods within the frame of the
> present, retro is able to "reread" them in ways that maximize their radical and
> transformative potential—to chart the affinities, for instance, between fashions
> of the forties and feminism in the eighties, or between fashions of the twenties
> and the "unisex look" of the late sixties. Vintage clothing is also a mechanism
> for crossing vestimentary, sexual and historical boundaries. (151)

18. Max Horkheimer and Theodor W. Adorno, *Dialectic of Enlightenment,* translated by John Cumming (New York: Continuum, 1972).

19. Mark Poster explores the "liberatory and repressive" effects of language-based electronic communication. Although Poster's argument about the "decentering" effects of these "modes of information" does not address visually-based subjectivity, his analysis could be extended to include electronic mediations of the gaze. See Mark Poster, *Modes of Information: Poststructuralism and Social Context* (Chicago: University of Chicago Press, 1990).

20. Lyotard, *Postmodern Condition.*

POST-SCRIPT

1. Jencks, *Language of Postmodern Architecture,* 5.

2. Freud's comment, "The sexual life of women is a 'dark continent' for psychology," from "The Question of Lay Analysis" (1926), was not, even metaphorically, more illuminating than his avowal in "Three Essays on the Theory of Sexuality" (1905): "[the sexual life of men] alone has become accessible to research. That of women . . . is still veiled in an impenetrable obscurity."

3. Lacan in "Guiding Remarks for a Congress on Feminine Sexuality" (written 1958, spoken in 1960, and published in 1964), offers a "Historical Introduction" of a "remarkable oversight." See *Feminine Sexuality,* edited by Juliet Mitchell and Jacqueline Rose (New York: W. W. Norton and Co., 1982).

4. "Answering the Question: What is Postmodernism?" originally appeared as "Reponse a la question: Qu'est-ce que le postmoderne?" in *Critique* and is now included in *Postmodern Condition.* See also Lyotard's "Defining the Postmodern," in *ICA Documents* 4 (1985).

5. In her book, *Feminism Without Women* (New York: Routledge, 1991), Tania Modleski has astutely described the ways in which this same process has been "acted out" in film culture.

6. Ibid.

7. Rosalind Krauss assiduously avoids the question of gender in her work on postmodernism. In the title essay of her book, *The Originality of the Avant-Garde and Other Modernist Myths* (Cambridge, Mass.: MIT Press, 1987), Krauss focuses on the example of Sherrie Levine's work, which "deconstructs the modernist notion of origin" (170). Levine's "appropriations" are not discussed in terms of a gendered theory of power. Kate Linker (see "Eluding Definition," *Artforum* 23, no. 4 [December 1984]): 61–67 and Abigail Solomon-Godeau (see "Living with Contradictions," *Screen* 28, no. 3 [Summer 1987]) have more precisely addressed these questions.

8. Craig Owens, "Discourse of Others: Feminists and Postmodernism," in *Anti-Aesthetic,* 59.

9. For feminist interventions in the postmodern debate, please see Nancy Fraser and Linda Nicholson, "Social Criticism without Philosophy: An Encounter between Feminism and Postmodernism," included in Nicholson's collection, *Feminism/Postmodernism* (New York: Routledge, 1990); Laura Kipnis, "Feminism: The Political Conscience of Postmodernism?" and Jacqueline Rose, "*The Man Who Mistook His Wife for a Hat* or *A Wife Is Like an Umbrella*—Fantasies of the Modern and Postmodern," both included in *Universal Abandon?;* Toril Moi, "Feminism, Postmodernism, and Style: Recent Feminist Criticism in the United States," *Cultural Critique,* no. 9 (Spring 1988); Linker, "Eluding Definition"; Barbara Creed, "From Here to Modernity: Feminism and Postmodernism," *Screen* 28, no. 2 (Spring 1987);

Abigail Solomon-Godeau, "Living with Contradictions: Critical Practices in the Age of Supply-Side Aesthetics," *Screen* 28, no. 3 (Summer 1987); Anne Friedberg, "Mutual Indifference: Feminism and Postmodernism," in *The Other Perspective*.

In book-length works, Hutcheon, *Politics of Postmodernism;* Meaghan Morris, *The Pirate's Fiancée* (London: Verso, 1988); Alice Jardine, *Gynesis: Configurations of Woman and Modernity* (Ithaca: Cornell University Press, 1985); and Jane Flax, *Thinking Fragments: Psychoanalysis, Feminism, and Postmodernism in the Contemporary West* (Berkeley: University of California Press, 1990) contend with feminism's role in postmodernism and postmodernity.

10. Moi, "Feminism, Postmodernism, and Style," 4. Moi is responding to criticism of her book *Sexual/Textual Politics* (London: Methuen, 1985) for its avoidance of French-inspired American feminism. She reviews Jardine's *Gynesis* and Jane Gallop's *Reading Lacan* (Ithaca: Cornell University Press, 1985).

Moi's polemic is constructed around a materialist critique of Jardine for her "untheorizable theoreticism" and her refusal to define feminism with an explicit antipatriarchal stance. "The naming of woman, or the textualization of femininity," Moi insists, "can only produce emancipatory effects if they are placed in an antipatriarchal context" (12). To be fair to Jardine, Moi is a bit overly snipish in her tone, chastizing Jardine for sidestepping materialist issues—historically constructed subjects—in her "transatlantic *pas-de-deux*":

> But to me, as to a whole tradition of American feminism, a feminist intellectual
> is one who seeks to stress her own politics, not one who seeks to replace it with
> geography. (10)

But Jardine does assert that the major new directions in French theory are "conceptually and in *praxis*, anti- and/or postfeminist" (20) and that she wants to clarify this without "getting overly caught up in explicit value judgements or polemics" (21).

11. Moi points out how Gallop engages in the paradoxical position that simultaneously questions mastery and asserts it: "Deliberately miming castration in language is precisely to reinscribe it in the realm of the transcendental signifier (Ibid., 17).

12. Ibid., 19.

13. Although the assumption that culture operates with these processes was only present in a limited way in Freud's own writing (in *Civilization and Its Discontents*), Marcuse (in *Eros and Civilization*) expanded these premises.

14. See J. Laplanche and J. B. Pontalis, *The Language of Psychoanalysis,* translated by Donald Nicholson-Smith (New York: Norton, 1974), 121–123.

15. Ibid., 81.

16. Silvia Bovenschen, "Is There a Feminine Aesthetic?," translated by Beth Weck-mueller, *New German Critique* 12 (1977). Reprinted in *Feminist Aesthetics,* edited by Gisela Ecker (Boston: Beacon Press, 1985), 47–48.

17. Lyotard, *Postmodern Condition,* 81.

18. Jardine, *Gynesis.* Jardine doesn't define feminism as antipatriarchal or political but as a movement "by, for, and about women."

19. Ibid., 25.

20. Ibid., 14, 22.

21. This coextensivity between feminist discourse and the feminine is found in much of feminist discourse and it is not unlike the assumed coextensivity between the map and the territory, an ontological assumption that is called into question by many theorists of the postmodern.

    See Elaine Showalter, "Critical Cross-Dressing: Male Feminists and The Woman of the Year," in *Men in Feminism,* edited by Alice Jardine and Paul Smith (New York: Methuen, 1987), 116–133.

22. Stephen Heath, "Difference," *Screen* 19, no. 3 (Autumn 1978): 53.

23. Victor Burgin, *The End of Art Theory: Criticism and Postmodernity* (Atlantic Highlands, N.J.: Humanities Press International, 1986), 204:

    The cultural theory of the 1970's—drawing predominately on feminism,
    Marxism, psycho-analysis and semiotics—demonstrated the impossibility of the
    modernist ideal of art

24. Owens, "Discourse of Others," 61.

25. Andreas Huyssen, "Mapping the Postmodern," *New German Critique* 33 (Fall 1984): 27.

26. Elaine Showalter, "Critical Cross-Dressing: Male Feminists and The Woman of the Year," in *Men in Feminism,* edited by Alice Jardine and Paul Smith (New York: Methuen, 1987), 116–133.

27. Owens, "Discourse of Others," 59.

28. See Fraser and Nicholson, "Social Criticism without Philosophy." Although Fraser points out that both feminism and postmodernism offer a philosophical critique, she describes both with univocal generalizations.

29. Teresa de Lauretis, "Feminist Studies/ Critical Studies: Issues, Terms, Contexts," in *Feminist Studies/Critical Studies* edited by Teresa de Lauretis (Bloomington: Indiana University Press, 1986), 7.

30. Huyssen, "Mapping the Postmodern," 27.

31. Owens, "Discourse of Others," 61.

32. Ibid., 58.

33. Charles Dickens, *A Tale of Two Cities,* opening pages.

■ INDEX

Designer:	Steve Renick
Compositor:	Impressions, a division of Edwards Brothers
Text:	10/13 Garamond, 10/13 Perpetua
Display:	Garamond, M. Gill Sans, Perpetua
Printer:	Edwards Brothers, Inc.
Binder:	Edwards Brothers, Inc.